Building
Science
Graphics

"Jen Christiansen's book is a compelling resource with helpful visual strategies and suggestions to create effective scientific illustrated explanatory diagrams. The extended step-by-step visual worksheets are must-haves for both expert and non-specialist audiences interested in visually communicating science. Her clarity and level of detail to articulate each step combined with her specialized guidance on how to work with design principles make this book one of its kind."
—Sheila Pontis, Sense Information Design,
and Massachusetts Institute of Technology

"This book will help readers and practitioners understand how to apply design principles during the process of developing and producing information graphics for diverse audiences, and offers perspectives about the design processes employed by graphics editors."
—Spencer Barnes, Associate Professor, Hussman School of Journalism and Media, University of North Carolina at Chapel Hill

"I love this approach—it's as methodical as good science. Breaking it down into manageable chunks is one thing; turning those chunks into an actual workflow is much more important, and that is in here. Trying to find resources that go through a methodical approach to designing information graphics is difficult. Trying to find ones that go beyond basic charts and into in-depth illustrations is even harder."
—Mark E. Johnson, Senior Lecturer, Grady College of Journalism and Mass Communication, University of Georgia

"Working with scientists and researchers myself, one of the many questions I get asked is where and how to start—this book will help to answer some of those questions and concerns. The fact that it is written by Jen Christiansen adds real value. The book is explained in a cohesive and logical way. This will allow the reader to follow the process, as you would for real, building an infographic from scratch—step-by-step."
—Nigel Hawtin, Information Design Consultant;
Former Graphics Editor, *New Scientist*

"The book provides a practical guide targeted at individuals without an explicit art/design background and tailored towards the need of science communication. I consider this a very worthwhile endeavor and believe that many scientists (including my graduate students and myself) will draw considerable utility from this book."
—Stefan Bruckner, Professor of Visualization,
Department of Informatics of the University of Bergen

Praise for *Building Science Graphics*

"Much like a successful science graphic, *Building Science Graphics* delivers compelling information on many different levels. From quick tips to deep dives, Christiansen shares well researched, clear examples, as well as actionable workflows and memorable anecdotes from her career. A great read and valuable resource for designers and researchers alike."
—Beth Rakouskas, Creative Director, *Science*

"This beautifully illustrated book is like a Swiss army knife—all the necessary tools of the trade are there and they fit together seamlessly. Communicating science visually has unique challenges and considerations, which makes this book a must-read for creators of science visuals. The step-by-step approach is accessible to all levels, from students to researchers to professional artists and designers."
—Kelly Krause, Creative Director, *Nature*

"Whenever Jen Christiansen was the art director for an article I was editing, I knew that no matter how imposing the illustrative challenge, she would find a visually stunning way to bring it to glorious, lucid life. In her hands, explanatory illustrations sing out a tale of discovery, one that inspires with the grace and elegance of its comprehension. With this marvelous book, Jen generously shares her approach to beautiful, informative design, and it does something I once wouldn't have imagined was possible: It makes me appreciate and love her work even more."
—John Rennie, Deputy Editor, *Quanta Magazine*;
Former Editor-in-Chief, *Scientific American*;
Adjunct Instructor, Arthur L. Carter Journalism Institute, New York University

"This book is a masterclass in the field of scientific visualization. Ms. Christiansen's approach is insightful, approachable, thorough, and inclusive. There is something here for everyone, from the true novice to those who have been practicing scientific visualization for years. Each page is bursting with useful and interesting content. As an unsurprising bonus, the book's design is a delight; it is a pleasure to read and peruse the images and layout. I strongly recommend this book for anyone interested in what it takes to create visuals that effectively and beautifully communicate science."
—Jill K. Gregory, MFA, CMI; President, Association of Medical Illustrators;
Associate Director of Instructional Technology,
Icahn School of Medicine at Mount Sinai

AK Peters Visualization Series

Visualization plays an ever-more prominent role in the world, as we communicate about and analyze data. This series aims to capture what visualization is today in all its variety and diversity, giving voice to researchers, practitioners, designers, and enthusiasts. It encompasses books from all subfields of visualization, including visual analytics, information visualization, scientific visualization, data journalism, infographics, and their connection to adjacent areas such as text analysis, digital humanities, data art, or augmented and virtual reality.

Series Editors:

Tamara Munzner, *University of British Columbia, Vancouver, Canada*
Alberto Cairo, *University of Miami, USA*

Recent titles:

Building Science Graphics
An Illustrated Guide to Communicating Science through Diagrams and Visualizations
Jen Christiansen

Joyful Infographics
A Friendly, Human Approach to Data
Nigel Holmes

Questions in Dataviz
A Design-Driven Process for Data Visualisation
Neil Richards

Making with Data
Physical Design and Craft in a Data-Driven World
Edited by Samuel Huron, Till Nagel, Lora Oehlberg, Wesley Willett

Mobile Data Visualization
Edited by Bongshin Lee, Raimund Dachselt, Petra Isenberg, Eun Kyoung Choe

Data Sketches
Nadieh Bremer, Shirley Wu

Visualizing with Text
Richard Brath

Interactive Visual Data Analysis
Christian Tominski, Heidrun Schumann

Data-Driven Storytelling
Nathalie Henry Riche, Christophe Hurter, Nicholas Diakopoulos, Sheelagh Carpendale

For more information about this series please visit:
https://www.routledge.com/AK-Peters-Visualization-Series/book-series/CRCVIS

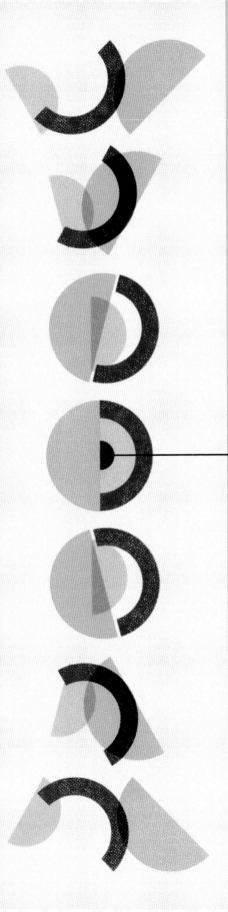

Building
Science
Graphics

**An illustrated guide to
communicating science
through diagrams
and visualizations**

JEN CHRISTIANSEN

AK Peters | CRC Press
Boca Raton and London

First edition published 2023
by CRC Press
6000 Broken Sound Parkway NW, Suite 300, Boca Raton, FL 33487-2742
and by CRC Press
4 Park Square, Milton Park, Abingdon, Oxon, OX14 4RN

© 2023 Jen Christiansen

CRC Press is an imprint of Taylor & Francis Group, LLC

Library of Congress Cataloging-in-Publication Data

Names: Christiansen, Jen, author.
Title: Building science graphics : an illustrated guide to communicating
   science through diagrams and visualizations / Jen Christiansen.
Description: First edition. | Boca Raton, FL : AK Peters/CRC Press, 2023. |
   Series: AK Peters visualization series | Includes bibliographical
   references and index.
Identifiers: LCCN 2022026513 (print) | LCCN 2022026514 (ebook) | ISBN
   9781032109404 (hardback) | ISBN 9781032106748 (paperback) | ISBN
   9781003217817 (ebook)
Subjects: LCSH: Scientific illustration. | Visual communication. |
   Communication in science. | Information visualization.
Classification: LCC Q222 .C47 2023 (print) | LCC Q222 (ebook) | DDC
   502.2/2--dc23/eng20221026
LC record available at https://lccn.loc.gov/2022026513
LC ebook record available at https://lccn.loc.gov/2022026514

ISBN: 9781032109404 (hbk)
ISBN: 9781032106748 (pbk)
ISBN: 9781003217817 (ebk)

DOI: 10.1201/9781003217817

Publisher's note: This book has been prepared from camera-ready copy provided by the author.

Cover image by Alli Torban, © 2022

Set in **Elena (Process Type Foundry),** Omnes (Darden Studio), and **Indivisible (Process Type Foundry)**

Design by Jen Christiansen

Dedicated to

George Christiansen and Marcia Christiansen
(my parents)

Joel Tolman
(my love)

Ed Bell
(my mentor)

Contents

Series Foreword

JEN CHRISTIANSEN KNOWS A THING OR TWO about designing science graphics; by the end of this book we're sure you'll agree with that.

This book is the most in-depth guide to designing effective, clear, and beautiful science visualizations and explanations we know. In it, Jen offers gentle, thorough, and practical advice on everything from structuring a visual narrative to making reasonable choices on typography, color, composition, visual style, and much, much more.

Jen draws from her own extensive experience in science communication; many of the examples in *Building Science Graphics* are her own designs. Having a formal background in both the sciences and the visual arts, you'll soon notice that Jen's graphics achieve a rare balance between accuracy, depth, and clarity.

If you are a scientist interested in communicating your research to the general public, or a designer who helps researchers do that, or a graphics reporter at a news publication, or a teacher or student in need of a great textbook, you're in for a treat.

**—Alberto Cairo and Tamara Munzner, Editors,
AK Peters Visualization Series**

This book is part of the AK Peters Visualization series, which aims to capture what visualization is today in all its variety and diversity, giving voice to researchers, practitioners, designers, and enthusiasts. Visualization plays an ever-more prominent role in the world, as we communicate about and analyze data. The series encompasses books from all subfields of visualization, including visual analytics, information visualization, scientific visualization, data journalism, infographics, and their connection to adjacent areas such as text analysis, digital humanities, data art, or augmented and virtual reality.

Preface

BUILDING SCIENCE GRAPHICS IS A PRACTICAL GUIDE for anyone—regardless of previous design experience and preferred drawing tools—interested in creating illustrated science diagrams. Starting with a clear introduction to the concept of science graphics and their role in contemporary science communication, it then outlines a process for creating illustrated explanatory diagrams using design strategies informed by perception science research. The heart of this book is composed of two extended worksheets: one designed to guide you through the process of building a graphic from the ground up, and another that guides you through the process of adapting an existing graphic for a different audience. Both are designed to help jump-start any new project, starting with the question, "Would a graphic be useful in this context?" Although the focus is on illustrated explanatory diagrams, the lessons and examples within are also relevant to the full spectrum of information graphics, including classic figurative illustration—such as specimen drawings—and data visualization. This is both a textbook and a practical reference for anyone that needs to convey scientific information in an illustrated form for articles, poster presentations, slide shows, press releases, blog posts, social media posts, and beyond.

My Point of View

As a science communicator of the visual variety, I've been producing science graphics professionally since 1996. My double-interest in science and art started at a pretty young age. I loved to draw, but almost always needed some sort of project brief, a prompt from someone else for a specific thing to depict. Science classes in school offered up a plethora of topics. My high school biology notebooks were filled with drawings. At Smith College, I double-majored in Geology and Studio Art. (Ask me about the trace fossil *Gyrolithes*, the star of my undergraduate honors thesis.[1]) I spent summers in the crustacea lab at the Natural History Museum of Los Angeles, sorting crustacea larvae and illustrating hydrothermal vent shrimp mouthparts.[2] Ultimately, I couldn't bear to follow one discipline at the expense of the other, and enrolled in the natural science illustration graduate program at the University of California, Santa Cruz. After a year of classroom training, I interned as an illustrator at *Scientific American* magazine. My education continued apprenticeship-style at the magazine under the tutelage of art director Ed Bell, and my internship led into an assistant art director position. I stayed with the magazine for a few years before heading south for a job at *National Geographic* magazine, first as an assistant art director/researcher hybrid, then a designer. Leaving *National Geographic* wasn't an easy decision, but the time was right to travel north again, and I started my own business. As a freelancer, I focused primarily on designing, art directing, and illustrating book and magazine projects for clients including McGraw Hill, The Cooking Lab, Intellectual Ventures, and The Rockefeller University. The pull of *Scientific American* was strong, however, and I returned to the magazine full time in 2007.

In my current role as a senior graphics editor at *Scientific American*, my goal with every project is to develop images that engage, inform, and inspire both specialist and non-specialist readers. Sometimes I create the final renderings myself. I also hire and collaborate with freelance illustrators, data designers, and researchers on a project-by-project basis, acting as a project manager of sorts.

I have been incredibly fortunate over the years to learn directly from a wide range of artists, designers, art directors, science journalists, scientists, researchers, and educators. That said, I cannot—and don't aim to—speak for all science graphic designers. My viewpoint is informed by research, but is rooted in a career of practice, not theory. The text that follows draws upon the work of many, and I hope that it provides a

---

1   Jennifer Christiansen, *The Trace Fossil* Gyrolithes: *Unwinding the Spiral Enigma in the St. Marys Formation (Miocene) of Maryland (*Smith College Department of Geology, 1995)

2   Joel Martin and Jennifer Christiansen, "A new species of the shrimp genus *Chorocaris* Martin & Hessler, 1990 (Crustacea: Decapoda: Bresiliidae) from hydrothermal vent fields along the Mid-Atlantic Ridge," *Proceedings of the Biological Society of Washington*, Vol. 108 (June 22, 1995)

sufficiently broad view of the topic. That said, I also present ideas, opinions, and frameworks that are my own. My thoughts do not necessarily reflect a consensus view within the science graphics community.

I should acknowledge that much of my personal experience is rooted in an era that is well described by Faith Kearns in *Getting to the Heart of Science Communication*:

> *Until recently, science communication advice was seemingly agnostic as to who the practitioner was, although the implicit assumption has been largely white, male, with tenure at an elite institution. Simultaneously, many science communicators spoke to a mythological 'general public,' in which everyone was lumped together. It was assumed the same strategies would work for all—practitioners and communities alike—and that factors such as race, gender, sexuality, age, ability, and class did not affect the communication and engagement process, much less power and authority.*[3]

I'm a cisgendered middle-class white woman born and raised in the United States who was in a position to take the unpaid internship that initiated my career in the mid-1990s. I certainly benefited from—and learned within—that era of science communication. My hope with this book is to share what I've learned about building science graphics as the field—and I—have grown over time. I am still learning. And the practices of science communication and information design are certainly still evolving. Throughout, I share references that are currently shaping my viewpoint and are challenging me to continue growing. This book is meant to be a benchmark. Not an endpoint.

Motivation

I wrote this book so that I'd finally have a singular and reasonably comprehensive reference to recommend to students and scientists who ask me how to create more considered diagrams for their scientific papers, articles, and presentations. I also wrote this book for designers, illustrators, and visual journalists who are struggling with how to approach content rooted in science; and to science communicators of all types looking to bolster their knowledge of the practice of creating graphics.

3   Faith Kearns, *Getting to the Heart of Science Communication: A Guide to Effective Engagement* (Island Press, 2021); © 2021 by Faith Kearns; Quote used by permission of Island Press, Washington, D.C.

Interest in science communication training is going up,[4] as have expectations for scientists and others to effectively communicate research findings to both broader and more well-defined audiences.[5] But most training materials focus on writing and oral presentations. There is a need for comprehensive, clear, and practical guides to communicating science through imagery.[6] Data visualization authors have been stepping up to the task in recent years, with books that run the gamut from chart-choosing guides, to design primers and data storytelling workbooks. This book aims to expand that corpus to include a different portion of the information graphics spectrum; illustrated explanatory diagrams. Scientists are expected to be able to create diagrams and figures for their papers. But they are not routinely trained in how to do so, and "visual material is typically treated as an add-on instead of being an integrated part of the whole."[7] That's not to say that webinars, guides, and references on the topic don't exist. Indeed, I'll nod to many of them in the pages that follow. But I am not aware of any other practical step-by-step guides to creating scientific illustrated explanatory graphics in book form. This text will help fill that gap on the bookshelf for not only scientists, but also journalists, authors, artists, and science communicators of all types.

Audience

The primary audience for *Building Science Graphics* is scientists and science communicators—students and researchers alike. The book presumes no previous formal design training. Familiarity with specific design or illustration computer programs is not required. The principles within can be applied to your drawing tools of choice. Designers, illustrators, visual journalists, and writers looking to become more

4   Toss Gascoigne et al., eds., *Communicating Science: A Global Perspective* (ANU Press, 2020)

5   Ilda Mannino et al., "Supporting Quality in Science Communication: Insights from the QUEST Project," *Journal of Science Communication*, Vol. 20 (May 10, 2021)

6   This topic is thoroughly cited by Karen J. Murchie and Dylan Diomede in "Fundamentals of Graphic Design—Essential Tools for Effective Visual Science Communication," *FACETS* (June 11, 2020).

7   Fabiola Cristina Rodríguez Estrada and Lloyd Spencer Davis, "Improving Visual Communication of Science Through the Incorporation of Graphic Design Theories and Practices Into Science Communication," *Science Communication*, Vol. 37 (February 1, 2015)

adept at conveying scientific content with graphics will also find the content useful, although a few chapters may cover familiar ground. This book is a natural fit for undergraduate and graduate-level science communication and journalism classes, and as a practical reference guide for anyone who needs to convey scientific information in an illustrated form.

What's in This Book

In this book, I use "graphics" as shorthand for the portion of the information graphics continuum that encompasses illustrated explanatory diagrams. Part 1 defines those terms, submits why they are useful for science communication, and explores concepts and principles that guide information design. I should point out that many of the fundamentals within this book lean quite heavily on design principles that come out of a very specific Western European and North American design tradition, destined for European and American audiences. Broader critiques of defaulting to those design systems are included. But the fact remains that this section leans heavily on a specific design canon.

Part 2 focuses more sharply on science graphics. It establishes a classification system of static science graphics types, and addresses topics that are particularly relevant to this sub-genre, including sections on complexity, uncertainty, and misinformation.

Part 3 is the crux. It outlines the process that I use to develop static science graphics, illustrated with real-world examples, including images of notes, concept sketches, tight sketches, and final products. This section includes two worksheets that I've designed to walk you through the process of building your own graphics. Although the guides describe specific *strategies*, they don't dictate specific solutions. Recommendations—rooted in fundamentals described in Parts 1 and 2—provide enough flexibility for you to directly address the needs of your specific audience.

Teams are often better suited to the task than individuals. Part 4 acknowledges that the project you have in mind may exceed your current skill level or schedule, and it provides tips on how to effectively collaborate with others.

In short, Part 1 explains the necessary underpinnings and frameworks. Parts 2, 3, and 4 focus on science graphics themselves and how to build them. This book is rooted in my experiences, and therefore leans heavily on what I've learned from collaborating with scientists and artists while creating science graphics for magazines and textbooks for over 25 years. Footnotes throughout nod to the work of others that have informed the text directly.

What's Not in This Book

Although many of the design principles and recommendations within are relevant across platforms and genres, this book is very much rooted in my experiences building static explanatory graphics. It does not directly address interactive explanatory graphics or animated graphics, topics that could easily fill entire books of their own.

This book also excludes tool-specific instructional guides. In case you're wondering, I usually start with a pencil and paper, and use Adobe Illustrator, Photoshop, and/or InDesign for my final graphics. Many other digital drawing programs exist, at a wide range of price points.

This book does not aim to teach you how to draw. It aims to get you thinking critically about how to organize and edit information within a set space. You may find that you're distracted by the task or challenge of drawing shapes, and unable to shift focus to the task of organizing those shapes into an explanatory diagram. If that's the case—and depending upon your needs—you may prefer to start with *Drawing on the Right Side of the Brain* by Betty Edwards.[8] Or you may prefer to make use of the extensive library of over 20,000 editable natural science icons available for use by BioRender,[9] organism silhouettes from PhyloPic,[10] or icons available for download by the Noun Project[11] (although the Noun Project isn't science-specific and some icons may include scientific inaccuracies).

I should admit that field research—the act of gathering evidence "from real people about how they think, feel, and behave in order to inform the design of effective solutions"[12]—is not a part of my regular practice. As a journalist working on tight deadlines, it sadly has not been practical or possible for me to step back and engage with my

---

8   Betty Edwards, *Drawing on the Right Side of the Brain*, The Deluxe Edition (TarcherPerigee, 2012)

9   *https://biorender.com/*

10 *http://phylopic.org/*

11 *https://thenounproject.com/*

12 Sheila Pontis, *Making Sense of Field Research: A Practical Guide for Information Designers* (Routledge, 2018)

intended audience during the design process for every graphic. My design decisions are informed by what I know about the magazine's subscribers as well as data on how readers interact with content on the magazine's website, and feedback in the form of letters from readers, communications with scientists and colleagues, and conversations within the design community. I always define my audience as a step in the design process. But it's important to note that this book does not include information based on my first-hand experience of how to collaborate with the intended audience as a part of the design process. For that reason, I largely rely on the expertise of others when addressing the topic in the pages that follow. Similarly, I still have much to learn on the accessibility front. The section that addresses this topic head-on in Chapter 12 is based on the expertise of others, and is limited in scope. These are both areas in which I'm committed to learn more. Many resources that I've found useful as I embark on that journey are cited within.

PART 1

Underpinning

CHAPTER 1

Introduction

AS A STUDENT, I was torn. Was I a scientist or an artist? I loved the clarity and order inherent to the scientific process: ask questions, set up methodologies, collect data, analyze. Research projects and papers I co-authored on the topics of trace fossils and hydrothermal vent species were immensely satisfying. No matter the result of the study, it gave me the chance to contribute a rigorously produced bit of knowledge to the world.

I also loved the idea of communicating through visuals rather than words. My studio arts classes encouraged me to question and morph methodologies. I couldn't stop making images. Nor could I imagine choosing one discipline at the expense of the other. Scientific illustration allowed me to merge those two identities. Finding the similarities between art and science, I honed in on observation and interpretation.

In college, I mimicked the style of vintage works rooted in direct observation.[1] Think Maria Sibylla Merian's botanical and entomological illustrations. I spent hours looking through a microscope, with a rapidograph

Image Credit: Maria Sibylla Merian; Metamorphosis of a Small Emperor Moth on a Damson Plum (plate 13 of the Caterpillar Book, 1679); Digital image courtesy of the Getty's Open Content Program.

---

1   It's important to acknowledge that colonization went hand-in-hand with expeditions that resulted in many classic scientific illustrations that are still lauded by lots of people today. I recommend reading "The Beauty and Violence of Ernst Haeckel's Illustrations," by John Kazior, *AIGA Eye on Design* (April 8, 2021).

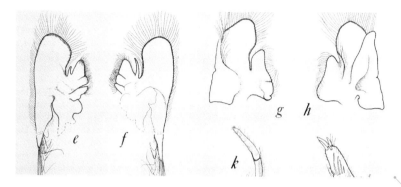

pen in-hand, counting hairs on mandibles and faithfully documenting crustaceans for species description papers.

My interest eventually shifted from illustrating objects toward trying to represent things that can't always be directly observed, like concepts and processes. Think Abū al-Rayḥān Muḥammad ibn Aḥmad al-Bīrūnī's moon phase diagram.

At the time, I thought of it as a natural extension of scientific illustration. In retrospect, I can see that I was simply striding toward the worlds of information design and data visualization. But I was lacking a clear guide.

Perhaps that's why in 1996 I was so taken by a required reading in graduate school: Edward R. Tufte's book, *The Visual Display of Quantitative Information*.[2] Not having had read much about information design up until that point, I devoured the pages, and moved on to other books by the same author. (I'm not alone. Tufte's writings were quite influential as the practice of data visualization and information design became more widespread in the late 1990s and early 2000s.) One of his classic and compelling "Principles of Graphical Excellence" stuck with me. It states concisely that, "Graphical excellence is that which gives to the viewer the greatest number of ideas in the shortest time with the least ink in the smallest space."[3]

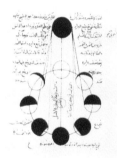

Soon after, I was swept into the publishing world, working for magazines that enthusiastically embraced extravagant, colorful, and remarkably detailed three-dimensional (3D) renderings. We were using a heck of a lot of printers' ink in as much space as we could carve out between columns of text. It made a lot of sense at the time.

---

2   Edward R. Tufte, *The Visual Display of Quantitative Information* (Graphics Press, 1983)

3   I should note that this is just one of five principles, and they appear in a book that is centered on visualizing quantitative, not qualitative, information.

Computer rendering programs were becoming more accessible to artists and designers, and digital 3D illustrations were elbowing out analog airbrush paintings and ink drawings. And the Web was starting to compete seriously for attention. The era called for lush, dynamic, and bold visuals in print media, and we delivered them. The trend influenced college-level science textbooks too, as imagery broke out of confined boxes and spilled into text columns, magazine-style. The work I was doing for *Scientific American*, *National Geographic*, and the science textbook market wasn't quite maximalism. But it certainly wasn't Tufte-esque minimalism.

But then the prevailing aesthetics began to shift in a minimalist direction again, and I was excited. The time felt right to consciously apply Tufte's principles. A 2011 *Scientific American* article on the topic of cosmic inflation by physicist Paul J. Steinhardt provided a great opportunity to see how far I could push it.

The original plan was to use simple and spare imagery. I hoped to introduce a visual vocabulary with shape and color, then use that visual vocabulary to explain several concepts related to the expansion of our universe. Although the content still needed to be vetted, I imagined the style of the final illustrations to be very similar to the concept sketches below; flat shapes and limited color. Every color, shape, and line would be imbued with meaning. Nothing extraneous. Cyan for the classic hypothesis, magenta for new ideas, and yellow zones to define the period of inflation.

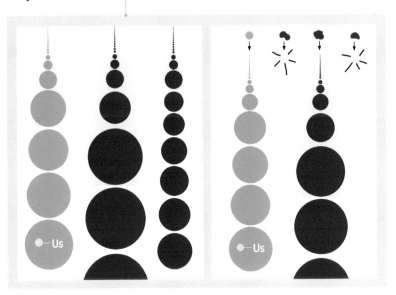

Image Credit: Concept sketches by Jen Christiansen

I was so caught up in developing a spare and efficient language to explain the science, that I was taken aback when editor-in-chief Mariette DiChristina asked for something richer and more engaging. I had completely lost sight of the context for the graphics. The illustrations were intended for an existing audience who loves articles about space. And a potential audience who might benefit from a familiar and comfortable visual hook as a welcoming counterpoint to the abstract concepts in the article. By stripping out figurative details, I had lost all visual references to space. And I may have pushed an already abstract concept further out of reach of a non-specialist audience.

So I pivoted, starting with color. Pure magenta, cyan, and yellow gave way to a color palette that evoked space—dark purples with bright white details, and warm globes that would eventually glow.

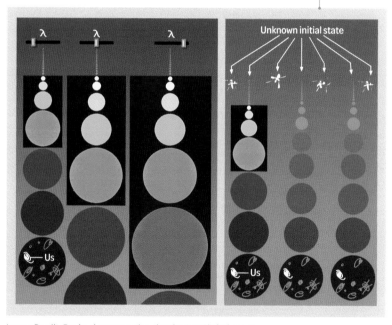

Image Credit: Revised concept sketches by Jen Christiansen

The final graphics remained more or less faithful to the original sketches in terms of content, but the spare iconography shifted toward a more figurative vibe. Ulitmately, artist Malcolm Godwin of Moonrunner Design brought the shapes to life. Intellectually, I resisted the shift in style at first. But in time I realized that the galaxy details and marble-like spheres provided a welcoming counterpoint to the abstract concepts in the article. I now like to think of those fanciful details as a

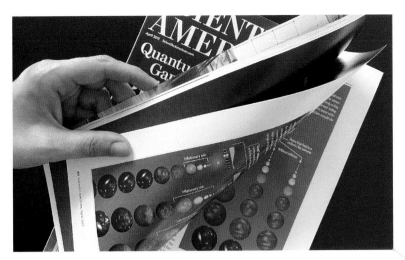

Image Credit: Photograph of magazine by Jen Christiansen. Detail of final illustrations by Malcolm Godwin (Moonrunner Design), as published in "The Inflation Debate," by Paul J. Steinhardt, *Scientific American* (April 2011).

welcoming gesture before blowing the reader's mind with counter-intuitive concepts. Sort of like a glass of wine alongside a challenging plate of tripe. The final lush imagery signals "space!" more directly than flat shapes for a casual reader flipping through the magazine.

I learned a few important things while working on that article. Those lessons continue to inform my graphics philosophy today:

- **Be wary of applying "principles of graphical excellence" without consideration of your particular project's ultimate audience and use;**
- **Nonetheless, there's still great value in critically considering the principles and ideas from folks who have come before.**

Although the final aesthetics of these cosmic inflation images don't reflect the spare concept I started with, approaching the project with a minimalist mindset forced me to prioritize how the information should be organized on the page. I wasn't leaning on visual style from the start, and I think the series of graphics is better for it.

I aim to honor those two lessons in this book. I will not offer my own "principles of excellence," as that depends upon who you're designing your images for, and how they'll be used. Those combined possibilities are endless. But I will present research findings and often-cited principles and ideas from others, as well as strategies for designing graphics that I have developed over time. My goal is to provide you with a solid foundation of knowledge about science communication and information design (Part 1), and a framework for thinking about—and building—science graphics of your own (Parts 2, 3, and 4).

As you'll see in Chapter 15, I start projects by establishing the goal of

Original Caption: "Schematic of the proposed solar powered water-splitting device incorporating two separate semiconductor rodarray photoelectrodes that sandwich an electronically and ionically membrane." Image Credit: As published in "Silicon and Tungsten Oxide Nanostructures for Water Splitting," by Karla R. Reyes Gil, Joshua M. Spurgeon, and Nathan S. Lewis, *Solar Hydrogen and Nanotechnology IV, SPIE Proceedings*, Vol. 7408, edited by Frank E. Osterloh (2009)

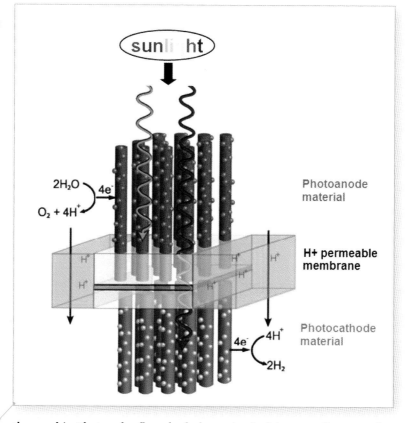

the graphic. That goal reflects both the project's ultimate audience, and the use to which it will be put. In my work for magazines, the context remains more or less consistent across a broad range of topics, so I don't always articulate it outright. But that context shapes every decision from content and composition to style. The following example shows how.

For an article on artificial photosynthesis, preliminary research uncovered a great reference figure published by Karla Reyes-Gil, Joshua Spurgeon, and Nathan Lewis. It's a schematic of a material their lab developed to mimic photosynthesis. This image is well suited to the context of a conference proceedings paper. The goal is clear: Show the components of the nanostructure and provide a basic sense of how it works. Color is used intentionally to represent different material types, labels are legible, and the schematic isn't overwhelming. It's not trying to accomplish too much in the space allotted, and it would also translate well into a slide deck or academic poster. It's a great example of a solid figure designed for the authors' peers in a book connected to a scientific conference.

When you change the audience and the outlet, you also shift the goal of the graphic. When presenting this same basic content to a non-specialist audience, I needed to not only engage non-specialist readers, but also help them more immediately see the parallels between this technology and natural photosynthesis. In an effort to make the parallels as explicit as possible, I started by drawing out the steps using the same composition for each approach—natural photosynthesis at the top, and artificial at the bottom. Then I used color to help highlight which parts correspond.

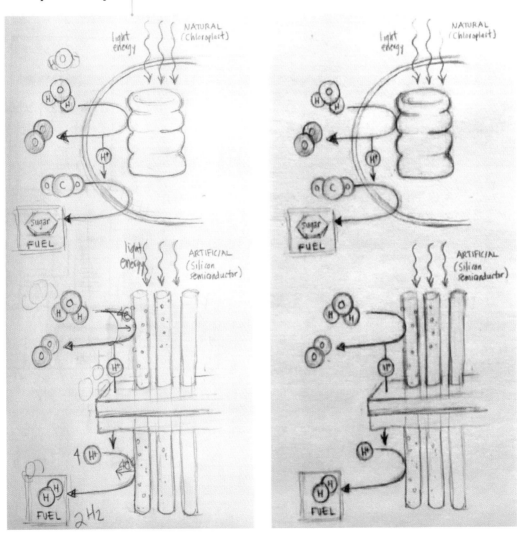

Image Credit: Jen Christiansen, sketches for "Reinventing the Leaf: Artificial Photosynthesis to Create Clean Fuel," by Antonio Regalado, *Scientific American* (October 2010)

But stacking things on top of each other meant that the reader's gaze would have to bounce from top to bottom and back again, searching for the corresponding steps. So I pulled the two approaches apart, and put them next to each other, leaving room for explanatory text between the two scenarios.

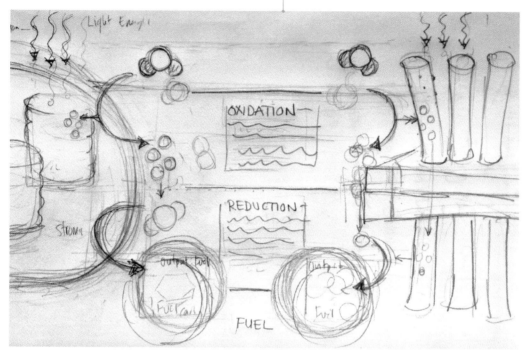

Image Credit: Jen Christiansen, sketch for "Reinventing the Leaf: Artificial Photosynthesis to Create Clean Fuel," by Antonio Regalado, *Scientific American* (October 2010)

Here's the final art box, as rendered by botanical artist Cherie Sinnen. As discussed in Chapter 10 on visual style (see page 127), the goal was to invite the reader in with a warm and welcoming aesthetic, keep them engaged with some basic primer information about photosynthesis that would likely feel a bit familiar, then have the reader build on that more familiar content by showing how the new technology works.

As demonstrated in this example, my initial solution was just that. An initial solution. I needed to draw it out to see what worked, and what didn't work. Once I realized that the composition—or position of objects on the page—didn't allow for a seamless comparison between scenarios, I was free to iterate. Knowledge of basic design concepts about composition, color, and visual style informed every decision along the way. But trial and error is a powerful teacher.

─────── **HOW IT WORKS** ───────

Solar Nanowires Mimic Nature

Plants harness the sun's energy to convert carbon dioxide and water into glucose—chemical fuel that can be used or stored (*left*). Researchers are devising artificial leaves that use sunlight to split water molecules, creating hydrogen fuel. Nathan Lewis's group at the California Institute of Technology is designing a small leaf with arrays of silicon nanowires that could produce hydrogen (*right*).

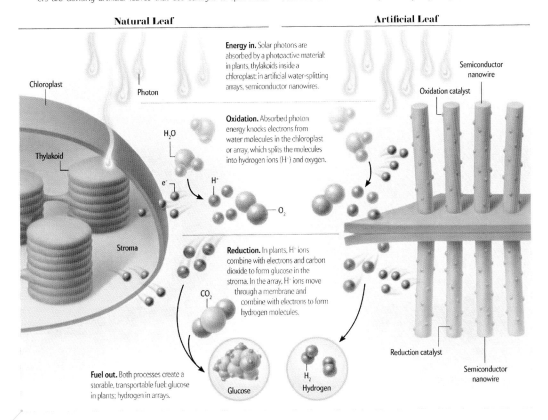

Natural Leaf   **Artificial Leaf**

Chloroplast

Photon

Energy in. Solar photons are absorbed by a photoactive material: in plants, thylakoids inside a chloroplast; in artificial water-splitting arrays, semiconductor nanowires.

Semiconductor nanowire

Oxidation catalyst

Thylakoid

H_2O

Oxidation. Absorbed photon energy knocks electrons from water molecules in the chloroplast or array, which splits the molecules into hydrogen ions (H^+) and oxygen.

e^- H^+ O_2

Stroma

Reduction. In plants, H^+ ions combine with electrons and carbon dioxide to form glucose in the stroma. In the array, H^+ ions move through a membrane and combine with electrons to form hydrogen molecules.

CO_2

Reduction catalyst

Semiconductor nanowire

Fuel out. Both processes create a storable, transportable fuel: glucose in plants; hydrogen in arrays.

Glucose

H_2 Hydrogen

The next two chapters take a step back, and provide a foundation for thinking about science graphics and science communication. Then you'll dive into basic concepts in design, lots of real-life examples, guides that aim to help you start—or continue—on your graphics-building journey, and tips on how to collaborate with others.

CHAPTER 2

What Are Science Graphics?

PRESUMABLY, FOLKS WHO PICK UP THIS BOOK—YOU!—are interested in learning more about using imagery to convey scientific information. But the language you use to describe those images is less predictable. Are they scientific figures? Science illustrations? Diagrams? Schematics? Visualizations? Science graphics, information graphics, or infographics? There are no wrong answers. Different communities use these terms with different levels of frequency to mean a variety of related things in different contexts. That said, it's not useful for me to use those words interchangeably and without clear intent within *this* context. So, let's start with defining some edges and words.

This book is about drawing and organizing lines and shapes to communicate a specific bit of science-related information to another person. The word "communication" is key. This book is about using imagery in the service of communication, not analysis. Although many of the lessons within apply to both motives.

In this book, I use "graphics" as shorthand for the portion of the information graphics continuum that encompasses illustrated explanatory diagrams. (In some contexts—outside of this book—I use the word graphics to refer to the entire information graphics continuum. But "illustrated explanatory diagrams" is a mouthful, so I'm hoping you'll be kind and indulge the modification.)

"Information graphics" is an umbrella term that encompasses the specific types of scientific figures, science illustrations, diagrams, schematics, and visualizations that are in this book. But the term is perhaps too broad and fuzzy, and doesn't quite efficiently and precisely describe the examples that follow. That said, it's a great place to start. (Jump to page 16 if you'd rather not linger too long on terminology.)

Information graphics are one of the products of a discipline referred to as information design.[1] Information design, as summarized by Sheila Pontis in 2018, is

> ...*the field concerned with facilitating understanding in order to help people achieve their goals by translating raw or disorganized data into forms that can be rapidly perceived, understood, processed, and used. Information design work of any kind seeks to enhance understanding —of a situation, concept, space, place, time, quantity, phenomenon— for an intended audience.* [2]

An incomplete list of other products of information design includes identification icons (such as food, camping, and bathroom symbols), wayfinding systems (such as subway or roadway direction signs), and static or interactive forms (such as voting ballots).[3]

But what, exactly, is an information graphic, other than one of several possible outputs of a particular genre of design that is centered on sharing information in a usable form? That's where things get a little fuzzy. Different practitioners and scholars have slightly different definitions. And I think it's fair to say that many of their definitions have shifted over time. Mine certainly have. And things get even more complicated when you throw in the related term "infographic." It's used by many as shorthand for "information graphic," and it nicely sets up the label of "infographer" to describe a person that makes them. But for others it evokes a very specific genre of vertical poster-like visual factoid displays. (Connie Malamed's wry 2011 blog post, "Infoposters Are Not Infographics: A Comparison"[4] remains one of my favorite readings on the topic.)

Some, like digital humanities researcher Johanna Drucker, have

---

1   For a really compelling meta-argument in favor of shifting thought away from the concept of information design and toward "sense-making," check out the work of Brenda Dervin. In "Chaos, Order, and Sense-Making: A Proposed Theory for Information Design" (in *Information Design*, edited by Robert Jacobsen, The MIT Press, 1999) she writes that "information is assumed to be natural but is in fact designed. And, because it is designed without attention to design, it fits the needs, struggles, and resources of the designers. This puts all others at a disadvantage." The practice of sense-making, in contrast, shifts focus to assisting human beings in *their* information design.

2   Sheila Pontis, *Making Sense of Field Research: A Practical Guide for Information Designers* (Routledge, 2018). Note that Pontis cites several works in connection to this definition, most directly: Richard Saul Wurman, Information Architects (Graphis Press, 1996). Quote reproduced by permission of Taylor & Francis Group, LLC, a division of Informa PLC. © 2018

3   Alison Black et al., eds., *Information Design: Research and Practice* (Routledge, 2017)

4   *https://understandinggraphics.com/visualizations/infoposters-are-not-infographics/*

defined the term as being data-specific. In 2014, for example, she described information graphics as "visualizations based on abstractions of statistical data."[5] But others reserve the term information graphic for non-data-specific content, and place abstractions of statistical data into a separate—albeit related—bin labelled "visualizations." And some go even further to suggest that the former implies that the image is a tool for communication, while the later implies that the image is a tool for analysis. In his book, *The Functional Art,*[6] Alberto Cairo discusses this tension, and describes a presentation/exploration continuum between the two endpoints.

Several authors have circled in on the idea that an information graphic is a multi-section visual display designed to communicate information using a combination of images and supporting text.[7] [8] [9] Sandra Rendgen emphasizes that the process is a transformative one, in which "certain characteristics of the source material are emphasized and visually encoded, while other characteristics are disregarded."[10]

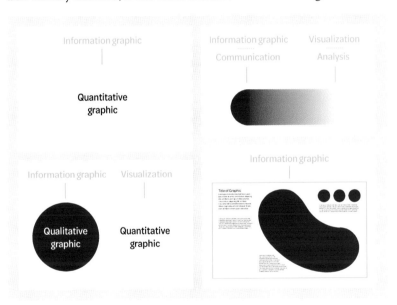

A variety of ways in which "information graphic" has been classified over time by different authors.

5   Johanna Drucker, *Graphesis: Visual Forms of Knowledge Production* (Harvard University Press, 2014)

6   Alberto Cairo, *The Functional Art* (New Riders, 2013)

7   Isabel Meirelles, *Design for Information* (Rockport Publishers, 2013)

8   Alberto Cairo, *The Truthful Art* (New Riders, 2016)

9   Sandra Rendgen, *History of Information Graphics*, ed. Julius Wiedemann (Taschen, 2019)

10   Ibid.

I think it's safe to say that there isn't a single clear definition that all agree upon, and you'll likely encounter folks who use the term in slightly different ways. And you may encounter some individuals who have a negative reaction to the term altogether, such as Edward Tufte, who in 1997 wrote of the "decorative clichés of 'info-graphics' (the language is as ghastly as the charts)",[11] despite beautifully reproducing and celebrating many gorgeous examples in his books that many would classify as infographics today.

Why don't I simply use the word "diagram," and avoid all of the ambiguities that go along with the words "infographic" and my use of "graphic"? Because diagram is a similarly slippery word,[12] and to my mind it doesn't effectively capture the multi-section possibilities described above.

That said, the question still remains. What exactly does "information graphic" mean? This is my succinct definition—and the way I'll use the term in this book: **Information graphics are images—built on a foundation of research—that are constructed primarily to convey information.**

For example, here's an information graphic from the pages of *Scientific American.* The team at Bryan Christie Design (including Violet Frances and Joe Lertola) use visual symbols and thoughtful composition to convey very specific information that is rooted in research. In this case, the goal is twofold: (1) show that a variety of different known microbe types reside in a variety of very specific parts of the human body, and; (2) show how one of the more thoroughly understood microbes interacts with the body.

For the title pages of that same article, they developed an image that is not a literal representation of the concept, but instead nods to the idea of a human as being defined by the microbes within. They are telling a story with visual symbols and thoughtful composition. But this is not an information graphic. Instead, it's an editorial illustration—a metaphorical image that represents the theme of the text, with a primary purpose of engaging the readers and priming them for the content to follow.

I tend to think of information graphics as a continuum, with figurative representations at one end and abstract representations on the other:

---

11   Edward Tufte, *Visual Explanations: Quantities, Evidence and Narrative* (Graphics Press, 1997)

12   Barbara Tversky, "Diagrams: Cognitive Foundations for Design," in *Information Design: Research and Practice,* ed. Alison Black et al. (Routledge, 2017)

Image Credit: Bryan Christie Design, as published in "The Ultimate Social Network," by Jennifer Ackerman, *Scientific American* (June 2012) (top and bottom); Reference: "Inside the Microbial and Immune Labyrinth: Gut Microbes: Friends or Fiends?" by Warren Strober, *Nature Medicine* (2010) (*B. fragilis* case study, top). Reproduced with permission from Bryan Christie Design.

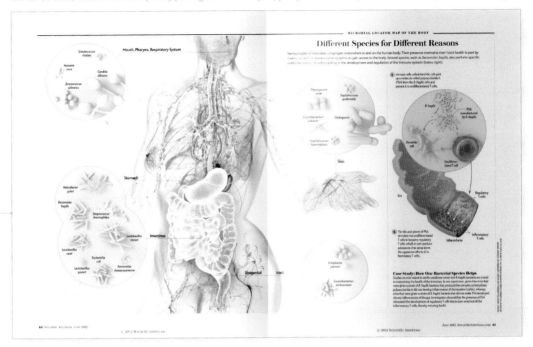

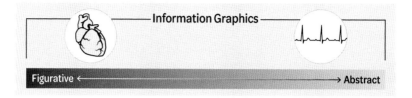

In the world of science, you could argue that the full continuum can also be referred to as data visualizations.[13] After all, essentially all of our work is rooted in data collection at some stage in the process; from bone length measurements in dinosaur reconstructions, to meticulously documented laboratory experiments that build up to a more complete understanding of processes like photosynthesis, to representations of mathematical expressions, like Feynman diagrams, to straight-up plotting of the raw data itself, in chart form.

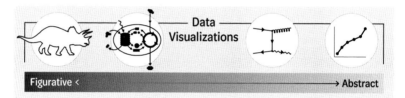

But, it's probably more useful in most cases to think of the continuum like this, with representative illustrations at one end, data visualizations on the other, and illustrated explanatory diagrams in the middle (see pages 20 and 21 for more examples).

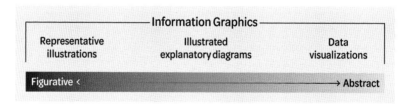

This book is focused on the center portion of this continuum—illustrated explanatory diagrams. Specifically, illustrated explanatory

13   I was introduced to this concept by Juan Velasco in his Show Don't Tell workshop presentation at the Malofiej International Infographics Summit in Pamplona, Spain (2011). He shared a Neanderthal reconstruction by Adrie Kennis and Alfons Kennis that he art directed for *National Geographic* Magazine, and argued that the final sculpture could be considered a data visualization: The shapes and volumes were based on dimensional plots of detailed and precise fossil measurements.

diagrams that aim to communicate information rooted in science. But that's a mouthful. So, for the purposes of this book, I use the shorthand "science graphics" or "graphics" to refer to that zone of the continuum.

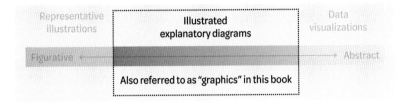

This book does not focus on representative illustrations (including specimen drawings, reconstructions, and scenes), as that portion of the continuum is a bit more rooted in the act of drawing, as opposed to designing, per se. To learn more about scientific illustration—with its emphasis on representative drawing and painting—check out *The Guild Handbook of Scientific Illustration.*[14]

This book does not focus on data visualizations (including line and bar charts, scatter plots, network diagrams, and beyond), although many of the principles within apply to that portion of the continuum. There is a growing pool of science-specific data visualization books that span the full range from theoretical to practical. See *https://Building ScienceGraphics.com* for an evolving list of my favorites.

The information graphics continuum—and this book—does not explicitly include photography, editorial illustrations (thematic illustrations generally inspired by text that entice readers to engage more fully with a publication's content), or fine art (in which aesthetics trump practicality). All of those genres can convey science content, for sure. Often quite powerfully. And there are fuzzy edges in which any and all of these genres can spill into another, as supporting imagery or as singular works that defy tidy definitions. However, those are all topics that aren't generally positioned within the information design umbrella, and are better suited to other authors.

Now that we have a mutual understanding of what I mean when I refer to "graphics" or "science graphics" in the pages that follow—the portion of the information graphics continuum that encompasses illustrated explanatory diagrams—let's get to the good stuff. Why are they useful, and how do you build them?

14   Elaine R.S. Hodges, ed., *The Guild Handbook of Scientific Illustration,* 2nd Edition
    (Wiley, 2003)

A CLOSER LOOK ──

The Information Graphics Continuum

The information graphics continuum places figurative representations on one end and abstract representations on the other. Here are a few examples, to give you a better sense of what I mean by each of the general categories.

Representative illustrations

Illustrated explanatory diagrams

Figurative

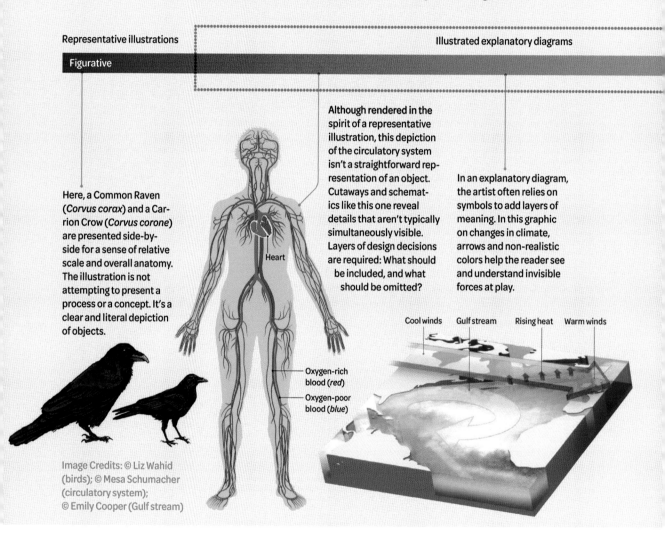

Here, a Common Raven (*Corvus corax*) and a Carrion Crow (*Corvus corone*) are presented side-by-side for a sense of relative scale and overall anatomy. The illustration is not attempting to present a process or a concept. It's a clear and literal depiction of objects.

Although rendered in the spirit of a representative illustration, this depiction of the circulatory system isn't a straightforward representation of an object. Cutaways and schematics like this one reveal details that aren't typically simultaneously visible. Layers of design decisions are required: What should be included, and what should be omitted?

In an explanatory diagram, the artist often relies on symbols to add layers of meaning. In this graphic on changes in climate, arrows and non-realistic colors help the reader see and understand invisible forces at play.

Heart

Oxygen-rich blood (*red*)

Oxygen-poor blood (*blue*)

Cool winds   Gulf stream   Rising heat   Warm winds

Image Credits: © Liz Wahid (birds); © Mesa Schumacher (circulatory system); © Emily Cooper (Gulf stream)

More to Explore

- *The Functional Art: An Introduction to Information Graphics and Visualization,* by Alberto Cairo (New Riders, 2013)
- *History of Information Graphics,* by Sandra Rendgen (Taschen, 2019)

This book is primarily concerned with the illustrated explanatory portion of the information graphics continuum. In this book, I generally use the shorthand "science graphics" or "graphics" to refer to this zone.

Data visualizations

Abstract

Although this graphic includes a few representative elements (such as the figure and clipboard), those objects are being used to help explain an abstract idea. The vignette doesn't depict an actual scenario. It's a visual metaphor that helps convey a quantum mechanics concept.

Electrical fields and magnetic fields can couple together to form electromagnetic waves, a concept depicted in this schematic. The peaks and valleys of the two fields are in sync and perpendicular. The concept—as depicted here—is not a quite a data visualization: It's a schematic representation of an equation.

In this depiction of global temperature, information (data) is completely removed from its physical context. Color represents temperature (blue is cooler, red is warmer), and position represents time (from 1850 on the left, to 2021 on the right).

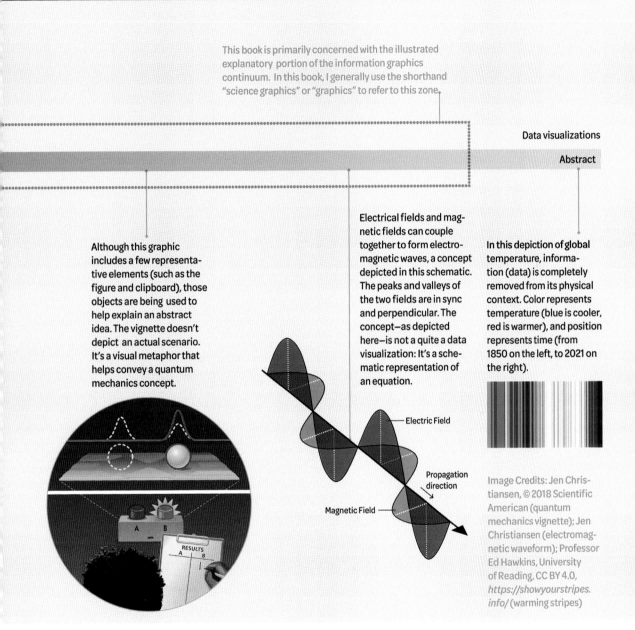

Electric Field

Propagation direction

Magnetic Field

Image Credits: Jen Christiansen, © 2018 Scientific American (quantum mechanics vignette); Jen Christiansen (electromagnetic waveform); Professor Ed Hawkins, University of Reading, CC BY 4.0, *https://showyourstripes. info/* (warming stripes)

- *Design for Information: An Introduction to the Histories, Theories, and Best Practices behind Effective Information Visualizations,* by Isabel Meirelles (Rockport Publishers, 2013)
- *Envisioning Information,* by Edward R. Tufte (Graphics Press, 1990)

CHAPTER 3
Science Communication Fundamentals

WHAT POPS TO MIND when you read the phrase "science communication"? My brain first flits back to around 1980, and memories of educational magazines, museums, and television shows. Specifically, flipping through collected copies of *Zoobooks*, gazing up at a wall of Ice Age animal skulls and a larger-than-life painting of a saber-toothed cat at the La Brea Tar Pits, and watching cinematic wildlife and space documentaries on television in my family's living room. Then my thoughts jump forward to the 2016 digital comic "A Timeline of Earth's Average Temperature"[1] by xkcd (also known as Randall Munroe), journalist-initiated COVID graphics and infection rate charts, and the 2020 social media video sensation *Antibodyody Antibody Song*[2] by Dr. Raven the Science Maven (also known as Raven Baxter).

Upon a quick read, the differences between those earlier and later associations may not seem significant—more of an indication of my age than anything else. But they also subtly reflect shifts in the broader practice of science communication over the last few decades. Public-facing "science communication" writ large in the US and UK was primarily considered to be an act of knowledge dissemination from an authoritative source (like a science institution or magazine), toward a broad and amorphous audience. More recently, a critical mass of science communication practitioners and researchers have been working toward recasting it as a conversation in the public sphere—an even exchange between many parties (not limited to scientists)—not a lecture by an institution.

That's not to say that participatory science communication efforts

1 *https://xkcd.com/1732/*
2 *https://www.youtube.com/watch?v=KBpQg6JMxSc*

didn't exist at all earlier, or that the unidirectional approach (characterized by one-way transmission of information) is now extinct. Being part of a robust museum research apprenticeship program in high school certainly engaged me as an active participant in my youth. And some researchers argue that the deficit model—a philosophy that leans on the idea that people simply don't know the facts, and that providing them with empirical evidence will impact their behavior and beliefs in a logical manner—is still alive and may work in some contexts.[3] (Although evidence shows that it's a futile form of unidirectional communication in most cases.)

Why is the state of the broader practice of science communication relevant to a book that's specifically focused on science graphics? Because it informs who is expected and encouraged to make science graphics and provides a framework for thinking about who they are for, and to what ends.

In retrospect, I can see more clearly how those variables have interacted with—and impacted—my relationship with science communication over time. My early career unfolded during a time characterized by the unidirectional model of science communication. I double majored in geology and studio art in college, then went to graduate school for science communication, in the field of natural science illustration. I refined my illustration technique skills, learned conventions of the field, and made connections in the industry. Observing things in person (drawing from life) supplemented by research was a key part of the process. I was a cheerleader for science, with laser-like focus on the content. Not the audience.

Although I was definitely trained to observe objects that I was illustrating with a critical eye, it wasn't until years later that I began to realize that I wasn't always viewing the bigger picture through that critical eye. I was working at a magazine at the time, but I didn't self-identify as a journalist. I considered myself a scientific illustrator and art director. I was working directly with scientists, using specialized skills to translate their findings into a visual language for a broader audience. Perhaps this is rooted in how I entered the field. I didn't go to journalism school. At the time, journalism school didn't feel like a good option for someone who wanted to draw about science.

---

3   Brian Trench, "Towards an Analytical Framework of Science Communication Models," in *Communicating Science in Social Contexts: New Models, New Practices,* ed. Donghong Cheng et al. (Dordrecht: Springer Netherlands, 2008)

Over time, I became more comfortable with applying a critical eye to the bigger picture, and with working as—and identifying as—a science journalist. As Teresa Carr states in an article about the role of science journalism within the science communication ecosystem: "Science journalists are beholden to their readers. Not the scientists whose work they are reporting on."[4] That entails asking tough questions, and not defaulting to science cheerleading mode. (That said, the boundary is fuzzy. Can an article written by a scientist about their own area of specialty be considered a journalistic endeavor, even if they adhere to journalistic standards? As Carr reports, there's not a consensus.)

By the early 2010s it had become clear to me that the new wave of folks entering the scene weren't contained by—or concerned with—specific roles within the structure of institutional science communication or science journalism. Magazine interns were emerging from journalism programs with data visualization and multimedia skills (not just reporting and writing chops). And scientists were routinely publishing blog posts on websites and networks hosted by news media companies.

My reaction at the time was something along the lines of: That's nice, but what's their priority, who are they beholden to, and what will they choose to ultimately pursue? Writing or illustration? Practicing science or science communication? I was being narrow-minded. After all, many folks drawn to science communication—like me—already actively resist categorization. We have at least two clear interests: For me it's one foot in science and one foot in the world of information design.

Before then, the tools of the publishing trade were expensive, and had steep learning curves. Drawing and design were just one part of the process. A whole other set of highly specific skills and bits of knowledge were needed when it came to preparing images for the printing press. I studied apprentice-style. The idea of learning desktop publishing skills and tools at the same time as juggling several other communication modes was daunting. This was reinforced and reflected by a hiring structure in the magazine world that rewarded medium specialization. Word people were reporters and editors—often with subject-matter areas of specialty—and image people were in the art department, working across all subject-matter areas.

But things are evolving. An example of those changes in journalism is *The New York Times* Climate Desk. Launched in 2017, it's a capsule team of journalists within a larger organization united by a specific

4   Teresa Carr, "Revisiting the Role of the Science Journalist," *Undark* (July 15, 2019)

subject matter (climate), not divided by mode of communication.

The landscape is also evolving beyond the world of journalism. Tools are now more varied and accessible. Fellowships and residencies are nurturing cross-disciplinary experiences and relationships. Anyone with a smartphone can push digital content out into the public arena. Online crowdfunding has become an option for garnering financial support for science communication projects that may not fit into classic funding models. The internet has made a multi-directional exchange about science more possible, at scale.[5]

My experiences as a science communicator underscore how easy it is to lose sight of the big picture when in the midst of practicing it. In this chapter, I take a step back and address science communication holistically. The frameworks that I describe in the pages that follow aren't the only guiding science communication philosophies. Nor are they mutually exclusive. My hope is that this section provides you with a general lay of the land. The practical advice for building graphics in the chapters that follow should be thought of as strategies and techniques that can be used to help you build graphics that work within broader-scale science communication frameworks, like the ones described below.

The Science of Science Communication

If you are reading this book and interested in science and science communication, you're likely invested in the idea of evidence-based decision making. So, naturally, you're looking for best practices as guided by rigorous research experiments. But the field, by many accounts, is quite young. And the variables are tremendous. I hate to break it to you, but there's not a single clear universal road map to science communication success rooted in empirical evidence.[6] [7] That said, there's still so much to be learned from the folks who are studying it. (TLDR: know your audience, treat them with respect, and tell stories.)

As a practitioner, it can be frustrating to navigate research findings

5   Monika Taddicken and Nicole Krämer, "Public Online Engagement with Science Information: On the Road to a Theoretical Framework and a Future Research Agenda," *Journal of Science Communication,* Vol. 20 (2021)

6   National Academies of Sciences, Engineering, and Medicine, *Communicating Science Effectively: A Research Agenda* (Washington, DC: The National Academies Press, 2017)

7   Sarah R Davies et al., "D1.1: Summary Report: European Science Communication Today" (QUEST, 2019) *https://questproject.eu/wp1-investigating-science-community-to-day-understanding-contemporary-practices-in-public-communication/*

to help guide decisions related to specific projects, as things depend so heavily on context. I'm hoping that this chapter, the sources cited within, discussions in subsequent chapters on uncertainty and misinformation, and the recommended readings on page 43 will be informative and useful. But perhaps I'm getting ahead of myself. Let's dive into what, exactly, science communication is.

Science communication encompasses a wide range of traditions and frameworks that vary across discipline, time, and space. At its broadest level, it generally refers to the idea of sharing information—and/or building knowledge with others—that is rooted in the practice or findings of science.[8] At a more granular level, it becomes complicated by who is—or who should be—participants in specific exchanges, the roles of the participants, and the goals of the exchanges.

The sheer number of possible combinations of those variables make it complicated to sort out clear best practices. For example, the language, style, and multimedia aids used by one scientist to communicate the results of an experiment to a peer through a research journal will be reasonably different than that used by a museum educator to communicate related information to an elementary school group, which will in turn be reasonably different from a dialogue on the same topic in a town hall setting. And each of these scenarios will be influenced by the community in which exchange takes place.

Many contemporary researchers and practitioners have been converging upon what's *not* effective, broadly speaking. Per a 2017 report by the National Academies of Sciences, Engineering, and Medicine: "A common assumption is that a lack of information or understanding of science fully explains why more people do not appear to accept scientific claims or engage in behaviors or support policies that are consistent with scientific evidence."[9] Known as the deficit model, the

---

8   Admittedly, this "practices or findings of science" framing is a bit lazy in that most likely brings to mind modern so-called "Western" scientific methodology, and excludes a history and the full breadth of science communication traditions rooted in sharing information related to technology and science-related observations outside of that model. For really interesting discussions of the topic, see Lindy Orthia and Elizabeth Rasekoala's post, "Anti-Racist Science Communication Starts with Recognising Its Globally Diverse Historical Footprint" (LSE Impact Blog; July 1, 2020) *https://blogs.lse.ac.uk/impactofsocialsciences/2020/07/01/anti-racist-science-communication-starts-with-recognising-its-globally-diverse-historical-footprint/*, and Stephanie Evergreen's post, "Decolonizing Data Viz" (Evergreen Data blog; January 6, 2021) *https://stephanieevergreen.com/decolonizing-data-viz/*

9   National Academies of Sciences, Engineering, and Medicine, *Communicating Science Effectively: A Research Agenda* (Washington, DC: The National Academies Press, 2017)

KNOWLEDGE GAP

solution under this assumption is to simply provide people with more information, in a one-way exchange. But, as the report goes on to describe, "people rarely make decisions based only on scientific information; they typically also take into account their own goals and needs, knowledge and skills, and values and beliefs."

As it turns out, adhering to the deficit model of science communication is probably not your best option—*especially* if your goal is to change people's minds—as exemplified by two projects related to vaccination behavior led by researcher Brendan Nyhan.

In a study published in 2014, Nyhan and his collaborators asked parents about intentions to have their children vaccinated for measles, mumps, and rubella (MMR). The parents then randomly received one of four interventions that either (1) corrected misinformation about vaccines, (2) presented information on disease risks, (3) used a dramatic narrative about the disease, or (4) employed visuals to make the risk of disease more tangible. Then they were asked about their intentions again.

You might expect that learning that a disease carries a higher risk than the vaccine would increase the probability of a parent having their kid vaccinated. Not so. "None of the pro-vaccine messages created by public health authorities increased intent to vaccinate with MMR."[10] (It should be said that the paper nods to a lot more nuance than that takeaway: Perhaps the construction of the educational materials themselves could've been improved. Notably, there were differences in the strength and type of reactions from parents that held different beliefs before the intervention.)

A subsequent study in 2015 on flu vaccines demonstrated that educational materials *could* help debunk the myth that the influenza vaccine can actually give people the flu. "However, the correction also significantly reduced intent to vaccinate among respondents with high levels of concern about vaccine side effects—a response that was not observed among those with low levels of concern."[11]

It's not hard to find examples of this disconnect in action today.

10   Brendan Nyhan et al., "Effective Messages in Vaccine Promotion: A Randomized Trial," *Pediatrics,* Vol. 133 (2014)

11   Brendan Nyhan and Jason Reifler, "Does Correcting Myths about the Flu Vaccine Work? An Experimental Evaluation of the Effects of Corrective Information," *Vaccine,* Vol. 33 (2015)

Despite the ever-growing proof that the available COVID-19 vaccines are effective and safe—and wide information campaigns to spread the word—many eligible folks in the US are refusing to be inoculated.

The erosion of confidence in the deficit model has occurred against a backdrop of large-scale changes in how lots of people relate to science, and how folks communicate with each other across all topics, as explored in a 2021 special issue of the *Journal of Science Communication*. In the introduction to that issue, Frank Kupper, Carolina Moreno-Castro, and Alessandra Fornetti assert that "the network of connections between science and society is becoming ever more complex, fragmented, heterogeneous and context-specific."[12] They nod to the digitalization of the public sphere, and its impact on how the public interacts with scientists and science communicators.

Some (including the authors mentioned above) write of an increasingly blurred boundary between science and society. But many view science and society as fundamentally interconnected, and have been shaping their communication efforts accordingly all along. Take African Gong, a "Pan-African Network for the Popularization of Science & Technology and Science Communication," founded in 2014. Their vision statement is "to realise a scientifically literate African citizenry driven and powered by its ownership of scientific knowledge."[13]

Elizabeth Rasekoala, president of the network, expands upon that idea in an interview by Cristina Sáez for "la Caixa" Foundation:

> *At African Gong we talk about social literacy, which is a synthesis of scientific and other types of literacy, like layers of knowledge. A person with basic scientific literacy is someone who can think critically that 'A causes B and so C.' Thus, if a politician or political party says 'No, first comes C and then A,' the person can question that message. If you are capable of equipping citizens with analytical, rational thought, you increase the country's democratic quality. And that's the link between scientific and social literacy.*[14]

Image Credit: Matteo Farinella; Originally produced for Lifeology (*lifeology.io/lifeology-univ-scicomm/*), and featured in the "What Is Science Communication?" Lifeology University SciComm Program course (*https://lifeomic.app.us.lifeology.io/viewer/lifeology/default/what-is-science-communication*). Reproduced with permission from the artist and Lifeology.

12   Frank Kupper, Carolina Moreno-Castro, and Alessandra Fornetti, "Rethinking Science Communication in a Changing Landscape," *Journal of Science Communication,* Vol. 20 (2021)

13   *https://www.africangong.org/* (accessed August 2, 2021)

14   Elizabeth Rasekoala, "Diversity Makes Science Better," The Social Observatory of the "la Caixa" Foundation, interview by Cristina Sáez (October 2019) *https://elobservatoriosocial.fundacionlacaixa.org/en/-/entrevista-elisabeth-rasekoala* (accessed August 2, 2021). Reproduced with permission from Elizabeth Rasekoala and "la Caixa" Foundation.

How do they work toward that vision? In part by empowering people through folding Indigenous knowledge systems into the practice of science communication.[15] It doesn't stop at simply considering the audience. It also reflects and actively involves everyone. As Summer May Finlay, Sujatha Raman, Elizabeth Rasekoala, Vanessa Mignan, Emily Dawson, Liz Neeley and Lindy A. Orthia assert, a respectful and level exchange of expertise between all parties should be prioritized, as opposed to an "us" to "them" flow of information:

> *...we hope to undermine models of inclusion that picture 'science commu-nicators' on one side and racialised, or otherwise-othered, 'communities' on the other. Such models risk sidelining the wealth of science communication practices occurring outside the mainstream, and can falsely characterise minoritised communities as resource poor, as if having nothing to offer, when in fact such communities produce relevant resources and are not in science or behavioural 'deficit.'*[16]

That approach is more in line with modern science communication models that emphasize *dialogue* or *participation*, as opposed to *deficien-cies*. All of these models are reflected/used to differing degrees in the mainstream science communication frameworks described below. (Note that the framework titles are, in some cases, my own charac-terizations. It is not an exhaustive, formal, or ubiquitous list.) When considering this selection of frameworks, it is important to keep in mind that—as highlighted by Finlay and co-authors—many of the concepts related to inclusivity have been authentically in play all along. As they put it (my emphasis), "Our examples show that outside the mainstream, this configuration is routine, **because communicators are working within their own communities.**"[17]

MODE-CENTRIC FRAMEWORK • The idea of a multi-directional exchange is baked into a concise definition by Massimiano Bucchi and Brian Trench, published in 2021: "science communication is the social conversation around science." They continue:

> *Two related usages of conversation are in play here: a mode of interactive*

---

15 *https://www.africangong.org/aboutus/* (accessed August 2, 2021)

16 Summer May Finlay et al., "From the Margins to the Mainstream: Deconstructing Science Communication as a White, Western Paradigm," *Journal of Science Communi-cation,* Vol. 20 (2021). Quote reproduced with permission from the authors.

17 Ibid.

communication that is set in contrast with dissemination or other hierarchical modes, and a concept that embraces all that is being said on a certain matter in society. ...The conversation we speak of is both singular—the social conversation—and plural—the dispersed conversations of communities and colleagues, including the behind-the-scenes conversations of scientists that come increasingly into public view through social networks.[18]

This framework—broken down in the table below—provides a few concrete ways to think about how science graphics can serve the social conversation around science. Some of those ways are familiar to me, like the concept of creating graphics by scientists for scientists in the context of academic journals. But it also leaves room for innovation in terms of thinking about how to create graphics that become part of larger-scale conversations and popular culture, as well as graphics that are designed to participate in specific conversations within more intimate groups of people.

Table restyled from: "Science communication as the social conversation around science," by Massimiano Bucchi and Brian Trench. In Massimiano Bucchi and Brian Trench, eds, *Routledge Handbook of Public Communication of Science and Technology*: 3rd ed. (Routledge, 2021). © 2021 by Routledge. Restyled with permission from Taylor & Francis Group.

Frameworks of the Social Conversation around Science

	Sci-Comm Applications	Aspects of Science	Public Uses	Social Perspectives	Orientation
DISSEMINATION	Deficit				Purposive, hierarchical, formal, closed
	Defense				
	Promotion	Findings: finished knowledge	Information, awareness, learning	Science literacy: scientism, technocracy	
	Popularization				
	Outreach				
DIALOGUE	Engagement	Issues: applications and implications of knowledge	Questioning, opinion, discussion	Science in society: post-normal, post-academic	
	Consultation				
	Interactivity				
	Deliberation				
PARTICIPATION	Chat	Processes: interpreting and (re-)constructing knowledge	Sharing, creating, enjoyment, critique	Society in science: civic science, citizen science	Non-purposive, participatory, informal, open
	Play				
	Co-creation				
	Film and Fiction				
	Art-Science				

18   Massimiano Bucchi and Brian Trench, "Rethinking Science Communication as the Social Conversation around Science," *Journal of Science Communication* Vol. 20 (2021). Quote reproduced with permission from the authors.

The table folds in the idea of co-creation, which lies at the very heart of many writings on truly inclusive science communication efforts.[19] Although, those writings also lead me to believe that the idea of co-creation should be prioritized across the full framework, and not relegated to the more "informal" end of the spectrum. Candidly, I'm not practiced in doing this myself. More on the topic of co-creation in the context of information design is on pages 164–165 and 304–306.

Key characteristics of the three models described by Lindy A. Orthia et al., in "Reorienting Science Communication towards Communities," *Journal of Science Communication,* Vol. 20 (2021). Image Credit: Jen Christiansen

COMMUNITY-CENTRIC FRAMEWORK • Bucchi and Trench certainly nod to the idea of conversations within communities in their work, but community orbs aren't overtly referenced in their table. Lindy A. Orthia, Merryn McKinnon, John Noel Viana, and Graham J. Walker address it head-on, with a way of thinking about the topic that can be used in tandem with other frameworks:

Community-Oriented Model Characteristics

Neighbourly Model

- Often geographically localized
- Not always a clearly identified communication partner at each end of the engagement (i.e. public events organized by a museum)
- Diffuse aim of science engagement

Problem-Solving Model

- Prioritizes practical solutions to problems
- May be initiated by either community members or external authorities
- Co-design is critical

Brokering Model

- Prioritizes the community's interests
- Initiated and implemented by people within the community
- May involve co-design
- Diffuse aim of science engagement

...we identified three models of existing community-oriented science communication, which we labelled neighbourly, problem-solving and brokering. The models complement rather than overlap familiar concepts such as one-way, dialogue or participatory science communication, any of which may be incorporated into community-oriented activities at different points. ...The primary difference between our three models is their priority: brokering science communication is primarily concerned with serving the community's interests, while neighbourly approaches tend to serve the interests of science, and problem-solving approaches prioritise practical solutions to a problem.[20]

They maintain that co-creation, relationship building, and relationship maintenance is key, and acknowledge that there isn't a clear, singular path to success.

19   Luisa Massarani and Matteo Merzagora, "Socially Inclusive Science Communication," *Journal of Science Communication,* Vol. 13 (2014)

20   Lindy A. Orthia et al., "Reorienting Science Communication towards Communities," *Journal of Science Communication,* Vol. 20 (2021). Quote reproduced with permission from the authors.

GOAL-CENTRIC FRAMEWORK • Yet another complementary framework is presented in the National Academies of Sciences, Engineering, and Medicine's research agenda on the topic.[21] This one argues that the end goal should drive the communication method. The five primary goals are (paraphrased by me):

- Share the findings and excitement of science.
- Increase appreciation for science in general, to enhance peoples' understanding of—and ability to navigate—the modern world.
- Increase knowledge and understanding of the science related to a specific issue, with an eye to personal decision making.
- Influence peoples' opinions, behavior, and policy preferences.
- Expand engagement so that a diverse set of perspectives about issues related to science and society can properly be considered when solving society-wide problems.

Clear best practices are not included, as the list of goals was presented as a prompt in 2017 for more research to help identify what communication methods best serve what goal(s).

INCLUSION-CENTRIC FRAMEWORK • Many of the frameworks above flirt with the idea of inclusivity, but it's worth stating things overtly, along with recommendations to help people work actively toward it. As Elizabeth Rasekoala put it in an interview with Stefan Skupien during the SciCOM 100 Conference in 2018:

> *The visioning...was that these issues of diversity, equity and social inclusion would also grow with the movement over time. However,...as the international science communication field/movement grew, it just seemed to carry on reinforcing a very Euro-centric and male hegemony. These issues somehow—once in a while they get discussed in conferences—in panel sessions, but are not really addressed as a mainstream drive, and are not really embedded into the consciousness of the movement.* [22]

Katherine Canfield and co-authors formalize a call for action on this front in their 2020 paper "Science Communication Demands a Critical

21   National Academies of Sciences, Engineering, and Medicine, *Communicating Science Effectively: A Research Agenda* (Washington, DC: The National Academies Press, 2017)

22   Elizabeth Rasekoala, as interviewed by Stefan Skupien in "Elizabeth Rasekoala on Science and Ownership," Sustainable Research Cooperation – A review (January 17, 2019), *https://sureco-review.net/2019/01/17/interview-elizabeth-rasakoka/* (accessed May 31, 2021). Quote reproduced with permission from Elizabeth Rasekoala.

Approach That Centers Inclusion, Equity, and Intersectionality." They center these eight points of reflection: [23]

EXCERPT FROM INTRODUCTION: We envision a fundamental shift in science communication whereby inclusion, equity, and intersectionality ground all research and practice. Eventually, we hope the term 'inclusive science communication' will be redundant. For now, however, the 'inclusive' descriptor is a valuable framing device to clarify objectives and speed this transition. To this end, we define ISC as an intentional and reflexive practice and research approach that:

- Recognizes historical oppressions, discrimination, and inequities and centers the voices, knowledge, and experiences of marginalized individuals and communities in STEMM dialogue.

- Acknowledges that each person's individual characteristics (e.g., gender, race, physical ability) overlap with one another (defined as "intersectionality" by Crenshaw, 1989) and that these intersectional identities affect their status in the world (Shimmin et al., 2017).

- Further acknowledges that explicit and implicit biases (historical, cultural, experiential) of science communication practitioners and scholars influence the design and implementation of their work (Reich et al., 2010; Dawson, 2014c).

- Rejects the oversimplifications of the deficit model (Trench, 2008; Simis et al., 2016), in which science communicators treat public audiences as lacking relevant knowledge or experience.

- Incorporates asset-based methods that respect and value the ideas, experiences, questions, and criticisms that diverse publics bring to conversations about STEMM (Banks et al., 2007).

- Aims to cultivate belonging and engagement of audience and collaborator perspectives (Wynne, 1992; Cheryan et al., 2013; Haywood and Besley, 2014; Leggett-Robinson et al., 2018).

- Offers a multi-scaled approach to shift organizational cultures and structures and redress the systemic problems of inequitable access to and engagement with STEMM (Anila, 2017; Bevan et al., 2018).

- Is relevant across formal and informal learning and engagement settings.

In summary, we urge a paradigmatic shift in science communication toward an overarching objective of expanding a sense of belonging in STEMM and approaches that embrace varied forms of expertise and ways of knowing. [23]

---

23   Katherine N. Canfield, Sunshine Menezes, Shayle B. Matsuda, Amelia Moore, Alycia N. Mosley Austin, Bryan M. Dewsbury, Mónica I. Feliú-Mójer, Katharine W. B. McDuffie, Kendall Moore, Christine A. Reich, Hollie M. Smith, and Cynthia Taylor, "Science Communication Demands a Critical Approach That Centers Inclusion, Equity, and Intersectionality," *Frontiers in Communication*, Vol. 5 (2020). Boxed excerpt is from an open-access article distributed under the terms of the Creative Commons Attribution License *https://creativecommons.org/licenses/by/4.0/* (CC BY 4.0). © 2020 Canfield, Menezes, Matsuda, Moore, Mosley Austin, Dewsbury, Feliú-Mójer, McDuffie, Moore, Reich, Smith, and Taylor.

These are not the only structured ways of thinking about science communication. And they don't necessarily dictate how strategies related to different models—like deficit, dialogue and participation—should be enacted within each structure. I present these four frameworks simply in the hopes that they'll help you (and me!) think through our collective science communication efforts more critically. And—particularly when taken together—they address many pertinent topics and open questions in the field. Looking for something more conclusive to dig your teeth into? Let's move on to a specific strategy: storytelling.

Storytelling

The last decade or so has been characterized by a resurgence in the popularity of narrative storytelling. Many folks—including data designers and scientific illustrators—have been exploring its potential, although research on its effectiveness in the service of science communication is still a work in progress.

What is narrative storytelling? As described by science communication researcher Michael Dahlstrom in 2014, "narratives follow a particular structure that describes the cause-and-effect relationships between events that take place over a particular time period that impact particular characters." [24] Liz Neeley and colleagues from The Story Collider emphasize their role as sensemaking devices. "They are means by which groups of people collectively reduce their uncertainty, resolve ambiguity, attribute consequences, and assign blame, among other things." [25] As story coach and author Lisa Cron says, "You can't change how someone thinks about something, without first changing how they feel about it." And, simply put, stories impact how people feel about things. [26]

The general consensus seems to be that thoughtfully crafted stories that feature the trajectory of a character (or characters) over time have the potential to encourage more people to care about—and connect with—topics related to science. But is that potential being realized? Some research indicates that it is, although the results are

24   Michael F. Dahlstrom, "Using Narratives and Storytelling to Communicate Science with Nonexpert Audiences," *Proceedings of the National Academy of Sciences* Vol. 111, Supplement 4 (2014)

25   Liz Neeley et al., "Linking Scholarship and Practice: Narrative and Identity in Science," *Frontiers in Communication* Vol. 5 (2020)

26   TEDx Talks, Wired for Story: Lisa Cron at TEDxFurmanU (2014) *https://www.youtube.com/watch?v=74uv0mJS0uM*

focused on very specific case studies, or are extrapolated from story-telling research that isn't necessarily limited to science communication applications. A few key evidence-supported findings on stories in general (not necessarily ones crafted specifically in service of science communication) are:

- Communications that absorb folks into a constructed world using descriptive language, characters, and a story arc are more engaging and are more likely to change people's behavior than those that do not.[27]
- This effect is particularly strong if the audience can identify or connect on some level with a character or social situation in the story.[28]
- Information is more memorable when served up in the form of a narrative story as opposed to expository forms.[29]

For more on storytelling (both narrative and expository) and design strategies for telling stories with—and about—graphics, see Chapter 11.

SciArt

If one of the strengths of stories—and their core power as a science communication strategy—lies in the ability to get people to feel things, then the same can be said of the arts more broadly. Works of art and performances[30] invite introspection and conversation. It follows that they can be used in the service of science communication.

"SciArt"[31]—as well as the addition of "A" in the classic STEM acronym, creating STEAM;[32] Science, Technology, Engineering, Art and Mathematics—are related to the idea of integrating the arts with sciences in fundamental ways. Not just as add-ons or exclusively as expository

27   Melanie C. Green and Timothy C. Brock, "The Role of Transportation in the Persuasiveness of Public Narratives," *Journal of Personality and Social Psychology,* Vol. 79 (2000)

28   This is well-cited and discussed in Liz Neeley et al., "Linking Scholarship and Practice: Narrative and Identity in Science," *Frontiers in Communication,* Vol. 5 (2020).

29   Arthur C. Graesser et al., "Advanced Outlines, Familiarity, and Text Genre on Retention of Prose," *The Journal of Experimental Education,* Vol. 48 (1980)

30   See Jamē McCray's 2017 SciVizNYC talk "Science on Stage" for more on how Superhero Clubhouse (*http://www.superheroclubhouse.org/*) uses the performing arts as a way to bridge the gap between scientific facts and the public consciousness *https://youtu.be/dmy7KHhKQHM*

31   A good entry point to the world of SciArt is *http://www.sciartinitiative.org/*

32   John Maeda, "STEM Art = STEAM," *The STEAM Journal,* Vol. 1 (2013)

communication tools. In some cases, the goal may be to infuse creative-arts thinking into the process of scientific research. For example, artist/scientist collaborations in the form of residencies. In other cases it may refer to science-inspired art. (This *can* take the form of a graphic, but also many things that are out of the scope of this book, like fashion.)

More often than not, the efforts result in visual artifacts or experiences that inform or instigate conversations about science. But the artifact shouldn't be thought of as the only act of "science communication" output. Co-creating the artwork opens up conversations between the collaborators: Those conversations are just as critical as the conversations sparked by the artwork ultimately shared with others.[33]

How do Graphics Fit in?

It's tempting to proclaim that visual languages are more universal than spoken and written languages, and that the very act of presenting information in the form of a drawing instead of words makes it more accessible. But that's not necessarily the case.[34] Visual jargon, for example, is just as prevalent as written jargon. Symbols that carry highly specific information within a specific context can be a really efficient way to communicate with others that are fluent in that visual language, like a peer group of scientists. But they simultaneously act as a brick wall to outsiders.

That said, think about how you experience a print newspaper or magazine. Do you flip through the pages first, scanning the images? What about social media? Once you start scrolling quickly down your timeline, what has the power to make you stop? Chances are, it's an image. There's generally a low initial barrier to entry when faced with an image. Color, form, and composition can trigger a reaction from the viewer without significant conscious effort. As perception researcher Colin Ware wrote, "visual media can support the perception of almost instantaneous scene gist, rapid explorations of spatial structure and relationships between objects, as well as emotions and motivations."[35]

33 Megan K. Halpern and Hannah Star Rogers, "Art–Science Collaborations, Complexities and Challenges," in Massimiano Bucchi and Brian Trench, eds., *Routledge Handbook of Public Communication of Science and Technology*, 3rd ed. (Routledge, 2021)

34 This is thoroughly explored by Neil Cohn in the context of sequential images in the book *Who Understands Comics? Questioning the Universality of Visual Language Comprehension* (Bloomsbury Academic, 2020).

35 Colin Ware, *Visual Thinking for Design*, 1st ed. (Morgan Kaufmann, Elsevier, 2008)

This ability to communicate quickly—before asking too much of the audience—is a powerful thing when vying for eyeballs. Especially if you prescribe to the idea of peoples' attention as being a limited resource. In science communication, a wide range of image types serve the purpose of engagement. Photographs, editorial illustrations, fine art, and graphics all have the potential to quickly capture the attention of people in different ways.

Under the "science communication is the social conversation around science" framework discussed earlier, each image type has a different role to play in nurturing those conversations. But to my mind, **science graphics are uniquely positioned as visual aids that have the power to both beckon folks in, *and* to provide concrete information to influence the conversations that follow.** At its best, engagement is followed by learning which then leads to continued engagement. All within the same frame.

Researchers have been chipping away at questions related to how graphics work—or don't work—in the service of science communication. But there are limitations. Many of the studies I highlight here focus on graphics that are created by scientists for an audience of their peers. Admittedly, that's a pretty narrow slice, and doesn't really speak directly to many of the points made earlier in this chapter about public-facing models and frameworks. But the results are still telling.

Several studies focus on graphical abstracts (also known as visual abstracts) from research journals. Graphical abstracts are summary figures that serve as a concise, image-driven preview of the paper. They're a handy subject. Many journals are starting to request them from paper authors, they generally adhere to a standard size (which also happens to fit well into many social media formats), and their goal is clear: Provide an easy-to-digest overview of the paper's findings to engage individuals who are scrolling through a lot of content.

According to a 2016 study by Eva-Maria Pferschy-Wenzig and colleagues, the mere presence of a graphical abstract in a paper is not associated with a higher rate of article downloads, abstract views, or total citations. (Citations are a nod in a paper to an earlier work—like many of the footnotes I use in this book—and are often used as a way to measure impact of an original article. The idea being that if a paper is cited in other papers quite a lot, it contains information notable enough to cause ripple effects in the field and impact the scholarship of others.) At least that was the case for 1,326 articles published from

March 2014 through March 2015 in the journal *Molecules*.[36]

A 2017 study by Andrew Ibrahim and colleagues paints a more complex picture. They found that social media engagement was higher with posts that included graphical abstracts, as opposed to posts about the articles that didn't include imagery. Specifically, tweets with graphical abstracts had about eight times as many impressions and retweets on Twitter, and 2.7 times as many click-throughs to the article. (Their study included 44 journal papers, and a set of graphical abstracts that were all created by a single designer—not the article authors themselves—using a consistent aesthetic.)[37]

Sandra Oska and colleagues built on this study by introducing another variable: posts on Twitter that included a figure from the paper other than the graphical abstract. Tweets that contained a graphical abstract had more than twice as many views as both citation-only tweets and non-abstract figure tweets, five times the engagements of citation-only tweets and more than 3.5 times the engagements of non-abstract figure tweets.[38]

What can we glean from that series of studies? Graphical abstracts don't necessarily boost engagement by simply existing. A strategy for using those graphics is also critical.

What about the impact of graphics on the perception of quality? Karen Cheng, Yeechi Chen, Kevin Larson, and Marco Rolandi investigated how graphical abstracts influenced reader impressions of the research paper and the authors that wrote it. They identified existing graphical abstracts that didn't adhere to design best-practices (in terms of making the best use of color, contrast, composition, and scale to boost legibility), gave them makeovers, and conducted a survey to see how people reacted to them. They found that the made-over graphical abstracts had a positive impact. The associated paper was perceived as "more interesting, more clearly written and more scientifically rigorous."[39]

36   Eva-Maria Pferschy-Wenzig et al., "Does a Graphical Abstract Bring More Visibility to Your Paper?" *Molecules,* Vol. 21 (2016)

37   Andrew M. Ibrahim et al., "Visual Abstracts to Disseminate Research on Social Media: A Prospective, Case-Control Crossover Study," *Annals of Surgery,* Vol. 266 (2017)

38   Sandra Oska et al., "A Picture Is Worth a Thousand Views: A Triple Crossover Trial of Visual Abstracts to Examine Their Impact on Research Dissemination," *Journal of Medical Internet Research,* Vol. 22 (2020)

39   Karen Cheng et al., "Proving the Value of Visual Design in Scientific Communication," *Information Design Journal,* Vol. 23 (2017)

Here's an example of one of the graphical abstracts, before the redesign:

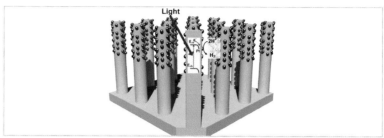

Here's the redesigned graphical abstract, for the same article:

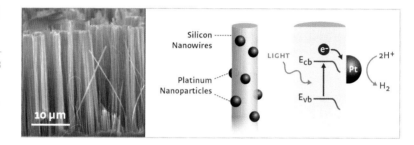

And here are results rooted in all 10 original and 10 redesigned graphical abstracts, according to 50 survey participants.

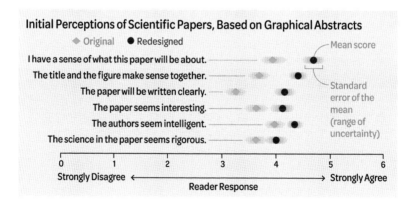

Although the presence of a graphical abstract in a paper isn't associated with higher citation rates (per the study discussed above), it seems that another measure related to graphics is. In a 2018 study, Po-shen Lee, Jevin D. West, and Bill Howe used computer vision and machine learning to count and classify nearly 7 million figures from 494,663 biomedical and life science research papers in the PubMed Central archive. They found that highly cited papers tend to have a larger number of diagrams and schematics per page than less-cited papers (by a greater measure than photographs, data visualizations, and tables). Although they didn't test for *why* that might be the case, they proposed a few possible explanations. Perhaps "visual information improves clarity of the paper, leading to more citations and higher impact, or that high-impact papers naturally tend to include new, complex ideas that require visual explanation."[40]

Large-scale studies like this one are possible in part due to the sharply focused and common primary goal of research papers—conveying experimental results to other researchers. They are also possible due to well-established traditions in scholarly scientific publishing—including routine use of citations—which provide a measure of the paper authors' success in their goal of reaching and influencing other researchers. I think it's fair to say that things get more complex when you step away from the clearly defined framework of the world of research journals. More complex, but not impossible.

The studies above highlight how science graphics can boost engagement and influence perceptions of the research and its authors. Tracie Curry and Ellen Lopez demonstrate how images can also provide context. They investigated the impact of including context-rich images—in this case, graphics and other visuals that reflected local and Indigenous knowledge—in reports designed for consideration by public sector resource management practitioners.

Their pilot study, conducted in collaboration with the Native Village of Wainwright (traditionally Ulʼguniq), focused on adaptation to climate change in northern Alaska. Interviews with environmental management agency employees made it clear that administrators would likely prefer summary images or tables over text-heavy documents, "due to time constraints." Curry and Lopez subsequently built three versions of a two-page informational report:

A. Standard with text that summarizes knowledge from the natural sciences, along with a few conventional graphics, including a sea ice extent timeline, and a pair of maps.

B. Same content as report A, with the addition of quotes from local residents.

C. Same content as report B, with the addition of context-rich images.

---

40 Po-Shen Lee, Jevin D. West, and Bill Howe, "Viziometrics: Analyzing Visual Information in the Scientific Literature," *IEEE Transactions on Big Data* Vol. 4 (2018)

The survey participants rated the reports that included quotes (B) and context-rich imagery (C) equally or more credible than reports that did not (A). Interviews with the study participants revealed some hesitations about the idea of including "context-rich" graphical content, as it was a bit outside of the norm within their agency. But they also acknowledged that ultimately the additional imagery and quotes helped underscore "the societal relevance of the science and [helped] readers understand what environmental conditions mean to people who live and work in the Arctic."[41]

Graphics allow for quantitative and qualitative presentation in a single image. And, as in the case of the figure shown here, they can provide context by presenting information in a way that nods to perspectives that may not otherwise be suitably represented in the text.

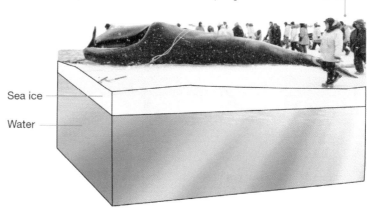

"Sea ice thickness and whaling. A minimum 3–4 feet of ice thickness is needed to support the weight of a whale." As published in "Images as Information: Context-Rich Images and the Communication of Place-Based Information Through Increased Representation in Environmental Governance," by Tracie Curry and Ellen D. S. Lopez, *Frontiers in Communication,* Vol. 5 (2020); Image reproduced without modification per CC BY 4.0 license (*https://creativecommons.org/licenses/by/4.0/*)

• • •

I SHOULD ADMIT that I'm a bit conflicted about how, exactly, science graphics fit in moving forward. The mainstream science communication mindset has clearly been shifting away from one-way communication with the public, and toward approaches centered on conversation, collaboration, and interaction. (Although I should be clear, the practice of

---

41 Tracie Curry and Ellen D. S. Lopez, "Images as Information: Context-Rich Images and the Communication of Place-Based Information Through Increased Representation in Environmental Governance," *Frontiers in Communication,* Vol. 5 (2020)

science itself has long been a conversation between scientists, in which researchers build on each others' work, document and repeat compelling observations by replicating experiments, and challenge each other with counter-arguments.) But what does that mean for static imagery that is often designed to be handed over to an audience, and digested in solitude (presentation aids and public exhibits notwithstanding)? Perhaps the answer lies in thinking of these sorts of static graphics as engaging and digestible content to help inform and spark conversations. Or perhaps they serve to document the conversations.[42] Or—more in line with what lies at the heart of the paradigm shift—it's time to grapple with how to flip things so that conversation, collaboration, and interaction with the intended audience can inform the graphic. Many folks are already doing this work. I'm still struggling with figuring out how to apply those lessons in a sustainable and meaningful way in the context of my own workflow and deadline schedules.

More to Explore

- *Getting to the Heart of Science Communication: A Guide to Effective Engagement,* by Faith Kearns (Island Press, 2021)
- *Routledge Handbook of Public Communication of Science and Technology,* Third Edition, edited by Massimiano Bucchi and Brian Trench (Routledge, 2021)
- *Communicating Science Effectively: A Research Agenda,* by National Academies of Sciences, Engineering, and Medicine (The National Academies Press, 2017)
- *Equity, Exclusion and Everyday Science Learning: The Experiences of Minoritised Groups,* by Emily Dawson (Routledge, 2020)
- **The Open Notebook:** The story behind the best science stories *https://www.theopennotebook.com/*
- **Lifeology University SciComm Program:** Free series of online flashcard courses, *https://lifeology.io/lifeology-univ-scicomm/*
- *A Tactical Guide to Science Journalism: Lessons From the Front Lines,* edited by Deborah Blum, Ashley Smart, and Tom Zeller Jr., (Oxford University Press, 2022)

---

42 Compelling meta-nods to the idea of documenting the conversation as a science communication tool include *The Dialogues: Conversations about the Nature of the Universe,* by Clifford V. Johnson (MIT Press, 2017), and *Equity, Exclusion and Everyday Science Learning* (Zine Edition) by Emily Dawson and Sophie Wang (*https://equityandeverydayscience.wordpress.com/zine*).

CHAPTER 4

Graphic Design Fundamentals

CHANCES ARE, AT SOME POINT IN SCHOOL—regardless of your ultimate educational or professional trajectory—you were formally taught writing fundamentals. Grammar, sentence structure, and different types of essays (including argumentative and narrative) are taught in American schools, and reinforced across many disciplines. That's not to say that you follow those rules strictly in all cases. (Shoot, as a fan of incomplete sentences, I break the rules a lot. Even in this book.) And many of those rules are contextual and continue to evolve. Think about how the rhythm of character-limited social media posts differ in style and tone from other short text forms. But in general, I'm guessing that you're aware of at least one set of formal writing fundamentals, and that you intentionally choose between different sets of writing guidelines—or consciously break them entirely—in different contexts.

I think it's safe to say that it's less common to formally learn graphic design fundamentals in school. And it's even rarer to have those guidelines reinforced across disciplines. Many folks aren't schooled in any system of design principles, much less more than one system. Chapters 4 through 9 aim to help fill that gap, for folks new to the topic.

Pause when you see a graphic that you particularly like, or don't like. Do you like it because it's easy to navigate? What about the image makes it easy to navigate? Do you find that it takes more energy to figure it out than you'd like to expend? Why do you think that is? Are there small changes in layout or color that might make it less complicated to figure out, or that might make it more accessible to more people? Does the design of the graphic resonate with its subject matter? Are there multiple ways in which the graphic can be interpreted? If so, does that seem like a feature or a bug?

Use that information to directly inform your own graphics. Is your image hard for other people to read? Perhaps you need a structure that helps make the flow of information more obvious. The details that follow can help you figure out how.[1]

For more context in terms of history and theory, I recommend the book *Graphesis*.[2] In it, Johanna Drucker presents a summary of the concept of graphic design—with a focus on work connected to Europe, Russia, and the United States—as a visual language of sorts, from the late 19th century to today. (Graphic design being distinct from the pictorial arts, which were rooted in representational forms.) She includes a discussion of the sharp rise in popularity of "visual abstraction as a formal system" in the early 20th century, along with a wave of formalized principles.

Many of the theoretical texts at this time had strong ties to the Bauhaus (a design movement spawned by a German school of the arts founded in 1919). The function-centric Swiss design movement followed (also with strong ties to the Bauhaus), with its grid-based organizational structure. Many of the principles that are held up as "best-practices" in American and European graphic design today are connected to these movements. Most notably, the idea that "form follows function," and pedagogical experiments related to practical unification of the arts, crafts, and manufacturing.

This book (*Building Science Graphics*) steps into the same territory as other recent instructional texts that Drucker squarely critiques as "gloss[ing over] their structural roots and formalist assumptions in favor of providing basic tools for production."[3] But I'm a practitioner[4] hoping to pass along concrete guidance to folks who may be unfamiliar with widely used design fundamentals. I can't imagine writing a book on the topic without summarizing conventions with regards to size, color, scale, and composition that are rooted in that Bauhaus-centric

The *NASA Graphics Standards Manual* designed by Richard Danne and Bruce Blackburn exemplifies the modernist vibe and philosophy of the Swiss design movement. (These pages are from the 1976 version.)

---

1   For a more expansive look at these topics—with lots of information graphics examples— see Connie Malamed's book *Visual Language for Designers: Principles for Creating Graphics That People Understand* (Rockport Publishers, 2009), Isabel Meirelles' book *Design for Information* (Rockport Publishers, 2013), and Edward R. Tufte's *Envisioning Information* (Graphics Press, 1990).

2   Johanna Drucker, *Graphesis: Visual Forms of Knowledge Production* (Harvard University Press, 2014)

3   Ibid.

4   Full disclosure: My classroom arts learning skewed toward studio classes: painting, illustration, and photography. So I didn't formally learn graphic design theory in depth— or the history of graphic design—in school.

history. Because, as Drucker goes on to write in *Graphesis*, "Somewhat tempered by issues of ethics, political and social conscience in design, and cultural studies approaches to analysis, the tenets of Gestalt psychology, semiotics, and formal composition remain standard elements of design practice, still applicable to contemporary work."

Herein lies the conundrum. As published in the book *Extra Bold*, "Eurocentric principles of modern design were conceived as egalitarian tools of social progress, yet they served to suppress differences among people across the globe."[5] **How can I resolve the tension between wanting to share design tips that are woven into the fabric of design education in America and Europe, without implying that it is the only system of design?**

The principles in the chapters that follow have served me well in the formal presentation of science graphics to broad American and European audiences, and are also well-suited to the current style of scientific journals. However, there are other design philosophies and histories that can provide guidance and inspiration, and may be better aligned with your goals and audience. It's important to be aware of several things:

- Many of the principles I present are representative of a particular trajectory rooted in so-called "western" graphic design.
- Some of these principles also have roots in non-European histories. (For example, the "golden ratio" concept associated with math-based composition grids popularized by the 1950s Swiss Design movement are often thought of as being traced back to ancient Greece. But, as graphic design scholar Audrey Bennett writes, there are several lines of evidence that suggest stronger ties to Africa.[6])
- There's an active, ongoing conversation about the need for scholars and practitioners to look beyond the Bauhaus for inspiration and guidance. (For example, Silas Munro and Ramon Tejada assert that "it is high time for a rethinking and remaking of the academic design studio into a 21st-century model. We are particularly interested in interrogating the colonial lineages of 20th-century formal aesthetics and structures for making." They prompted workshop attendees to make/design "from a personal place that

5   Ellen Lupton et al., *Extra Bold: A Feminist, Inclusive, Anti-Racist, Nonbinary Field Guide for Graphic Designers* (Princeton Architectural Press, 2021)

6   Audrey Bennett, "Follow the Golden Ratio from Africa to the Bauhaus for a Cross-Cultural Aesthetic for Images," *Critical Interventions,* Vol. 6 (January 1, 2012), and Audrey G. Bennett, "The African Roots of Swiss Design," *The Conversation* (March 16, 2021)

engages and tells stories—that forms can inherit unconventional ways for designers and people to share, inform, and live." [7])

For more about that conversation, check out these resources:

- ***Scratching the Surface*, episode 183:** Dori Tunstall, dean of design at Ontario College of Art and Design, talks with podcast host Jarrett Fuller about anthropology, design, sharing knowledge, and the work of decolonizing design programs. [8]
- ***Decolonizing Design Reader*** (initiated by Ramon Tejada): There are a few versions of this organic collection of resources. The living, collaborative project is currently online as a Google Document. A pdf version of the list captured at a moment in time also exists, accessible through Tejada's website. [9] For more context, and a direct link to the open document, see "Disrupting Design with Capital 'D,'" an interview with Ramon Tejada by Luana de Almeida. [10]
- ***Extra Bold: A Feminist, Inclusive, Anti-Racist, Nonbinary Field Guide for Graphic Designers*** (by Ellen Lupton, Farah Kafei, Jennifer Tobias, Josh A. Hallstead, Kaleena Sales, Leslie Xia, and Valentina Vergara.) [11]
- **BIPOC Design History:** A series of BIPOC-centered design courses—with classes including queer Blackness, the rise of hip hop's graphic language, urgent protest graphics of Black Lives Matter movement, and the 21st century data activism of the collective Data for Black Lives—facilitated by Polymode East. [12]

That's all to say that all of the principles I outline in the chapters that follow are not necessarily universal. But they are incredibly useful. Being aware of these concepts will help you be a more thoughtful and

7   From the description of the "It's Time to Throw the Bauhaus Under the Bus" workshop, presented by Letterform Archive, *https://www.typeroom.eu/content/letterform -archive-presents-it-s-time-throw-bauhaus-under-bus-workshop* (post dated September 19, 2019; accessed April 27, 2022)

8   *https://scratchingthesurface.fm/183-dori-tunstall* (released April 14, 2021)

9   *https://ramongd.net/*

10   Luana de Almeida, "Disrupting Design with Capital 'D,'" *Futuress* (February 24, 2021) *https://futuress.org/magazine/disrupting-design-with-capital-d/*

11   Ellen Lupton et al., *Extra Bold: A Feminist, Inclusive, Anti-Racist, Nonbinary Field Guide for Graphic Designers* (Princeton Architectural Press, 2021)

12   *https://bipocdesignhistory.com/* (A related book—*Black Design in America*—is expected to be published by Princeton University Press in 2023.)

intentional designer of graphics that connect with people. As Audrey G. Bennett writes in the introduction to *Design Studies: Theory and Research in Graphic Design*, "Traditionally graphic design theory has privileged intuition and creativity over empirical research." But, she goes on to write,

> *It can be argued that the art-based principles of graphic design—including (but not limited to) contrast, hierarchy, repetition, alignment, and color— are in fact theories proven through a long history of successful experimentation in practice. Indeed, graphic designers—through professional practice—have tested and retested to the point where it makes sense to refer to these theories as laws or principles.*[13]

So, if the field is to move forward in a productive way, especially when it comes to communicating with heterogeneous audiences, Bennett argues that more designers need to intentionally engage in a research-oriented practice.

Let's return to Edward Tufte's proclamation that "graphical excellence is that which gives to the viewer the greatest number of ideas in the shortest time with the least ink in the smallest space."[14] Is that true? And if it is true in one context, is it true in another? Thankfully, research scientists are steadily chipping away at these sorts of questions. This leads me to the next chapter: What—broadly—can designers learn from the field of cognitive neuroscience?

More to Explore

- *Graphesis: Visual Forms of Knowledge Production,* by Johanna Drucker (Harvard University Press, 2014)
- *Design Studies: Theory and Research in Graphic Design,* edited by Audrey Bennett (Princeton Architectural Press, 2006)
- *Graphic Design: The New Basics,* 2nd edition, by Ellen Lupton and Jennifer Cole Phillips (Princeton Architectural Press, 2015)
- *Design Justice: Community-Led Practices to Build the Worlds We Need,* by Sasha Costanza-Chock (MIT Press, 2020)
- *Data Feminism,* by Catherine D'Ignazio and Lauren F. Klein (MIT Press, 2020)

13   Audrey G. Bennett, "The Rise of Research in Graphic Design," in *Design Studies: Theory and Research in Graphic Design* (Princeton Architectural Press, 2006). Quote reproduced with permission from Princeton Architectural Press; permission conveyed through Copyright Clearance Center, Inc.

14   Edward R. Tufte, *The Visual Display of Quantitative Information* (Graphics Press, 1983)

CHAPTER 5

Perception Science

WHEN I WAS A STUDENT making decisions about pursuing research science or visual science communication, it didn't occur to me that there was another way to integrate those two interests. Some folks—like me—make images about science. Other folks—like some perception researchers—conduct studies that test how different visuals impact how we understand, remember, and reason with information.

The science of how we see—and more to the point for our purposes, how we make sense of what we see—is an active area of research. Sadly, there's a practitioner-researcher gap. Lots of designers are familiar with classic works, like the Gestalt findings (for more on this, see page 62). But keeping abreast of the latest vision and perception research isn't always a priority in the day-to-day deadline scramble. And academic researchers aren't always in tune with the questions that practicing designers are most interested in having answered.[1] For those reasons, I love the sentiments of Audrey G. Bennett (see page 49) and Sheila Pontis (see page 231) with regards to encouraging designers to embrace a research-oriented practice. Keeping up with academic literature on the topic is useful, but it's also important to carve out time to test the success of our own projects.

This chapter is an introduction to some perception research findings that are particularly relevant to information designers, followed by a list of recommended readings, conferences and podcasts.

---

1   Cognitive scientist Steve Franconeri and I had a conversation about this at the 2021 IEEEVIS conference VisComm workshop moderated by Jonathan Schwabish. A recording is available as PolicyViz Podcast episode 205 (published November 16, 2021). *https://policyviz.com/podcast/episode-205-steve-franconeri-and-jen-christiansen-a-viscomm-workshop/*

Vision versus Perception

The basic science of **vision**, centered on light entering the eye, and signals traveling to the brain via the optic nerve, may be familiar to you.

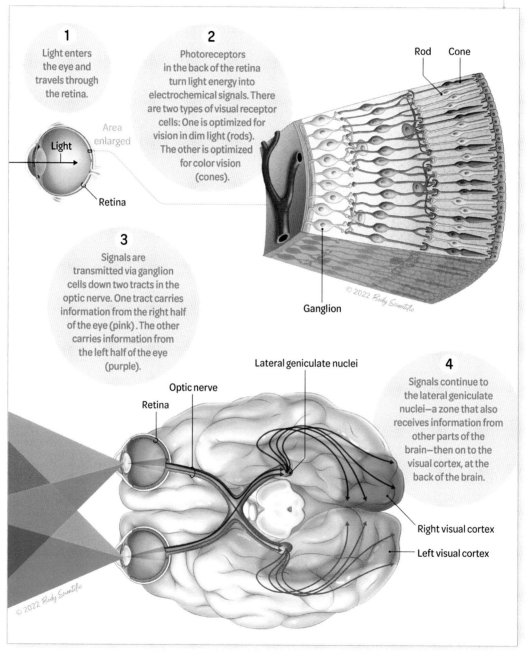

1 Light enters the eye and travels through the retina.

2 Photoreceptors in the back of the retina turn light energy into electrochemical signals. There are two types of visual receptor cells: One is optimized for vision in dim light (rods). The other is optimized for color vision (cones).

Light

Area enlarged

Retina

Rod   Cone

Ganglion

3 Signals are transmitted via ganglion cells down two tracts in the optic nerve. One tract carries information from the right half of the eye (pink). The other carries information from the left half of the eye (purple).

Lateral geniculate nuclei

Optic nerve

Retina

4 Signals continue to the lateral geniculate nuclei—a zone that also receives information from other parts of the brain—then on to the visual cortex, at the back of the brain.

Right visual cortex

Left visual cortex

© 2022 Body Scientific

How we make sense of what we see—also known as the science of visual **perception** (a sub-field of cognitive neuroscience)—is generally less familiar to folks than the physiology of seeing. Let's pick things up where step 4 in the graphic on page 52 leaves off. The leading view is that visual function continues from the visual cortex along two general processing streams, with some signalling overlap. (This was first described by scientists Leslie G. Ungerleider and Mortimer Mishkin in 1982).

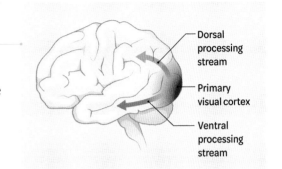

Dorsal processing stream

Primary visual cortex

Ventral processing stream

But not all cognitive scientists agree on the best way to characterize those two streams. Ungerleider and Mishkin's initial framework described the ventral (lower) stream as being characterized by processes that help answer the question "What?" This includes functions related to features and identity. The dorsal (upper) stream was characterized by processes that help answer the question "Where?" Subsequent studies sharpened focus on the variables being processed, as opposed to the category of question that they help to answer. In this view, the ventral (lower) stream is concerned with form and color. The dorsal (upper) stream is concerned with motion. But it has since been shown that each stream processes both types of information. Yet there *are* key differences between the two streams, including size and processing speed.

As George Mather writes in *Foundations of Sensation and Perception*, building evidence suggests that the "two streams are not strictly segregated modules dedicated to processing separate stimulus attributes. They may specialize in different tasks (action guidance, shape analysis, and so on), rather than in attribute processing."[2]

And it's likely not as hierarchical and unidirectional as the brain diagram above suggests. The model shown here emphasizes a "bottom-up" view, in which perception is driven by sensory inputs: It implies that the object you're looking at initiates a sequential domino effect that ultimately leads to object recognition. It does not directly address the "top-down" forces also in play, in which previous experiences help shape the interpretation of new sensory inputs.

The brain diagram above is one way of representing the bottom-up

2   George Mather, *Foundations of Sensation and Perception*, 3rd ed. (Psychology Press, 2016)

signalling pathways. Those bottom-up singalling pathways are also represented here, collapsed into red arrows in the graphic below. Some researchers prefer to think of things as a more dynamic, multi-directional network model, in part because sweeping unidirectional arrows on brains don't properly address the idea that many things are happening simultaneously. For example, as Michael W. Eysenck and

Origins of Perception

The classical view of perception (*blue panel*) holds that it is a direct window onto an external reality. Sensory signals flow from the bottom up, entering the brain through receptors in our eyes, ears, nose, tongue and skin to reveal the outside world to us as it is. Top-down signals within the brain serve only to finesse what is perceived. In the prediction machine view of perception (*green panel*), in contrast, perceptual content is carried by top-down predictions made by the brain based on prior experience. Bottom-up signals function mainly to convey prediction errors, which rein in the brain's hypotheses. Perception is thus a controlled hallucination in this model.

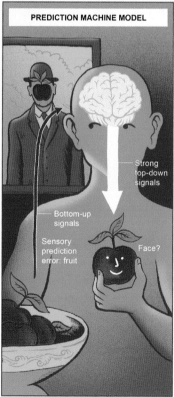

Mark T. Keane write (with a nod to the work of neurobioloist Semir Zeki), "a green object may be a car, a sheet of paper or a leaf, and a car can be red, black or green. Thus, we often need to process all of an object's attributes for accurate perception."[3]

Why am I presenting this information? To demonstrate that **perception involves a bunch of discrete parts of the brain that specialize in processing different types of incoming signals from the retina.** David H. Hubel and Torsten N. Wiesel received a Nobel Prize in 1981 for their work from a few decades earlier that helped establish this concept. Previously it was widely thought that the back of the brain acted more like a screen, receiving signals from the retina like a movie projection. Hubel and Wiesel demonstrated that the information is processed in columns of cells in the primary visual cortex, with each column corresponding to a tiny area of the retina.[4] **The cells in each of those columns extract some simple information about the image in that part of the retina and pass it on to other regions of the brain to build increasingly complex and complete representations of what we see. That concept can help inform how to build graphics in a way that can be more easily perceived and interpreted.**

Image Credit: Modified from a figure published in *Information Visualization: Perception for Design*, 4th ed., by Colin Ware (Morgan Kaufmann, Elsevier, 2020) © 2021—with permission from Elsevier.

Here's an example of this idea in practice, from the book *Information Visualization*, by Colin Ware. Some notations are easier to read than others. Ware explains, "lines that connect the various components, for example, are a notation that is easy to read, because the visual cortex of the brain contains mechanisms specifically designed to seek out continuous contours."[5] Other notations, such as the use of discrete symbols, are harder to parse.

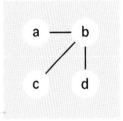

Attention

Many of the design principles that follow are related to the idea of making it as easy as possible for a reader to make sense of your graphic. In most cases, it's likely that you'll want the audience to pay attention to the *information* that you're presenting as opposed to being preoccupied

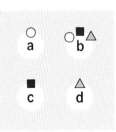

3   Michael W. Eysenck and Mark T. Keane, *Cognitive Psychology: A Student's Handbook*, 8th edition (Psychology Press, 2020)

4   Nobel Prize Outreach (October 9, 1981) *https://www.nobelprize.org/prizes/medicine/1981/press-release/*

5   Colin Ware, *Information Visualization: Perception for Design*, 4th ed. (Morgan Kaufmann, Elsevier, 2019)

with cutting through distractions or trying to figure out how to navigate through or translate the visual cues that you're using. The concept of visual working memory helps explain why there's a trade-off: We have a limited capacity for making sense of novel sensory inputs on the fly.

Long-term memory holds things we have already learned. We rely on working memory—and short-term memory[6]—to learn a new task. Critically, working memory is limited. (Some of that information may ultimately be established in long-term memory.) It follows that effective and efficient instruction aims to use working memory strategically, by guiding attention to focus on the learning task at hand.[7]

Some research suggests that working memory limitations are object-specific. For example, in a study published in 2001, Edward K. Vogel, Geoffrey F. Woodman, and Steven J. Luck hypothesized that the number of objects that can be stored in working memory are feature-independent. (Feature variables included color and orientation.) They conducted a set of 16 experiments in which images of a set of symbols or objects were presented in sequence. Study participants indicated if the second image was identical or different from the first.

The memory test results supported their hypothesis: Only about four simple objects or items were retained from image to image and identified correctly in sequence. But, "participants could retain multifeature objects in WM [working memory] just as easily as single-feature objects, allowing as many as 16 features to be retained when distributed across four objects."[8]

It's tempting to jump on this as evidence that generally supports Tufte's concept that "graphical excellence is that which gives to the viewer the greatest number of ideas in the shortest time with the least ink in the smallest space."[9] After all, it seems pretty efficient to encode one object with several meanings, right?

---

6   "Working memory has been conceived and defined in three different, slightly discrepant ways: as short-term memory applied to cognitive tasks, as a multi-component system that holds and manipulates information in short-term memory, and as the use of attention to manage short-term memory." —Nelson Cowan, "What Are the Differences between Long-Term, Short-Term, and Working Memory?" *Progress in Brain Research*, Vol. 169 (2008)

7   John Sweller, "Cognitive Load Theory," in *Encyclopedia of the Sciences of Learning*, ed. Norbert M. Seel (Springer US, 2012)

8   Edward K. Vogel, Geoffrey F. Woodman, and Steven J. Luck, "Storage of Features, Conjunctions, and Objects in Visual Working Memory," *Journal of Experimental Psychology: Human Perception and Performance*, Vol. 27 (2001)

9   Edward R. Tufte, *The Visual Display of Quantitative Information* (Graphics Press, 1983)

Not so fast. More recent research contradicts that finding. An experiment published in 2004 by G.A. Alvarez and P. Cavanagh demonstrated that as the information load of objects went up, the number of objects held in memory went down. Study participants remembered more of some objects (including colored squares) than of other objects (including Chinese characters and polygons), suggesting that "there is a trade-off between the complexity of the objects and the total number of objects that can be stored in memory."[10] (The authors nod to critical differences in methodology, and differing levels in the complexity of objects as possible reasons for the contradictory results.)

Steve Haroz and David Whitney showed that these capacity limits directly impact the effectiveness of information visualizations, especially with regards to the ability to detect unexpected information within two layout configurations. They tested peoples' abilities to: detect a unique and known target (find the red object); detect an unknown target (find the oddball object); and determine the number of categories present. One configuration grouped like objects together. The other configuration had a random arrangement. Their three primary conclusions: "(1) Grouping is far more beneficial for oddball search compared with known-target search. (2) Accessing overall information (like heterogeneity or number of categories) is better for grouped displays. (3) For difficult tasks, aim to reduce variety in the entire view rather than optimizing small regions."[11]

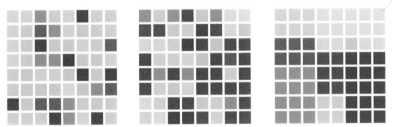

Original Caption: "These images each have one colored square that is unique within that image. How long does it take you to find each? How many color categories are there in each panel? Why does grouping make both tasks substantially easier?" Image Credit: © 2012 IEEE. Reprinted, with permission, from "How Capacity Limits of Attention Influence Information Visualization Effectiveness," by Steve Haroz and David Whitney, *IEEE Transactions on Visualization and Computer Graphics*, Vol. 18 (December 2012)

How might that knowledge play out in a graphic designed to convey information, as opposed to a graphic designed for perception tests? Here's an example of the same information, presented in two different

10   G.A. Alvarez and P. Cavanagh, "The Capacity of Visual Short-Term Memory Is Set Both by Visual Information Load and by Number of Objects," *Psychological Science,* Vol. 15 (February 1, 2004)

11   Steve Haroz and David Whitney, "How Capacity Limits of Attention Influence Information Visualization Effectiveness," *IEEE Transactions on Visualization and Computer Graphics,* Vol. 18 (December 2012)

ways. Which of these two panels allows you to more easily assess the relative proportion of cells over time?

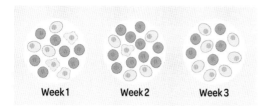

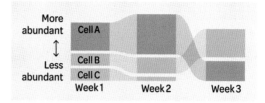

I'm betting it's the one on the right. Likes are grouped, quantities are ordered, and connecting lines help guide attention.

We should also keep in mind that different graphics have different goals, and therefore these findings don't provide a recipe for design success in all situations. For example, extrapolating from working memory research, you could surmise that decorative details or complex and novel encodings may not be beneficial. Why weigh down attention with superfluous marks? Well, they may be worth it, if your goal is to create a graphic that lingers in your audience's mind, or that they can recall as having seen before.

Michelle Borkin and her colleagues conducted an experiment in which participants were presented with a sequence of visualizations, and were asked to press a button when they encountered an image they had seen earlier in the sequence. The results showed that visualizations that contained pictograms (photographs, cartoons, or symbols of recognizable objects) were recalled more readily than those that did not, more colorful images were recalled more readily than less colorful ones, unique forms were recalled more readily than standard forms, and that "visualizations with low data-to-ink ratios and high visual densities (i.e., more chart junk and 'clutter') were recalled more readily than minimal, 'clean' visualizations."[12] The authors make it clear that reader comprehension was not measured: Visualizations were present-ed briefly as images to be seen, not properly read.

More to Explore

For more information about the basics of how we see and perceive things, as well as a window into the latest research:

12   Michelle A. Borkin et al., "What Makes a Visualization Memorable?," *IEEE Transactions on Visualization and Computer Graphics*, Vol. 19 (December 2013)

- *Cognitive Psychology: A Student's Handbook,* 8th edition, edited by Michael W. Eysenck and Mark T. Keane (Psychology Press, 2020): This textbook folds in many of the newer findings that older texts don't cover, citing papers copiously, but maintaining readability.
- *Information Visualization: Perception for Design,* 4th edition, by Colin Ware (Morgan Kaufmann, Elsevier, 2019): A super and comprehensive reference about "what the science of perception can tell us about visualization."

For more on the topic, with an emphasis on data visualization:

- **"The Science of Visual Data Communication: What Works,"** by Steven L. Franconeri, Lace M. Padilla, Priti Shah, Jeffrey M. Zacks, and Jessica Hullman, *Psychological Science in the Public Interest* (December 15, 2021): A comprehensive report that "presents research-backed guidelines for creating powerful and intuitive visualizations oriented toward communicating data to students, coworkers, and the general public."
- **"39 Studies about Human Perception in 30 Minutes,"** by Kennedy Elliott: A written version of talk presented at OpenVisConf in April 2016 (Medium blog post published May 2, 2016), *https://medium.com/@kennelliott/39-studies-about-human-perception-in-30-minutes-4728f9e31a73*
- **Multiple Views,** "A blog about visualization research, for anyone, by the people who do it," edited by Jessica Hullman, Danielle Szafir, Robert Kosara, and Enrico Bertini, *https://medium.com/multiple-views-visualization-research-explained*
- Interviews with perception researchers on the **Data Stories** podcast, hosted by practitioner Moritz Stefaner and researcher Enrico Bertini (*https://datastori.es/*), and the **PolicyViz Podcast,** hosted by Jonathan Schwabish, *https://policyviz.com/podcast/*

Selected conferences that include sessions that aim to bridge the practitioner-researcher gap:

- **IEEE VIS conference:** The Premier Forum for Advances in Visualization and Visual Analytics, *http://ieeevis.org/*
- **Gordon Research Conference on Visualization in Science and Education,** *https://www.grc.org/visualization-in-science-and-education-conference/*
- **Information+:** Interdisciplinary Practices in Information Design & Visualization, *https://informationplusconference.com/*

CHAPTER 6

Making Sense of Visual Complexity

I'M SIMULTANEOUSLY ENTRANCED WITH and somewhat befuddled by the simple lines, patterns, and flat shapes that dutifully make an appearance in information design books like this one. It's pretty much required that I include a discussion of visual Gestalt principles from decades ago, and present Jacques Bertin's visual variables. But it can all feel so academic. It's sometimes hard to see how small panels that present idealized variations of single design variables can inform how to build multi-part graphics that aim to convey complex stories.

After all, more often than not, scientific content is complex. Most of the design and editing strategies in this book aim to guide you toward helping your audience make sense of complexity. Your first instinct may be to simplify the information in order to make it more broadly accessible. Yet simplification may erase the latest key finding, distilling things in a way that doesn't honor the cool new discovery you're trying to highlight. In general, I find it more productive to focus on clarifying, not simplifying (with a nod to designer Nigel Holmes, Alberto Cairo,[1] and many others who have spoken and written about this idea).

So why, then, are there so many examples of the simplest of panel comparisons in this chapter? Where's the complexity?

The complexity is yet to come. This chapter presents time-tested ideas, principles, and tools that you can use to help clearly convey information as the level of complexity goes up. The concepts seem simple, but they're powerful. They can be employed to clarify relationships between objects, and reduce distracting visual noise.

1   Alberto Cairo, "We Mustn't Simplify Stories; We Must Clarify Them" (accessed November 19, 2021) http://www.thefunctionalart.com/2016/09/we-mustnt-simplify-stories-we-must.html

Relationships

Gestalt Psychology is more or less rooted in the idea that the whole is greater than the sum of its parts. The Berlin school's Gestaltists—a cohort of German psychologists including Max Wertheimer (1880-1943), Kurt Koffka (1886-1941), and Wolfgang Köhler (1887-1967)—focused specifically on the idea that the *relationships* between those parts inform how we perceive the whole.

The most general concept from the original Gestaltists was the law of Prägnanz, which maintains that, in general, we default to the simplest possible visual explanation for what we see. The other principles fall into two primary themes: groupings, and figure-ground relationships. Many of the original principles have held up, and others have since been added. Some of the assumptions of the original Gestaltists have been shaken by subsequent research. For example, when these ideas first crystalized, it

A CLOSER LOOK

Visual Gestalt Principles

The following selection of concepts and visual effects—often associated with Gestalt Psychology—are particularly relevant for static graphics.

Perceptual Grouping refers to effects that cause people to perceive elements within an image as belonging with each other. These associations can result in perceived pairings, patterns, or dominant shape and path interpretations.

 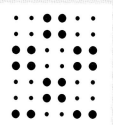 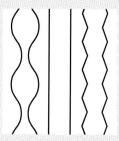 

Proximity • Equally spaced dots are generally perceived as a uniform block. When spacing is irregular, we perceive the dots that are closer to each other as belonging to the same sub-unit.

Similarity (of color, of size, of orientation) • All else being equal, we perceive objects that share a common visual attribute (color, size, or orientation for example) as belonging to the same group.

Symmetry • All else being equal, we tend to perceive lines that are symmetrical as a unit.

Parallelism • All else being equal, we tend to perceive lines that are parallel as a unit.

was assumed that the processes involved were innate to the brain. Since then, the importance of learning and experience (top-down influences) have been shown to play an important role.[2]

Most of the principles were originally demonstrated with two-dimensional abstract drawings. Things get quite a bit more complex when the principles are tested against natural three-dimensional scenes. But lucky for us, science graphics are often two-dimensional abstract drawings: Many of the ideas can be directly applied to great effect in information design.

2   Eysenck and Keane include a concise critique and summary of Gestalt-centric research in *Cognitive Psychology: A Student's Handbook,* 8th edition (Psychology Press, 2020). For a much more in-depth analysis, see Johan Wagemans et al., "A Century of Gestalt Psychology in Visual Perception I. Perceptual Grouping and Figure-Ground Organization," *Psychological Bulletin,* Vol. 138 (November 2012).

Continuity • We tend to favor tracking smooth and continuous lines, rather than following a path that includes abrupt angles.

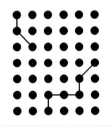

Closure • We tend to complete closed shapes, seeing this arc as a full circle behind a triangle.

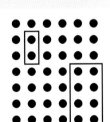

Common region • We tend to perceive elements that lie within the same bounded area as a unit.

Element connectedness • We tend to perceive elements that are connected as a unit.

Figure-Ground Effects describe how we distinguish primary objects of interest from the background: The item we identify as the primary object is thought to have "form." The background lacks form. In general, regions that are relatively small, symmetrical, and/or convex (curve outward) are perceived as objects that are distinct from the background. The example below shows one of those variables in action. The white concave shapes generally read as backgound. The black convex shapes read as objects in the foreground. To my mind, this class of Gestalt principles is less directly useful than perceptual groupings when it comes to designing science graphics.

Symbols

For the purposes of this book, it's probably most useful to think of semiotics (the study of signs and symbols, and how they impart meaning) in terms of *conventions*. Each scientific discipline has its own set of conventions when it comes to the abstract and graphical representation of objects and processes. I like to think of it as visual jargon. Scientific visualization relies on it a lot. Symbols and colors can carry highly specific information within a specific context, and allow the illustrator to efficiently communicate complex information with others who are fluent in that visual language.

Flip through any science textbook, and you'll see symbols rolling out along with new concepts. For example, students learn to interpret and use ribbon diagrams in biochemistry, electron orbital diagrams in chemistry, and Feynman diagrams in particle physics. (For more on visual jargon—along with a plea to avoid relying on it too much when creating graphics for non-specialist audiences—see page 178.)

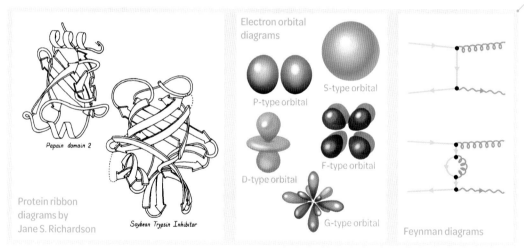

Protein ribbon diagrams by Jane S. Richardson

Papain domain 2

Soybean Trypsin Inhibitor

Electron orbital diagrams

P-type orbital

S-type orbital

D-type orbital

F-type orbital

G-type orbital

Feynman diagrams

Some core conventions transcend discipline, like the visual variables outlined in Jacque Bertin's classic *Semiology of Graphics.*[3] Originally intended for cartographers, it's also an often-cited work in the broader field of data visualization. (Equally intriguing, but less lushly illustrated, is Fernande Saint-Martin's *Semiotics of Visual Language.*[4])

---

3   Jacques Bertin, *Semiology of Graphics,* trans. William J. Berg, 1st ed. (Esri Press, 2010). Originally published in French as *Sémiologie Graphique* in 1967.

4   Fernande Saint-Martin, *Semiotics of Visual Language,* 1st edition (Bloomington: Indiana University Press, 1990)

Bertin's Visual Variables

Jacques Bertin isn't the only person who has compiled a set of visual features. But his set is pretty famous. He outlines eight primary variables for static, two-dimensional representation. (Strictly speaking, he refers to six of those as proper "variables." He refers to position as "planar dimensions," and bound to the content.) The book *Semiology of Graphics* includes many examples and visual summaries of these concepts. Here's a breakdown of the different ways he maintains that a mark in a plane can be encoded with information. More recent visual variable lists for static imagery by other authors include size, color, and orientation (well-supported by research); as well as luminance, pictorial depth cues, shape, line termination, closure, curvature, shading, luster, number, and aspect ratio (somewhat supported by research).[5]

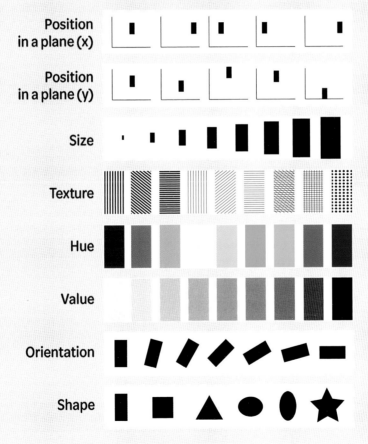

Position in a plane (x)

Position in a plane (y)

Size

Texture

Hue

Value

Orientation

Shape

---

5   Jeremy M. Wolfe, "Approaches to Visual Search: Feature Integration Theory and Guided Search," in Anna C. Nobre and Sabine Kastner, eds., *The Oxford Handbook of Attention* (OUP Oxford, 2014)

Arrows

One of the most ubiquitous symbols used in science graphics is the arrow. When Bang Wong surveyed a single 85-page issue of the scientific journal *Nature Methods*, he tallied 300 of them: More than half of all figures included at least one arrow.[6]

When used in graphics, arrows often suggest a change in state or position (things go from A to B) A→B, or causality (C leads to, activates, or triggers D) C→D. Both endpoints may not be explicitly defined. For example, it's generally accepted that when used like this: ●→ , the dot is about to move (or in the process of moving) to the right.

There are lots of subtle variations on that idea, including arrows that indicate rotation direction (⤴), relative values (more ↑, and less ↓), expanded view ⑤ ➤ ⑤, and a whole suite of discipline-specific uses. For example, as Wong notes with regards to the field of genetics, an "arrow with a right-angle line segment is understood as a transcription start site or promoter, and a short arrow placed parallel to a line usually indicates a PCR primer."[7] Discipline-specific uses of arrows may be useful when communicating with folks immersed in that field, but I recommend treating them as the visual jargon that they are. If your intended audience doesn't know the jargon, the arrow won't be meaningful. Come up with another solution, or label things carefully.

Since arrows imply directionality, I generally recommend that you avoid using them as a way to connect labels with objects, or as a way to connect expanded views to their origin. (This is rooted in my opinion as a practitioner that sees a *lot* of arrows, not the academic literature.) Save them for instances that make full use of their power! Some arrow alternatives for label leader lines include using a bullet at the end to help ground the leader in the object being labelled, or lassoing the target object. For enlarged views, consider using swoop lines to connect the framed origin and enlarged views.

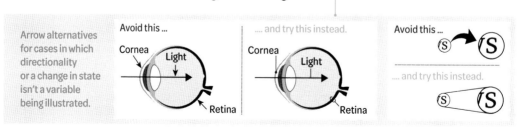

Arrow alternatives for cases in which directionality or a change in state isn't a variable being illustrated.

Avoid this ...

Cornea · Light · Retina

.... and try this instead.

Cornea · Light · Retina

Avoid this ... ⑤ ➤ ⑤

.... and try this instead. ⑤ ⑤

6   Bang Wong, "Arrows," *Nature Methods,* Vol. 8 (September 2011)

7   Ibid.

Bertin's *Semiology of Graphics* [8] has a really lovely section on arrows. Here are a couple of his particularly useful opinions on the matter:

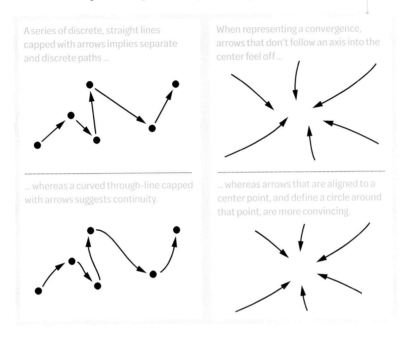

A series of discrete, straight lines capped with arrows implies separate and discrete paths ...

When representing a convergence, arrows that don't follow an axis into the center feel off ...

... whereas a curved through-line capped with arrows suggests continuity.

... whereas arrows that are aligned to a center point, and define a circle around that point, are more convincing.

● ● ●

NOW, LET'S CRANK UP THE COMPLEXITY. The following chapters build upon these ideas, and show how things play out in real-world science graphics. Don't lose sight of the principles and design tips from this chapter as attention shifts to other variables, and the content being illustrated. Subtle position adjustments that reinforce relationships between objects, and line and arrow refinements can make your graphic much easier to read.

8   Jacques Bertin, *Semiology of Graphics*, trans. William J. Berg, 1st ed. (Esri Press, 2010). Originally published in French as *Sémiologie Graphique* in 1967.

CHAPTER 7

Organization and Emphasis

MY FAVORITE PART OF WORKING ON A GRAPHIC is when I draw a series of small frames in my sketchbook and start scribbling in the possibilities. How should the information be partitioned? Where will the reader's gaze enter the space? What piece of information do they need first, second, and third? How can I direct their attention through that series in an intuitive manner? How can the position of the elements reinforce the story I'm trying to tell?

Brainstorm doodle series for a graphic about stars.

After years of working on graphics, these sorts of decisions become second-nature. But it can be helpful to pause and think through organization and attention-guiding strategies one at a time, rather than falling back on the same solutions over and over again. This chapter outlines the fundamentals.

Composition

In design and the visual arts, composition refers to how elements are organized on the page, or within a frame. It's about the relative position of points, lines, shapes and objects: When designing graphics, it's where form meets function. How you place objects within a space directly impacts the path your audience takes when reading through a graphic, and can reinforce the main point of the graphic.

When dealing with quantitative information, chart form carries this burden. Datapoint coordinates are predetermined by their underlying values: Choosing a chart form becomes the primary decision related to composition. Different chart forms are appropriate for highlighting different types of relationships. For example, line charts are good for tracking changes over time. Bar charts are suited for comparing discrete categories. There are lots of references to help you sort this out when it comes to quantitative information.[1]

Things are more nebulous when organizing qualitative information on a page. But here are some helpful guidelines. Think about taking a reader by the hand, and walking them through your graphic, one step at a time. What information do they need to encounter first, in order to understand the rest of the figure? What information should they encounter second? How can you help the reader follow the correct path effortlessly on their own, if you aren't there to walk them through it?

Audiences who read written languages that are oriented from left to right have been trained to start at the top, left corner of the page, and then will tend to read from left to right, and top to bottom. Audiences who read written languages that are oriented from right to left may be more likely to start in the top right corner.

"How mRNA COVID-19 Vaccines Work" public service announcement posters from the CDC (Centers for Disease Control and Prevention) in English (*left*) and Arabic (*right*). Image Credit: CDC; National Center for Immunization and Respiratory Diseases (NCIRD), Division of Viral Diseases (*content source*); Downloaded October 10, 2021.

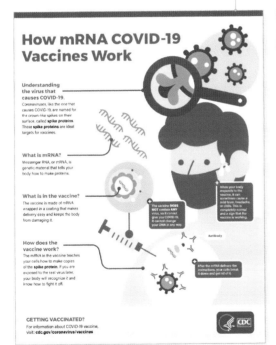

1   Guides include Stephanie Evergreen's *Effective Data Visualization: The Right Chart for the Right Data* (SAGE Publications, 2016), Andy Kirk's *Data Visualization: A Handbook for Data Driven Design*, 2nd edition (SAGE Publications Ltd, 2019), and Jonathan Schwabish's *Better Data Visualizations: A Guide for Scholars, Researchers, and Wonks* (Columbia University Press, 2021).

I often start with that in mind, but also provide a clear path for a reader to follow. Designer Lucy Reading-Ikkanda uses that approach in this graphic for *Quanta Magazine*, reinforcing the sequence of events with arrows, zig-zagging across the page with a clear left-to-right, and top-to-bottom flow of information.

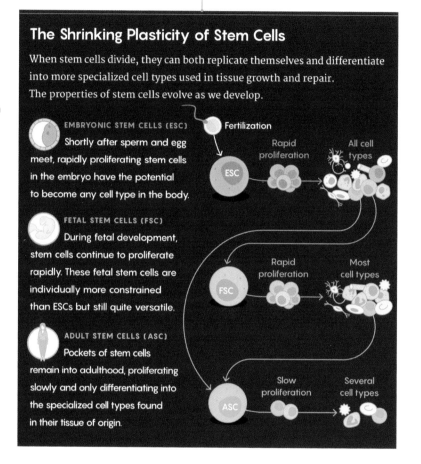

That composition works particularly well when showing a step-by-step process. And it's a good default position. But you can also use the position of objects on the page to help highlight second-level points you are trying to make. For example, if the process is cyclical, reinforce it with a cyclical composition, as in this example on the topic of malaria, by Pierre Chassany. Here, a natural entry point into the cycle is the mosquito highlighted in a contrasting color (green) at the "noon" position at top, with arrows reinforcing a clockwise flow for the main cycle.

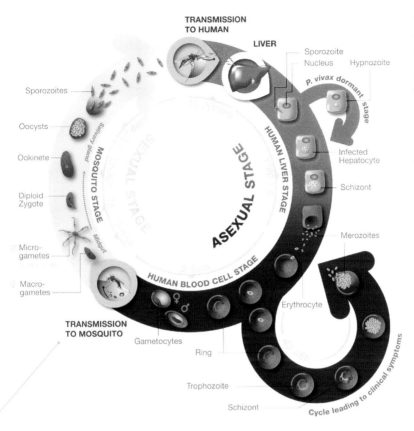

When comparing and contrasting variations on the same process, it can be useful to keep the orientation of each vignette exactly the same, and aligned. When the objects are presented in this way, you've set up the reader to quickly spot the differences between the scenarios, as with this before and after view by Raoul Rañoa, for the *Los Angeles Times*.

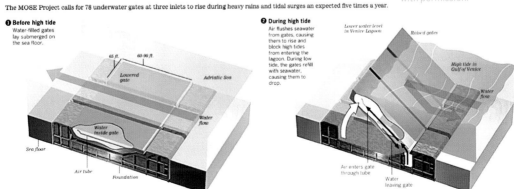

The MOSE Project calls for 78 underwater gates at three inlets to rise during heavy rains and tidal surges an expected five times a year.

Multiply that concept many times, and you'll create a *small multiples* composition (a term popularized by Edward Tufte). The audience learns how to read one element, then can efficiently apply that knowledge to the other elements. Per Tufte, "as our eye moves from one image to the next, this constancy of design allows viewers to focus on changes in information rather than changes in graphical composition."[2] It can be used to great effect, as in this example by Ed Hawkins, in which he displays global changes in temperature over time.

Image Credit: Professor Ed Hawkins (@ed_hawkins), National Centre for Atmospheric Science, University of Reading; Data: HadCRUT5.0.

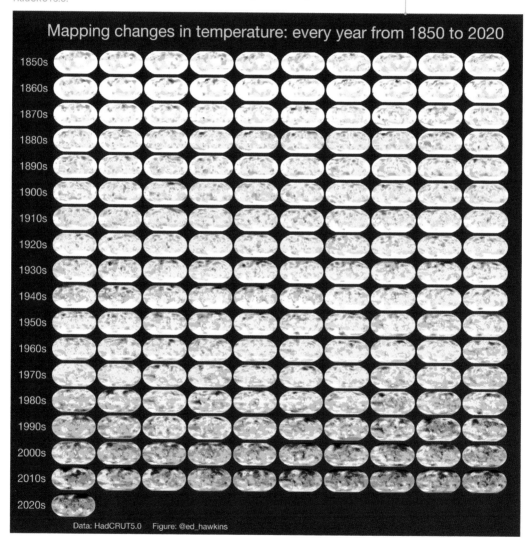

Mapping changes in temperature: every year from 1850 to 2020

Data: HadCRUT5.0   Figure: @ed_hawkins

2   Edward R. Tufte, *Envisioning Information* (Graphics Press, 1990)

That said, if the series of objects you're presenting don't share a variable that you're trying to compare directly, things can feel a bit overwhelming in this sort of grid. Lots of elements of the same size presented in a block without a compositional anchor may cause the reader's eyes to glaze over. It's akin to trying to read many pages of running text without paragraph breaks, subheads, or chapter breaks. Sometimes your eye just needs a break, or a natural place to re-enter the scene.

Which brings me to the sections below. I'll start with grid systems, then move on to how you can introduce negative space, visual hierarchy, and other visual cues to help guide the reader's attention through your graphic.

Grids and Alignments

The concept of a grid in design is probably familiar to you: Books, newspapers and websites are often organized according to them. The larger plane is divided into smaller boxes, with clear bands (or gutters) running between them. Those gutters of negative space prevent images or text from colliding into each other. The overall effect is logical and modular. Alignment lines are built into the structure. The grid lines don't exist as marks on the final product. Rather, they are temporary lines that help in the planning stages.

Although simple and straightforward in concept, grid system discussions can get incredibly detailed and complex. For our purposes—designing graphics within a defined space—I think we can keep it pretty high-level. But please keep in mind that this is a simplified glimpse at the topic. There's a lot more to grid systems, including the mathematics behind them, careful accommodation of different fonts in terms of column widths and letter heights, setting up multi-page documents or consistent grids for branding purposes, and design solutions that both honor and destabilize the form.[3]

3   For an incredibly detailed and strict guide to grids, see Josef Müller-Brockmann's *Grid systems in graphic design: A visual communication manual for graphic designers, typographers and three dimensional designers.* (Niggli Verlag, Bilingual Edition 18, 2021; originally published in German in 1981). For a great broader introduction to the topic—including non-Swiss histories and examples that push its boundaries—see *The Swiss Grid* virtual exhibit and online learning tool hosted by Poster House in New York City (*https://swissgrid.posterhouse.org/*). One of my favorite examples of a grid system that unifies publications across an organization is from the U.S. National Park Service. Read more about their award-winning and long-lasting Unigrid System at *https://www. nps.gov/subjects/hfc/a-brief-history-of-the-unigrid.htm* .

On this page, I've made the grid visible. This pattern of guidelines was used throughout this book, made visible to me while organizing pages. Many programs (like Adobe InDesign, the tool I used to design this book) allow you to set up custom guides, or choose from existing templates. The guides can be made visible or invisible easily, and aren't set up to print. But you don't need assistance from a program to use grid-system thinking in your work. My sketchbooks are filled with aligned shapes, as I map out content in a rudimentary hand-drawn modular grid of sorts.

Some grids are symmetrical and quite dense, allowing for a wide range of solutions while still maintaining a clean structure throughout designs within a series. Others are a bit less dense, and perhaps not even symmetrical, but still provide clear guides for image modules and alignments.

As a cold reader of this graphic about the sun by Chris Bickel for *Science*, it's clear to me that a grid system is in play. The material is chunked up and organized in a logical manner. Sub-sections are easy to distinguish. I have a clear sense of which captions are associated with each image or group of images. Labels are also aligned. It's possible that the labels are not positioned according to the primary grid, but the regularity of their positions make them easy to find, and reinforces an overall sense of clarity.

Intentionally breaking the "rules"—in this case, the grid— can can be used to great effect to draw attention, or to create drama or an additional level of hierarchy. This is particularly effective when a grid is otherwise clearly established. This paragraph, for example, breaks from the grid. Yes, it's a circle. But more importantly, it defies the defined boundaries, spanning more than one column (but not extending to two), and extending into the margins.

The content in this multi-part graphic is organized into clear modules. There are a range of possible underlying grid structures that led to this design solution. I made a guess at one possibilty, shown on the following page. Image Credit: C. Bickel/Science; From "The Calm before the Storms," by Sarah Scoles, *Science,* Vol. 364 (May 31, 2019). Reproduced with permission from AAAS.

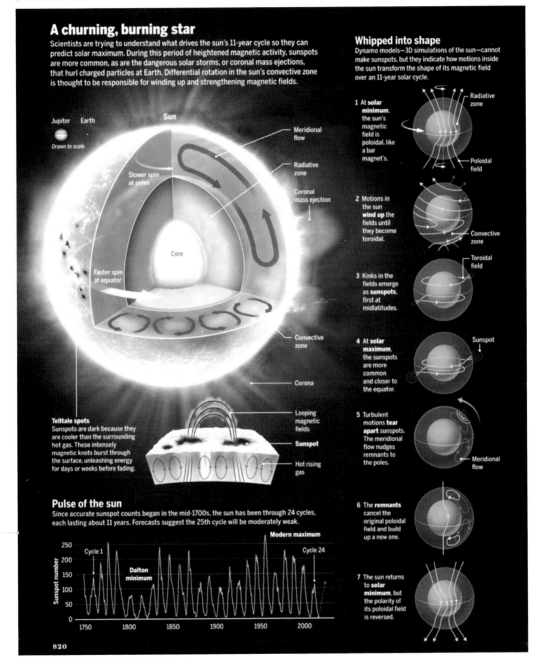

A churning, burning star

Scientists are trying to understand what drives the sun's 11-year cycle so they can predict solar maximum. During this period of heightened magnetic activity, sunspots are more common, as are the dangerous solar storms, or coronal mass ejections, that hurl charged particles at Earth. Differential rotation in the sun's convective zone is thought to be responsible for winding up and strengthening magnetic fields.

Jupiter   Earth   Sun
Drawn to scale

Slower spin at poles

Faster spin at equator

Core

Meridional flow

Radiative zone

Coronal mass ejection

Convective zone

Corona

Looping magnetic fields

Sunspot

Hot rising gas

Telltale spots
Sunspots are dark because they are cooler than the surrounding hot gas. These intensely magnetic knots burst through the surface, unleashing energy for days or weeks before fading.

Whipped into shape
Dynamo models—3D simulations of the sun—cannot make sunspots, but they indicate how motions inside the sun transform the shape of its magnetic field over an 11-year solar cycle.

1 At **solar minimum**, the sun's magnetic field is poloidal, like a bar magnet's.

Radiative zone

Poloidal field

2 Motions in the sun **wind up** the fields until they become toroidal.

Convective zone

3 Kinks in the fields emerge as **sunspots**, first at midlatitudes.

Toroidal field

4 At **solar maximum**, the sunspots are more common and closer to the equator.

Sunspot

5 Turbulent motions **tear apart** sunspots. The meridional flow nudges remnants to the poles.

Meridional flow

6 The **remnants** cancel the original poloidal field and build up a new one.

7 The sun returns to **solar minimum**, but the polarity of its poloidal field is reversed.

Pulse of the sun
Since accurate sunspot counts began in the mid-1700s, the sun has been through 24 cycles, each lasting about 11 years. Forecasts suggest the 25th cycle will be moderately weak.

Modern maximum

Cycle 1

Cycle 24

Dalton minimum

Sunspot number

250
200
150
100
50
0

1750   1800   1850   1900   1950   2000

820

A possible organizational grid (dotted, magenta), with labels aligned with a secondary-level guides (dashed, cyan). Magenta and cyan lines are not in the original image file. They are added here to highlight alignments. Image Credit: C. Bickel/Science; From "The Calm before the Storms," by Sarah Scoles, *Science,* Vol. 364 (May 31, 2019). Base image reproduced with permission from AAAS.

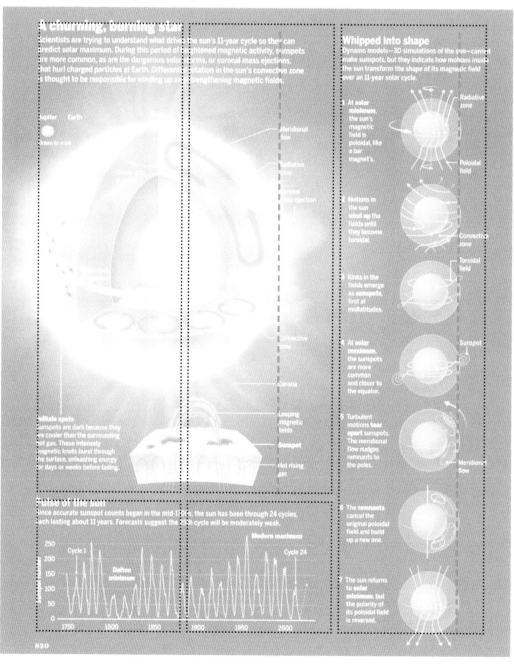

Smaller graphics—or graphics that don't include a lot of sub-sections or elements—may not need much compartmentalizing at all, and a complex grid system may be more than you need. But the concepts of alignments and clear organization of objects on a page still hold. For example, here's a less dense graphic that appeared in *Nature Reviews*. Each element is defined by the empty space around it, and those elements are aligned in a way that reinforces the content. Here, I added an overlay of dashed cyan lines to highlight the vertical alignment connecting different views of the same condition, and magenta dotted boxes to highlight the horizontal alignment that connects information that can be compared across conditions.

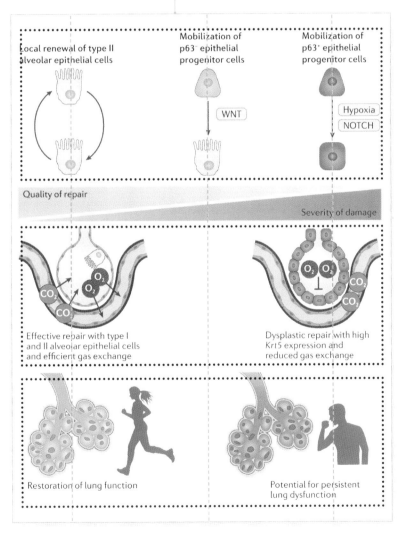

Magenta dotted rectangles and cyan dashed lines are not in the original image file. They are added here to highlight alignments. Image Credit: Reproduced with permission from Springer Nature: as published in "Influenza Virus and SARS-CoV-2: Pathogenesis and Host Responses in the Respiratory Tract," by Tim Flerlage et al. *Nature Reviews Microbiology* (April 6, 2021); © 2021.

Even in an example with fewer elements, a clear horizontal alignment axis makes for a clean and clear flow of information.

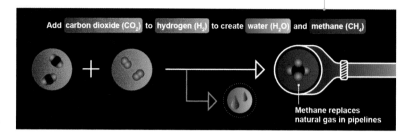

As you can see with all of the examples above, using a grid system doesn't mean that your graphic is dominated by a series of squares printed on the page, with each square holding a bit of the content. Rather, it's a way of thinking about how to divide up and organize your information in a way that feels cohesive and clear.

Negative Space

Negative space (the empty zones around elements) can be used to frame objects and create groupings, as in the sun example. Although the imagery spills out a bit in the background in this case, the text blocks define "positive" or active space, leaving gutters of apparent negative space between them. You may be tempted to use a line as a square frame around a set of objects to define them as a unit. If so, stop and try using a buffer of negative space instead. Lines and frames can be useful, especially if you're cropping in on a detail within a larger scene. But if you're simply hoping to corral objects together, negative space may do the trick without introducing additional visual noise. Remember the Gestalt law of proximity? Items that are positioned closely together tend to be perceived as a group. Thoughtful use of space buffers around those groupings can help reinforce their proximity.

Negative space can also serve as a break for the eye. Consider this graphic by Adrian Leung for *Bloomberg.* The imagery and text is given some space to breathe. There's a lot of negative space on the right side in particular. But the label alignments make it feel intentional, and not haphazard. Every bit of space in this graphic has been considered, but not activated with marks.

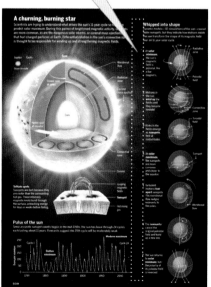

Negative space (deliniated here with a yellow dotted box)

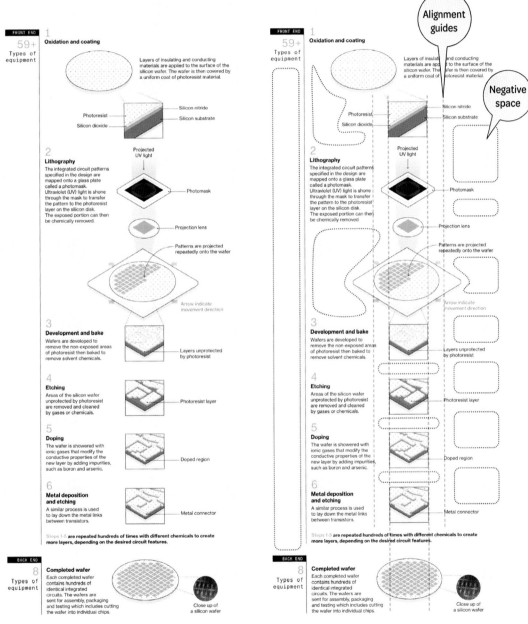

Objects are not positioned to fit as much as possible into the space. Rather, objects are positioned along a few strong vertical guidelines that help retain balance and reinforce the flow of information, from top to bottom.

Visual Hierarchy

As Ellen Lupton and Jennifer Cole Phillips put it in *Graphic Design: The New Basics*, hierarchy can be:

> *...conveyed visually, through variations in scale, value, color, spacing, placement, and other signals. Expressing order is a central task of the graphic designer. Visual hierarchy controls the delivery and impact of a message. Without hierarchy, graphic communication is dull and difficult to navigate. ...Hierarchy can be simple or complex, rigorous or loose, flat or highly articulated. Regardless of approach, hierarchy employs clear marks of separation to signal a change from one level to another.*[4]

Some commonly used "marks of separation" that can help delineate changes in levels of importance are the focus of this section, starting with **position**. As discussed above, readers of written languages that flow left to right and top to bottom are trained to start in the top left portion of an image frame. It's often handy to include your graphic's title and introductory caption in that spot. All other things being equal, it's the information that your reader is most likely to encounter first. Following that logic, it's also a handy spot for setup imagery that applies to the rest of the graphic.

Here, for example, a broad-level caption and a brain illustration span the full width of the graphic, in the dominant position at the top of the page. That band includes the takeaway point of the graphic, in words. It also includes a visual that acts as a locator map for the rest of the graphic: The information that's represented in that detail applies to all of the content below. When taken together, the title, introductory caption, and brain illustration prime the reader for the more detailed information to follow. When material is positioned at the top of the space, spanning the content below like an umbrella, it visually reinforces its role as the first thing that readers should absorb.

Small variations in position can also draw attention to particular el-

4   Ellen Lupton and Jennifer Cole Phillips, *Graphic Design: The New Basics*, 2nd edition (Princeton Architectural Press, 2015). Quote republished with permission of Princeton Architectural Press, LLC, © 2015. Permission conveyed through Copyright Clearance Center, Inc.

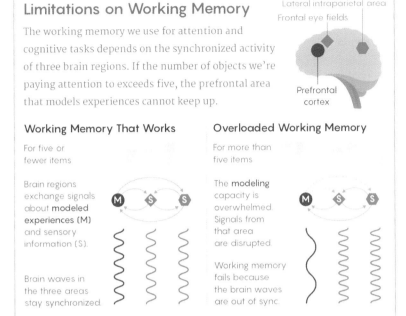

Limitations on Working Memory

The working memory we use for attention and cognitive tasks depends on the synchronized activity of three brain regions. If the number of objects we're paying attention to exceeds five, the prefrontal area that models experiences cannot keep up.

Lateral intraparietal area
Frontal eye fields
Prefrontal cortex

Working Memory That Works

For five or fewer items

Brain regions exchange signals about **modeled experiences (M)** and sensory information (S).

Brain waves in the three areas stay synchronized.

Overloaded Working Memory

For more than five items

The **modeling** capacity is overwhelmed. Signals from that area are disrupted.

Working memory fails because the brain waves are out of sync.

Image Credit: Lucy Reading-Ikkanda/Quanta Magazine, as published in "Overtaxed Working Memory Knocks the Brain Out of Sync," by Jordana Cepelewicz, *Quanta Magazine* (June 6, 2018). Reproduced with permsision of *Quanta Magazine*.

ements within a graphic. For example, if you wanted to draw attention to a specific decade in the small multiples example introduced on page 74, a slight offset of that set of globes attracts the eye. In the panel on the right, the 1980s panel is elevated to a position of prominence. This sort of position trick only works when a clear structure is in place for

Image Credit: Professor Ed Hawkins (@ed_hawkins), National Centre for Atmospheric Science, University of Reading; Data: HadCRUT5.0 (*left*): Jen Christiansen (*right*).

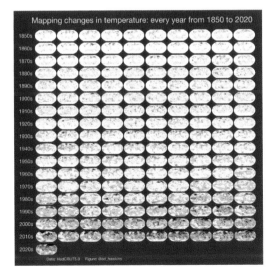

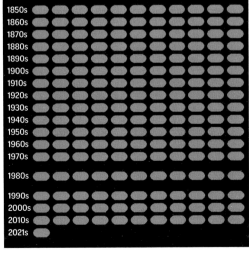

the rest of the graphic, and when used sparingly. The critical underlying idea being that our eyes are drawn to areas of contrast. It works in this example because there's a clear pattern in play, and then a distinct break from that pattern. When it comes to science graphics, it's generally a good idea to also clearly indicate why the position of prominence is warranted. This may be a mention of the 1980s in an introductory caption, or—even better—with an annotation that addresses the significance directly linked to the highlighted area.

Variation in **size** adds visual interest to a graphic. In science graphics, the largest element should be chosen wisely, however, as it plays a few roles. It's not only an anchor for the composition, but it also suggests some sort of prominence in terms of content. Here, illustrator Daisy Chung draws your attention to a mechanism that changes carbon waste into usable graphene. The object is large and detailed, helping to underscore that the graphic is about a flash heating system

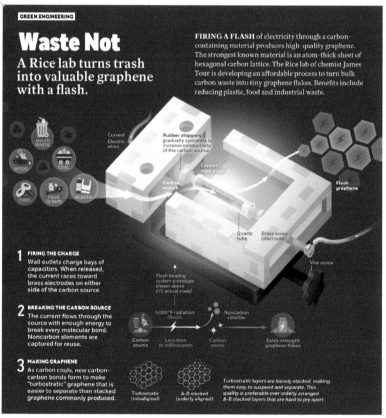

Image Credit: Daisy Chung, *Rice Magazine* (Office of Public Affairs, Rice University; Spring 2020).

that is in development. The page isn't about theory. It's about transitioning from theory into technology; that bit of technology dominates the graphic, primarily due to its scale. Supporting information follows with smaller schematics, helping a reader to more fully understand the process and output.

Variation in size also applies to line thickness. Here, Katie Peek uses thick lines to emphasize telescope baselines on a globe. Geography details provide background context in thinner lines. If all line thicknesses were the same in this illustration, it would be difficult to distinguish telescope connectors from the latitude and longitude lines.

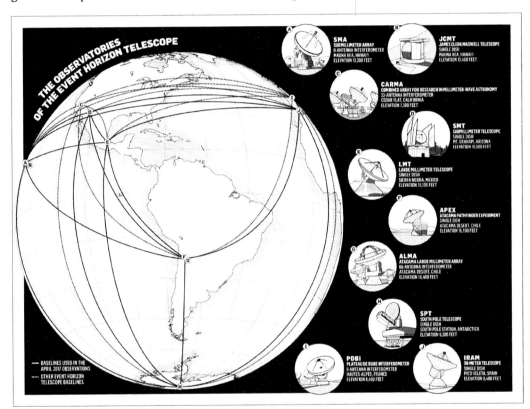

Image Credit: Katie Peek, from *Einstein's Shadow* by Seth Fletcher (Ecco, 2018). Published with permission of the artist.

Color variation is a powerful and elegant way to introduce contrast—and therefore multiple levels, or hierarchy—to an image. For example, in an article on visualization in science-policy, the authors include a graphic that presents six ways that interactive displays can allow the audience to explore a dataset. They use tints (lighter versions of a color) and shades (darker versions of a color) to draw your attention to the critical elements. The lighter elements provide critical context for the emphasized details, but they don't fight for attention. Further emphasis is added with a blue glow, underscoring that the highlighted zone-of-interest has been selected. It's not a static inset.

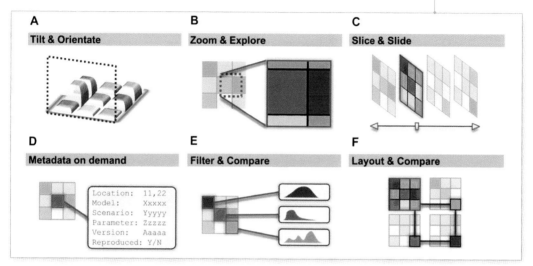

Color is used for a few purposes in this graphic by Amanda Montañez and Tami Tolpa, but most critically, it literally highlights the most important zone of the data visualization. The full chart is needed for context, but the small vertical strip from zero to $50,000 per year holds the crux. A strip of yellow draws attention to that zone without obfuscating the underlying data. (See Chapter 8 for more on color.)

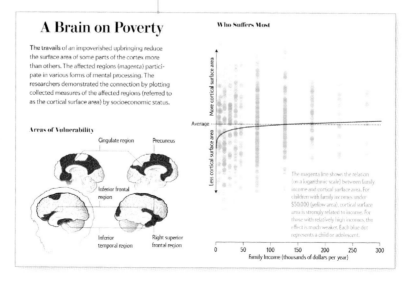

Flow of Information

Signalling different levels of importance by varying position, scale, or color is powerful in its own right. But things get really exciting when two or more of those variables work in concert. For example, designer John Grimwade intentionally guides the reader's eye through this graphic on cloud seeding by setting up the flow of action in a way that reinforces the flow of information. The thoughtful composition is reinforced by careful use of all three variables discussed above: scale, position, and color. Each important element leads to the next important element, directing audience attention through the information by dialing visual levels up and down as you proceed through the image. Here's a breakdown of some of the strategies in play.

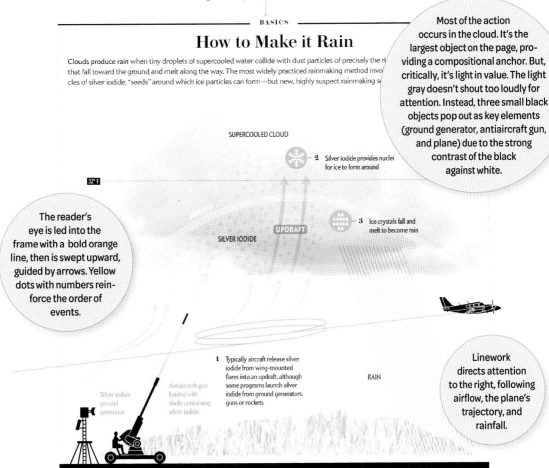

——— BASICS ———

How to Make it Rain

Clouds produce rain when tiny droplets of supercooled water collide with dust particles of precisely the ri[...] that fall toward the ground and melt along the way. The most widely practiced rainmaking method invo[...] cles of silver iodide, "seeds" around which ice particles can form—but new, highly suspect rainmaking s[...]

Most of the action occurs in the cloud. It's the largest object on the page, providing a compositional anchor. But, critically, it's light in value. The light gray doesn't shout too loudly for attention. Instead, three small black objects pop out as key elements (ground generator, antiaircraft gun, and plane) due to the strong contrast of the black against white.

SUPERCOOLED CLOUD

2   Silver iodide provides nuclei for ice to form around

32° F

UPDRAFT

SILVER IODIDE

3   Ice crystals fall and melt to become rain

The reader's eye is led into the frame with a bold orange line, then is swept upward, guided by arrows. Yellow dots with numbers reinforce the order of events.

Linework directs attention to the right, following airflow, the plane's trajectory, and rainfall.

1   Typically aircraft release silver iodide from wing-mounted flares into an updraft, although some programs launch silver iodide from ground generators, guns or rockets

RAIN

Silver iodide ground generator

Antiaircraft gun loaded with shells containing silver iodide

DEMONSTRATION

Composition Makeover (part one of three)

This is the first installment of a demonstration that takes part in three stages. Context and content remain steady throughout the makeover: It's is a hypothetical graphic destined for a hypothetical academic journal. The redesigned images are all for the same audience and outlet as the original version. The content is completely made up. (It's a somewhat generic product of my imagination.) The initial graphic includes less-than-ideal design choices that are not

BEFORE

Figure 1. Pathogenesis of classical cat treat disease and paradoxical cat treat disease. (A) Classical: Protein one, which is produced by the gut upon the ingestion of a treat, forms complexes with protein two. These complexes trigger alpha cells to produce large amounts of protein three. Protein three stimulates beta cells, which releases proteins four and five. Protein four triggers gamma cells to start massing in the gut's lining. Gamma cells then release protein six, pushing gut lining cells into a hypergrowth state, resulting in a grumpy cat. This condition can be confirmed by testing for levels of proteins three, four, and six. (B) Paradoxical: The introduction of drug A successfully blocked classical cat treat disease in most cats, by inhibiting the production of protein four. However, some cats were still grumpy. In 1 to 3 percent of cats, paradoxical cat treat disease may arise due to an increase in production of protein five, a side effect of drug A. The full pathway of paradoxical cat treat disease is not yet understood, but can be confirmed by testing for levels of proteins three and five.

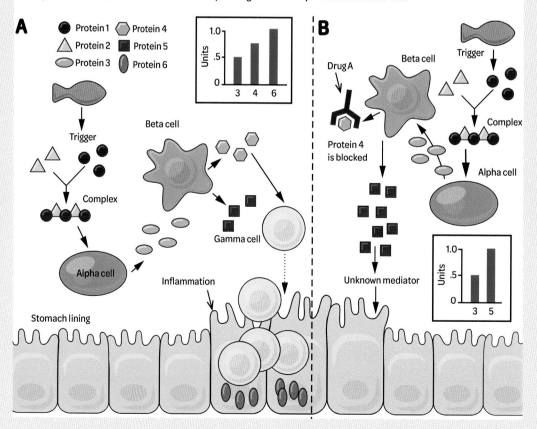

made up. I've seen a lot of figures that are organized in this manner. The makeover stage on this spread is limited to changes in composition. Color and general approaches to type remain unchanged. Stage two folds in color (see pages 110–111). Stage three folds in typography (see pages 124–125). Rendering style is the same throughout—and fairly standard—to avoid distracting from the other core design changes with razzle dazzle.

Composition changes here are primarily in the service of (1) clearly showing the linear flow of the process, and (2) facilitating an easy and direct comparison between each scenario.

AFTER

Figure 1. Pathogenesis of classical cat treat disease and paradoxical cat treat disea ___ one, which is produced by the gut upon the ingestion of a treat, forms complexes with prot ___ plexes trigger alpha cells to produce large amounts of protein three. Protein three stimulates beta ___ ich releases proteins four and five. Protein four triggers gamma cells to start massing in the gut's lining. Gamma cells then release protein six, pushing gut lining cells into a hypergrowth state, resulting in a grumpy cat. This condition can be confirmed by testing for levels of proteins three, four, and six. (B) Paradoxical: The introduction of drug A successfully blocked classical cat treat disease in most cats, by inhibiting the production of protein four. However, some cats were still grumpy. In 1 to 3 percent of cats, paradoxical cat treat disease may arise due to an increase in production of protein five, a side effect of drug A. The full pathway of paradoxical cat treat disease is not yet understood, but can be confirmed by testing for levels of proteins three and five.

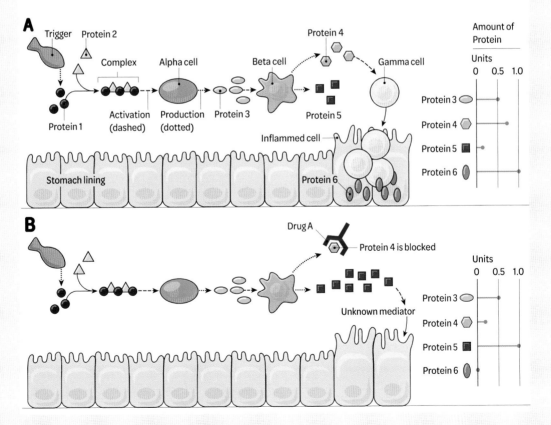

DEMONSTRATION ——————————————————————————

Academic Poster Design

Academic conference poster trends and templates come and go,[1] but the ritual of mingling at conferences (both virtual and in-person) to share research—with the help of science-fair-esque visual aids—persists. I encourage you to think of your conference poster as a large graphic. Step back from the frame, and employ the design principles described in this book to the whole poster space, not just the graphics boxes within it. Start with a grid across the whole poster, as a guide for text block and image alignments. Use negative space to help create section groupings. Create visual hierarchy with variations in color, scale, and position of objects. And please spend time carefully considering your typography. Are

1   Eva Amsen, "A Graphic Design Revolution For Scientific Conference Posters," *Forbes* (June 2019)

BEFORE

Poster Title in the Space Right Here
This is a faux academic poster that could use some design love.
By Author One, Author Two, Author Three, and Author Four
Affiliation Here

Section One
Lorem ipsum dolor sit amet, consectetuer adipiscing elit, sed diam nonummy nibh euismod tincidunt ut laoreet dolore magna aliquam erat volutpat. Ut wisi enim ad minim veniam, quis nostrud exerci tation ullamcorper suscipit lobortis nisl ut aliquip ex ea commodo consequat. Duis autem vel eum iriure dolor in hendrerit in vulputate velit esse molestie consequat, vel illum dolore eu feugiat nulla facilisi at vero eros et accumsan et iusto odio dignissim qui blandit praesent luptatum zzril delenit augue duis dolore te feugait nulla facilisi. Lorem ipsum dolor Lorem ipsum dolor sit amet, consectetuer adipiscing elit, sed diam nonummy nibh euismod tincidunt ut laoreet dolore magna aliquam erat volutpat. Ut wisi enim ad minim veniam.

Mostrud exerci tation ullamcorper suscipit lobortis nisl ut aliquip ex ea commodo consequat. Duis autem vel eum iriure dolor in hendrerit in vulputate velit esse molestie consequat, vel illum dolore eu feugiat nulla facilisis at vero eros et accumsan et iusto odio dignissim qui blandit praesent luptatum zzril delenit augue duis dolore te feugait nulla facilisi.

Lorem ipsum dolor sit amet, cons ectetur adipiscing elit, sed diam nonummy nibh euismod tincidunt ut laoreet dolore magna aliquam erat volutpat. Ut wisi enim ad minim veniam, quis nostrud exerci tation ullamcorper suscipit lobortis nisl ut aliquip ex ea commodo consequat.Lorem ipsum dolor sit amet, consectetuer adipiscing elit, sed diam nonummy nibh euismod tincidunt ut laoreet dolore magna aliquam erat volutpat. Ut wisi enim ad minim veniam, quis nostrud exerci tation ullamcorper suscipit lobortis nisl ut aliquip ex ea commodo consequat. Duis autem vel eum iriure dolor in hendrerit in vulputate velit esse molestie consequat, vel illum dolore eu feugiat nulla facilisis at vero eros et accumsan et iusto odio dignissim qui blandit praesent luptatam

Section Three
Lorem ipsum dolor sit amet, consectetuer adipiscing elit, sed diam nonummy nibh

Euismod tincidunt ut laoreet dolore magna aliquam erat volutpat. Ut wisi enim ad minim veniam, quis nostrud

Section Two
Lorem ipsum dolor sit amet, consectetuer adipiscing elit, sed diam nonummy nibh euismod tincidunt ut laoreet dolore magna aliquam erat volutpat. Ut wisi enim ad minim veniam, quis nostrud exerci tation ullamcorper suscipit lobortis nisl ut aliquip ex ea commodo consequat. Duis autem vel eum iriure dolor in hendrerit in vulputate velit esse molestie consequat, vel illum dolore eu feugiat nulla facilisis at vero eros et accumsan et iusto odio dignissim qui blandit praesent luptatum zzril delenit augue duis dolore te feugait nulla facilisi. Lorem ipsum dolor Lorem ipsum dolor sit amet, consectetuer adipiscing elit, sed diam nonummy nibh euismod tincidunt ut laoreet dolore magna aliquam erat volutpat. Ut wisi enim ad minim veniam.

Mostrud exerci tation ullamcorper suscipit lobortis nisl ut aliquip

THIS IS A TABLE

	CATEGORY A	CATEGORY B	CATEGORY C	CATEGORY D
TOPIC ONE	notes	notes	notes	notes
TOPIC TWO	notes	notes	notes	notes right here
TOPIC THREE	notes in this space	notes here	notes	notes here
TOPIC FOUR	notes	notes	notes right have	notes
TOPIC FIVE	notes	notes in this space	notes	notes in this space

Lorem ipsum dolor sit amet, consectetuer adipiscing elit, sed diam nonummy nibh euismod tincidunt ut laoreet dolore magna aliquam erat volutpat. Ut wisi enim ad minim veniam, quis

Section Four
Lorem ipsum dolor sit amet, consectetuer adipiscing elit, sed diam nonummy nibh euismod tincidunt ut laoreet dolore magna aliquam erat volutpat. Ut wisi enim ad minim veniam, quis nostrud exerci tation ullamcorper suscipit lobortis nisl ut aliquip ex ea commodo consequat. Duis autem vel eum iriure dolor in hendrerit in vulputate velit esse molestie consequat, vel illum dolore eu feugiat nulla facilisis at vero eros et accumsan et iusto odio dignissim qui blandit praesent luptatum zzril delenit augue duis dolore te feugait nulla facilisi. Lorem ipsum dolor Lorem ipsum dolor sit amet, consectetuer adipiscing elit, sed diam nonummy nibh euismod tincidunt ut laoreet dolore magna aliquam erat volutpat. Ut wisi enim ad minim veniam.

Section Five
Lorem ipsum dolor sit amet, consectetuer adipiscing elit, sed diam nonummy nibh euismod tincidunt ut laoreet dolore magna aliquam erat volutpat. Ut wisi enim ad minim veniam, quis nostrud exerci tation ullamcorper suscipit lobortis nisl ut aliquip ex ea commodo consequat. Duis autem vel eum iriure dolor in hendrerit in vulputate velit esse molestie consequat, vel illum dolore eu feugiat nulla

Section Six
Lorem ipsum dolor sit amet, consectetuer adipiscing elit, sed diam nonummy nibh euismod tincidunt ut laoreet dolore magna aliquam erat volutpat. Ut wisi enim ad minim veniam, quis nostrud exerci tation ullamcorper suscipit lobortis nisl ut aliquip ex ea commodo consequat. Duis autem vel eum iriure dolor in hendrerit in vulputate velit esse molestie consequat, vel illum dolore eu feugiat nulla facilisis at vero eros et accumsan et iusto odio dignissim qui blandit praesent luptatum zzril delenit

your columns too wide for the font size you're using? Does a person have to stand very close to your poster and shuffle back and forth in order to read the text? Are you simply trying to put too much information into the space that you have allotted, given the manner in which your audience will encounter it? Remember, your poster isn't a paper that will be consumed by a single person in isolation, under a reading light. It may need to capture the attention of a person striding by many feet away, in the midst of a sea of other posters tacked to room dividers, in a space with unknown lighting. Be kind to your audience. Make the flow of information clear, and the content legible. Here are three poster redesigns to show you how some of the design concepts covered in Chapters 7 through 9 can help you step up your poster game.

Design changes here are primarily in the service of (1) legibility, and (2) delineating a clear and logical path through the information. Note that I eliminated a lot of text. It's okay to dedicate more space to imagery than words! Body text should be at least 24 pts; labels should be at least 18 pts.

AFTER

Poster Title in the Space Right Here

This is the redesigned version of a faux academic poster.

By Author One, Author Two, Author Three, and Author Four

Affiliation Here

——— Section One ———

Lorem ipsum dolor sit amet, consectetuer adipiscing elit, sed diam nonummy nibh euismod tincidunt ut laoreet dolore magna aliquam erat volutpat. **Ut wisi enim ad minim veniam, quis nostrud exerci tation ullamcorper suscipit lobortis nisl ut aliquip ex ea commodo consequat.** Duis autem vel eum iriure dolor in hendrerit in vulputate velit esse molestie consequat, vel illum dolore eu feugiat nulla facilisis at vero eros et accumsan et iusto odio dignissim qui blandit praesent luptatum zzril delenit augue duis dolore te feugait nulla facilisi. Lorem ipsum dolor Lorem ipsum dolor sit amet, consectetuer adipiscing elit, sed diam nonummy.

——— Section Two ———

Lorem ipsum dolor sit amet, consectetuer adipiscing elit, sed diam nonummy nibh euismod tincidunt ut laoreet dolore magna aliquam erat volutpat. Ut wisi enim ad minim veniam, quis nostrud exerct.

Lorem ipsum dolor sit amet, consectuer adipiscing elit mica two

Lorem ipsum dolor sit amet, con sectuer adipiscing elit mica two

Lorem ipsum dolor sit amet, con sectuer adipiscing elit mica two

Lorem ipsum dolor sit amet, con sectuer adipiscing elit mica two

Lorem ipsum dolor sit amet, con sectuer adipiscing elit mica two

——— Section Three ———

Lorem ipsum dolor sit amet, consectetuer adipiscing elit, sed diam nonummy nibh euismod tincidunt ut laoreet dolore magna aliquam erat volutpat. Ut wisi enim ad minim veniam (Ⓐ), Quis nostrud exerci tation ullamcorper suscipit lobortis nisl ut aliquip ex ea commodo consequat. Duis autem vel eum iriure dolor. (Ⓑ) In hendrerit in vulputate velit esse molestie consequat, vel illum dolore eu feugiat nulla facilisis at vero eros et accumsan et iusto odio dignissim qui blandit praesent luptatum.

——— Section Four ———

Lorem ipsum dolor sit amet, consectetuer adipiscing elit, sed diam nonummy nibh euismod tincidunt ut laoreet dolore magna aliquam erat volutpat. Ut wisi enim ad minim veniam, quis nostrud exerci tation ullamcorper suscipit lobortis nisl ut aliquip ex ea commodo consequat.

Scenario A

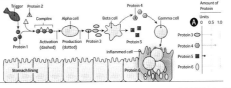

Scenario B

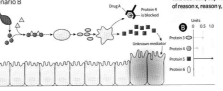

This was really suprising, because of reason x, reason y, and reason z.

——— Section Five ———

Lorem ipsum dolor sit amet, consectetuer adipiscing elit, sed diam nonummy nibh euismod tincidunt ut laoreet dolore magna aliquam erat volutpat. Ut wisi enim ad minim veniam, quis nostrud exerci tation ullamcorper suscipit lobortis nisl ut aliquip ex ea commodo consequat. Duis autem vel eum iriure dolor in hendrerit in vulputate velit esse molestie consequat, vel illum dolore eu feugiat nulla facilisis at vero eros et accumsan et iusto odio dignissim qui blandit praesent luptatum zzril delenit augue duis dolore te feugait nulla facilisi. Lorem ipsum dolor Lorem ipsum dolor sit amet, consectetuer adipiscing elit, sed diam nonummy nibh euismod tincidunt ut laoreet dolore magna aliquam erat volutpat. Ut wisi enimint ad minim ven Mostrud exerci tation ullamcorper.

——— Section Six ———

Lorem ipsum dolor sit amet, consectetuer adipiscing elit, sed diam nonummy nibh euismod tincidunt ut laoreet dolore magnateum aliquam erat volutpat. Ut wisi enim ad minim veniam, quis nostrudexerci tation ulla mcorper suscipit lobortis nisl ut aliquip ex eacomm odo consequat. Duis autem vel eum iriure dolor in hendrerit in vulputate velit esse molestie consequat, vel illum dolore eu feugiat nulla facilisis at vero eros et. **Accumsan et iusto odio dign issim qui blandit praesent luptatum zzril delenit augue duis dolore.**

BEFORE

Poster Title in the Space Right Here
This is a faux academic poster that could use some design love.
By Author One, Author Two, Author Three, and Author Four
Affiliation Here

SECTION 1

Lorem ipsum dolor sit amet, consectetuer adipiscing elit, sed diam nonummy nibh euismod tincidunt ut laoreet dolore magna aliquam erat volutpat. Ut wisi enim ad minim veniam, quis nostrud exerci tation ullamcorper suscipit lobortis nisl ut aliquip ex ea commodo consequat. Duis autem vel eum iriure dolor in hendrerit in vulputate velit esse molestie consequat, vel illum dolore eu feugiat nulla facilisis at vero eros et accumsan et iusto odio dignissim qui blandit praesent luptatum zzril delenit augue duis dolore te feugait nulla facilisi. Lorem ipsum dolovolutpat. Ut wisi enim ad minim veniam.Mostrud exerci tation ullamcorper suscipit lobortis nisl ut aliquip ex ea commod. Ut wisi enim ad minim veniam, quis nostrud exerci tation ullamcorper suscipit lobortis nisl ut aliquip ex ea commodo consequat.

SECTION 2

Lorem ipsum dolor sit amet, consectetuer adipiscing elit, sed diam nonummy nibh euismod tincidunt ut laoreet dolore magna aliquam erat volutpat. Ut wisi enim ad minim veniam, quis nostrud exerci tation ullamcorper suscipit lobortis nisl ut aliquip ex ea commodo consequat. Duis autem vel eum iriure dolor in hendrerit in vulputate velit esse molestie consequat, vel

illum dolore eu feugiat nulla facilisis at vero eros et accumsan et iusto odio dignissim qui blandit praesenis dolore te feugait nrem ad minim veniamLorem ipsum dolor sit amet, consectetuer adipiscing elit, sed diam nonummy nibh euismod tincidunt ut laoreet dolore magna aliquam erat volutpat. Ut wisi enim ad minim veniam, quis nostrud exerci tation ullamcorper suscipit lobortis nisl ut aliquip ex ea commodo consequat.

SECTION 3

Lorem ipsum dolor sit amet, consectetuer adipiscing elit, sed diam nonummy nibh euismod tincidunt ut laoreet dolore magna aliquam erat volutpat. Ut wisi enim ad minim veniam, quis nostrud exerci tation ullamcorper suscipit lobormsan et iusto odio dignissim qui blandit praesenis dolore te feugait nrem ad minim veniamLorem ipsumtis ex ea commodo consequat.

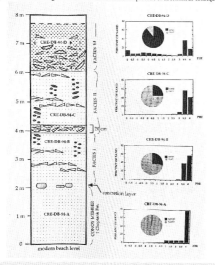

SECTION 4

Lorem ipsum dolor sit amet, consectetuer adipiscing elit, sed diam nonummy nibh euismod tincidunt ut laoreet dolore magna aliquam erat volutpat. Ut wisi enim ad minim veniam, quis nostrud exerci tation ullamcorper suscipit lobortis nisl ut aliquip ex ea commodo consequat. Duis autem vel eum iriure dolor in hendrerit in vulputate velit esse molestie consequat, vel illum dolore eu feugiat nulla facilisis at vero eros et accumsan et iusto odio dignise dolor in hendrerit in vsim qui blandit praesent luptatum zzril delenit augue duis dolore te feugait nulla facilsi. Lorem ipsum dolor Lorem ipsum dolor sit amet, consectetuer adipiscing elit, sed diam nonummy nibh euismod tincidunt ut laoreet dolore magna aliquam erat volutpat. Ut wisi enim ad Ut wisi enim ad minim veniam. Lorem ipsum dolor sit amet, consectetuer adipiscing elit, sed diam nonummy nibh euismod tincidunt ut laoreet dolore magna aliquam erat volutpat. Ut wisi enim ad minim veniam, quis nostrud exerci tation ullamcorper suscipit lobortis nisl ut aliquip ex ea commodo consequat.

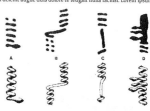

Lorem ipsum this is placeholding text. Aliquam erat volutpat. Ut wobortis nisl ut aliquiquat.

SECTION 5

Lorem ipsum dolor sit amet, consectetuer adipiscing elit, sed diam nonummy nibh euismod tincidunt ut laoreet dolore magna aliquam erat volutpat. Ut wisi enim ad minim veniam, quis nostrud exerci tation ullamcorper suscipit lobortis nisl ut aliquip ex ea commodo consequat. Duis autem vel eum iriuresequancorper suscipit lobortis nisl ut aliquip ex ea commodo consequat.Lorem ipsum dolor sit amet, consmsan et iusto odio dignissim qui blandit praesent luptatum zzril delenit augue duis dolore te feugait nullaLorem ipsum dolor sit amet, consectetuer adipiscing elit, sed diam nonummy nibh euismod tincidunt ut laoreet dolore magna aliquam erat volutpat. Ut wisi enim ad minim veniam, quis nostrud exerci tation ullamcorper suscipit lobortis nisl ut aliquip ex ea commodo consequat.

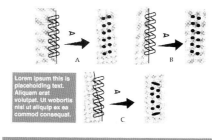

Lorem ipsum this is placeholding text. Aliquam erat volutpat. Ut wobortis nisl ut aliquip ex ea commod consequat.

SECTION 6

Lorem ipsum dolor sit amet, cons ectetuer adipiscing elit, sed diam nonummy nibh euismod tincidunt ut laoreet dolore magna aliquam erat volutpat. Ut wisi enim ad minim veniam, quis noad minim veniam, quis nostrud exerci tation ullamcorper suscipit lobortis nisl ut aliquip ex ea commodo consea facilisis at veoreet dolore magna aliquam erat volutpat. Ut wisi enim ad mini Lorem ipsum dolor sit amet, consectetuer adipiscing elit, sed diam nonummy nibh euismod tincidunt ut laoreet dolore magna aliquam erat volutpat. Ut wisi enim ad minim veniam, quis nostrud exerci tation ullamcorper suscipit lobortis nisl ut aliquip ex ea commodo consequat.

Adhere to the poster guidelines provided by your conference organizers, and include the information they require. But avoid overloading your poster with too much information. Edit down to the critical bits, and prominently feature particularly pertinent text and images.

AFTER

Poster Title in the Space Right Here
This is the redesigned version of a faux academic poster.

By Author One, Author Two, Author Three, and Author Four
Affiliation Here

Section One

Lorem ipsum dolor sit amet, consectetuer adipiscing elit, sed diam nonummy nibh euismod tincidunt ut laoreet dolore magna aliquam erat volutpat. Ut wisi enim ad minim veniam, quis nostrud exerci tation suscipit lobortis nisl ut aliquip ex ea commodo consequat. Duis autem vel eum iriure dolor in hendrerit in velit esse consequat, vel illum dolore eu nulla facilisis at vero. Lorem ipsum dolor sit amet, consectetuer adipiscing elit, sed diam nonummy nibh euismod tinci copperdunt ut laoreet dolore magna aliqua.

Section Two

Lorem ipsum dolor sit amet, consectetuer adipiscing elit, sed diam nonummy nibh euismod tincidunt ut laoreet dolore magna aliquam erat volutpat. Ut wisi enim ad minim veniam, quis nostrud exerci tation ullamcorper suscipit lobortis nisl ut aliquip ex ea commodo consequat. Duis autem vel eum iriure dolor in hendrerit in vulputate velit esse molestie consequat, vel illum dolore u feugiat nulla facilisis at vero eros.

Quis nostrud exerci tation ullamcorper suscipit lobortis nisl ut aliquip ex ea commodo consequat. Duis autem vel eum Lorem ipsum this is a caption

Section Three

Lorem ipsum dolor sit amet, consectetuer adipiscing elit, sed diam nonummy nibh euismod tincidunt ut laoreet dolore magna aliquam erat volutpat. Ut wisi enim ad minim veniam, quis nostrud exerci tation ullamcorper suscipit lobortis nisl ut aliquip ex ea commodo consequat. Duis autem vel eum iriure dolor in hendrerit in vulputate velit esse molestie consequat, vel illum dolore eu feugiat.

Section Four

Lorem ipsum dolor sit amet, consectetuer adipiscing elit, sed diam nonummy nibh euismod tincidunt ut laoreet dolore magna aliquam erat volutpat. Ut wisi enim ad minim veniam, quis nostrud exerci tation ullamcorper suscipit lobortis nisl ut aliquip ex ea commodo consequat. Duis autem vel eum iriure dolor in hendrerit in vulputate velit esse molestie consequat, vel illum dolore eu feugiat nulla facilisis at vero eros et accumsan et iusto odio dignissim qui bland.

Quis nostrud exerci tation ullamcorper suscipit lobortis nisl ut aliquip ex ea commodo consequat. Duis autem vel eum Lorem ipsum this is a caption Quis nostrud exerci tation ullamcorper susc

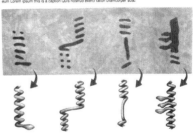

Section Five

Lorem ipsum dolor sit amet, consectetuer adipiscing elit, sed diam nonummy nibh euismod tincidunt ut laoreet dolore magna aliquam erat volutpat. **(A)** Ut wisi enim ad minim veniam, quis nostrud exerci tation ullamcorper suscipit lobortis nisl ut aliquip ex ea commodo consequat. Duis autem vel eum iriure dolor in hendrerit in vulputate velit esse molestie consequat. **(B)** Vel illum dolore eu feugiat nulla facilisis at vero eros et accumsan et iusto odio dignissim qui blandit praesent. **(C)** Luptatum zzril delenit augue duis dolore te feugait nulla facilisi. Lorem ipsum dolor Lorem ipsum dolor sit amer.

Quis nostrud exerci tation ullamcorper suse ipit lobortis nisl ut aliquip ex ea commodo consequat. Duis autem vel euomrem ipsum

Quis nostrud exerci tation ullamcorper suse ipit lobortis nisl ut aliquip ex ea commodo consequat. Duis autem vel

Quis nostrud exerci tation ullamcorper suse ipit lobortis nisl ut aliquip ex ea commodo consequat. Duis autem vel eumorem ipsum.

Section Six

Lorem ipsum dolor sit amet, consectetuer adipiscing elit, sed diam nonummy nibh euismod tincidunt ut laoreet dolore magna aliquam erat volutpat. Ut wisi enim ad minim veniam, quis nostrud exerci tation suscipit lobortis nisl ut aliquip ecom.

BEFORE

Poster Title in the Space Right Here
This is a faux academic poster that could use some design love.
By Author Name

Affiliation Here

Caterpillar Photo Credit: Ryan Hagerty, USFWS (public domain)

Section Four

Lorem ipsum dolor sit amet, consectetuer adipiscing elit, sed diam nonummy nibh euismod tincidunt ut laoreet dolore magna aliquam erat volutpat. Ut wisi enim ad minim veniam, quis nostrud exerci tation ullamcorper suscipit lobortis nisl ut aliquip ex ea commodo consequat. Duis autem vel eum iriuresequancorper suscipit lobortis nisl ut aliquip ex ea commodo consequat.Lorem ipsum dolor sit amet, consemsan et iusto odio dignissim qui blandit praesent luptatum zzril delenit augue duis dolore te feugait nullaLorem ipsum dolor sit amet, consectetuer adipiscing elit, sed diam nonummy nibh euismod tincidunt ut laoreet dolore magna aliquam erat volutpat. Ut wisi enim ad minim veniam, quis nostrud exerci tation ullamcorp

Section One

Lorem ipsum dolor sit amet, consectetuer adipiscing elit, sed diam nonummy nibh euismod tincidunt ut laoreet dolore magna aliquam erat volutpat. Ut wisi enim ad minim veniam, quis nostrud exerci tation ullamcorper suscipit lobortis nisl ut aliquip ex ea commodo consequat. Duis autem vel eum iriure dolor in hendrerit in vulputate velit esse molestie consequat, vel illum dolore eu feugiat nulla facilisis at vero eros et accumsan et iusto odio dignissim qui blandit praesent luptatum zzril delenit augue duis dolore te feugait nulla facilisi. Lorem ipsum dolovolutpat. Ut wisi enim ad minim veniam.Mostrud exerci tation ullamcorper suscipit lobortis nisl ut aliquip ex ea commod. Ut wisi enim ad minim veniam, quis nostrud exerci tation ullamcorper suscipit lobortis nisl ut aliquip ex ea commodo consequat.

Section Two

Lorem ipsum dolor sit amet, consectetuer adipiscing elit, sed diam nonummy nibh euismod tincidunt ut laoreet dolore magna aliquam erat volutpat. Ut wisi enim ad minim veniam, quis nostrud exerci tation ullamcorper suscipit lobortis nisl ut aliquip ex ea commodo consequat.Lorem ipsum dolor sit amet, consemsan et iusto odio dignissim qui blandit praesent luptatum zzril delenit augue duis dolore te feugait nullaLorem ipsum dolor sit amet, consectetuer adipiscing elit, sed diam nonummy nibh euismod tincidunt ut laoreet dolore magna aliquam erat volutpat. Ut wisi enim ad minim veniam, quis nostrud exerci tation ullamcorper suscipit lobortis nisl ut aliquip ex ea commodo consequat.

Section Three

Lorem ipsum dolor sit amet, consectetuer adipiscing elit, sed diam nonummy nibh euismod tincidunt ut laoreet dolore magna aliquam erat volutpat. Ut wisi enim ad minim veniam, quis nostrud exerci tation ullamcorper suscipit lobortis nisl ut aliquip ex ea commodo consequat.Lorem ipsum dolor sit amet, consemsan et iusto odio dignissim qui blandit praesent luptatum zzril delenit augue duis

Section Five

Lorem ipsum dolor sit amet, consectetuer adipiscing elit, sed diam nonummy nibh euismod tincidunt ut laoreet dolore magna aliquam erat volutpat. Ut wisi enim ad minim veniam, quis nostrud exerci tation ullamcorper suscipit lobortis nisl ut aliquip ex ea commodo consequat. Duis autem vel eum iriure dolor in hendrerit in vulputate velit esse molestie consequat, vel illum dolore eu feugiat nulla facilisis at vero eros et accumsan et iusto odio dignissim qui blandit praesent luptatum zzril delenit augue duis dolore te feugait nulla facilisi. Lorem ipsum dolovolutpat. Ut wisi enim ad minim veniam.Mostrud exerci tation ullamcorper suscipit lobortis nisl ut aliquip ex ea commod. Ut wisi enim ad minim veniam,

Engaging photos and drawings can help hook people and give them a quick sense of the subject matter of your poster. But I don't recommend crowding out the rest of your content with them. For academic conferences, make sure that the key take-home message of your research doesn't get lost in the midst of generic imagery.

AFTER

Poster Title in the Space Right Here
This is the redesigned version of a faux academic poster.

Author Name, Affiliation here

Section One

Lorem ipsum dolor sit amet, consectetuer adipiscing elit, sed diam nonummy nibh euismod tincidunt ut laoreet dolore magna aliquam erat volutpat. Ut wisi enim ad minim veniam, quis nostrud exerci tation ullamcorper suscipit lobortis nisl ut aliquip ex ea commodo consequat. Duis autem vel eum iriure dolor in hendrerit in vulputate velit esse molestie consequat, vel illum dolor

Section Two

Lorem ipsum dolor sit amet, consectetuer adipiscing elit, sed diam nonummy nibh euismod tincidunt ut laoreet dolore magna aliquam erat volutpat. Ut wisi enim ad minim veniam, quis nostrud exerci tation ullamcorper suscipit lobortis nisl ut aliquip ex ea commodo consequat. Duis autem vel eum iriure dolor in hendrerit in vulputate velit esse molestie consequat, vel illum dolore eu feugiat nulla facilisis at vero eros et accumsan et iusto odio dignissim qui blandit praesent luptatum zzril delenit augue duis dolore te feugait nulla facilisi. Lorem ipsum dolor Lorem ipsum dolor sit amet, consectetuer adipiscing elit, sed diam nonummy.

Section Three

Lorem ipsum dolor sit amet, consectetuer adipiscing elit, sed diam nonummy nibh euismod tincidunt ut laoreet dolore magna aliquam erat volutpat. Ut wisi enim ad minim veniam, quis nostrud exerci tation ullamcorper suscipit lobortis nisl ut aliquip ex ea commodo consequat. Duis autem vel eum iriure dolor in hendrerit in vulputate velit esse molestie consequat, vel illum dolore eu feugiat nulla facilisis at vero eros et accumsan et iusto odio dignissim qui blandit praesent luptatum zzril delenit augue duis dolore te feugait nulla facilisi. Lorem ipsum dolor Lorem ipsum dolor sit amet, consectetuer adipiscing elit, sed diam nonummy.

Section Four

Lorem ipsum dolor sit amet, consectetuer adipiscing elit, sed diam nonummy nibh euismod tincidunt ut laoreet dolore magna aliquam erat volutpat. Ut wisi enim ad minim veniam, quis nostrud exerci tation ullamcorper suscipit lobortis nisl ut aliquip ex ea uismod tincidunt ut laoreet dolore magna aliquam erat volutpat. Ut wisi enim ad minim veniam, quis nostrud exerci tation ullamcorper suscipea commodo consequat. Duis autem vel eum iriure dolor in hendrerit in vulputate velit esse molestie consequat, vel illum dolore eu feugiat nminim veniam, quis nostrud exerci tation ullamcorper suscipit lobortis nisl ut aliquip exulla facilisis at vero eros et accumsan et iusto odio dignissim qui blandit praesent luptatum zzril delenit augue duis dolore te feugait nulla facilisi. Lorem ipsum dolor Lorem ipsum dolor sit amet, consectetuer adipiscing elit, sed diam nonummy.

Time

Section Five

Lorem ipsum dolor sit amet, consectetuer adipiscing elit, sed diam nonummy nibh euismod tincidunt ut laoreet dolore magna aliquam erat volutpat. Ut wisi enim ad minim veniam, quis nostrud exerci tation ullamcorper suscipit lobortis nisl ut aliquip ex ea commodo consequat. Duis autem vel eum iriure dolor in hendrerit in vulputate velit esse molestie consequat, vel illum dolore eu feugiat nulla facilisis at vero eros et accumsan et iusto odio dignissim.

Caterpillar Photo Credit: Ryan Hagerty, USFWS (public domain)

CHAPTER 8

Color

IT'S WELL ESTABLISHED THAT COLOR VISION is enabled by so-called cone cells in the retina. But many finer points of how humans perceive color are still active areas of research.

Trichromacy theory describes how three distinct types of cone cells respond to different light wavelengths (S-cones detect short wavelengths, M-cones detect medium wavelengths, and L-cones detect long wavelengths). Relative stimulation of those different cell types allows us to perceive a wide range of colors. Cells are sensitive to overlapping wavelengths. But this theory stops short of explaining what happens after the cones are activated.

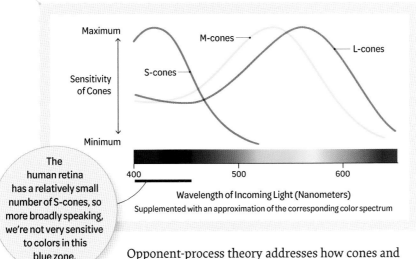

The human retina has a relatively small number of S-cones, so more broadly speaking, we're not very sensitive to colors in this blue zone.

Supplemented with an approximation of the corresponding color spectrum

Opponent-process theory addresses how cones and rods interact with other neurons in the retina (specifically bipolar cells and ganglions). This model suggests that there are three

opponent channels: red/green (courtesy of cones), blue/yellow (cones), and black/white (rods). Differences in the signals from the rods and cones are processed down the line by bipolar cells and ganglions. It also helps to explain negative afterimage optical illusions. Stare intensely at the blue square in the box at the top for a spell, and then shift your gaze to the empty box below it.

Are you seeing a yellow after image? That's the blue/yellow channel at work.

Dual-process theory suggests that the processes in trichromacy theory and opponent-process theory are not at odds. Rather, they work in tandem: distinct cone cells that respond to different wavelengths feed into opponent cells. Exactly how they might work in tandem is still not clear.[1]

Light wavelengths and cell responses to stimuli can be measured, and studied by physiologists focused on mechanism and function. How a color *appears* to us is a slightly different beast, and addressed more directly by psychophysicists, who bridge the gap between stimuli and sensations. Colors—as we perceive them—aren't absolute; they vary from person to person. As researcher Karen Schloss explains, color is also subject to perceptual issues (variations in our ability to see and discriminate colors in different settings), aesthetic issues (different people have different preferences), and semantics (different people associate different concepts with different colors).[2]

For our purposes, it's probably more useful to address the idea of *why* we see color: Color vision allows humans to more easily distinguish things from one another, remember those objects, and communicate with others about them.[3] It follows that color can be used in information design as a way to selectively isolate and highlight objects and information. But first we should dive more deeply into the language of color, and color theory as it relates to design. After all, words like yellow and green are helpful, but they aren't very precise.

1   Michael W. Eysenck and Mark T. Keane, *Cognitive Psychology: A Student's Handbook,* 8th edition (Milton Park, Abingdon, Oxon ; New York, NY: Psychology Press, 2020), with a nod to Steven K. Shevell and Paul R. Martin, "Color Opponency: Tutorial," *JOSA A,* Vol. 34 (July 1, 2017)

2   Enrico Bertini and Moritz Stefaner, "Color with Karen Schloss," *Data Stories,* podcast episode 119 (April 27, 2018)

3   Christoph Witzel and Karl R. Gegenfurtner, "Color Perception: Objects, Constancy, and Categories," *Annual Review of Vision Science,* Vol. 4 (2018)

See "A Closer Look: Color Jargon, Translated" on page 100 for helpful ways of thinking about, talking about, and adjusting color.

The language and cultural connotations of color vary across time and space. For that reason, I don't recommend optimum color palettes in this book, as this depends on the content you're presenting, the ultimate context, and your audience. Rather, I simply encourage you to pause and think about how you're using color in your graphic. It's a powerful tool for helping your audience isolate and track pertinent objects or information within a graphic. Are you using it in your favor?

Approaching Color Critically

Many scientific disciplines lean on color palette conventions that are generally not optimized for human perception. And many designers faithfully adhere to those conventions when otherwise redesigning the same information for non-specialist audiences. (I've certainly been guilty of doing it.) One infamous example is the rainbow colormap.

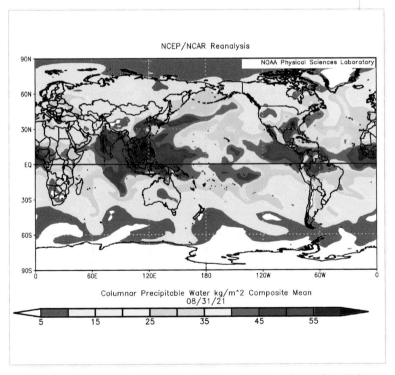

Image Credit: NOAA/ESRL Physical Sciences Laboratory, Boulder, Colorado, *http://psl. noaa.gov/*; Data analysis model: "The NCEP/NCAR Reanalysis 40-Year Project," by E. Kalnay et al., *Bulletin of the American Meteorological Society*, Vol. 77 (March 1996)

Color Jargon, Translated

What's the difference between hue and value? How about chroma and saturation? Lots of terms related to color are a bit slippery, and often interchanged, sometimes incorrectly. And different color spaces (see page 157) come with different conventions and language traditions. The Munsell System (developed by Albert H. Munsell, culminating in a color atlas published in 1915[1]) provides a handy way to break things down. Here's a modern rendering of part of his tree model, annotated with definitions. Many wedges are removed in this view, so you can see how the variables play out for a few spokes.

Hue refers to the general color category. For example, all of these might be classified as blue:

And these as red:

White

Yellow

Green-yellow

Yellow-red

Red

Green

Red-purple

Blue-green

Purple

Blue

Value indicates the lightness or darkness of a color. Tints are lighter, more luminous and brighter versions (at the top of the Munsell tree); shades are darker, less luminous versions (at the bottom).

Purple-blue

Black

Chroma refers to the strength or weakness of a color. It ranges from desaturated or dull (ring center) to saturated or intense (ring edge).

Image Credit: Universal Images Group North America LLC / Alamy Stock Photo (central tree)

1   Albert. H. Munsell, *Atlas of the Munsell Color System* (Wadsworth, Howland & Co., Inc., Printers, 1915), *https://library.si.edu/digital-library/book/atlasmunsellcol00muns*

What's the problem, other than a palette that may feel too intense for some tastes? The full rainbow spectrum isn't generally *perceived* as a smooth gradient. A few transition points are more prominent than others. (This effect is often much stronger when viewed on a screen, as opposed to a print page. See page 157 for more on the differences between subtractive and additive color spaces.)

Some zones have larger perceived jumps in hue than others. The jump from yellow to orange here, for example, seems larger than the jump from green to, well...green. Even though the distance between swatches is the same in both cases.

These perceived irregularities are particularly evident when viewed next to a continuous grayscale gradient.

Rainbow color gradients have been falling out of favor in recent years for this reason,[4] but conventions are hard to shake. In the meantime, retain a critical eye and question default color palettes. A good rule of thumb to help identify color palettes that may be doing more harm than good is to try printing things out on a black and white printer, or simply converting your digital file to grayscale. If you're seeing patterns in your color legend that don't honor the nature of what the gradient aims to represent, change your color palette. Here's how the rainbow spectrum fares in that test:

That said, a straightforward grayscale gradient, like this one, comes with issues of its own.

4   S. Zeller and D. Rogers, "Visualizing Science: How Color Determines What We See," *Eos* (May 21, 2020) *http://eos.org/features/visualizing-science-how-color-determines-what-we-see*

Monochromatic color palettes (like a simple grayscale gradient) are particularly at risk of an optical illusion that can make a single color look different in two different positions, depending upon the color of its immediate neighbor. The effect is called simultaneous contrast. All six of these dots are the same color.

The rainbow color palette skirts this effect. It's easier to isolate and correctly identify discrete colors as your eye travels from the key to the image. Luckily, there are ways of making the most of both approaches. One way to do that is demonstrated by Bang Wong in *Nature Methods*. Here, he shows how a linear change in lightness with a simultaneous change in hue and saturation can play out.[5]

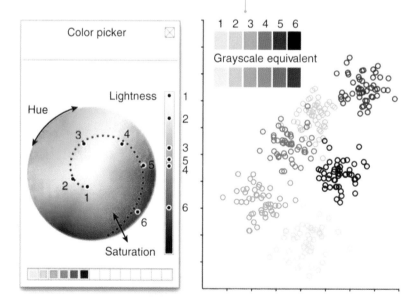

In the case of a gradient, or to otherwise represent continuous values, those numbered color picker dots would ideally be equidistant from one another on the lightness scale. As demonstrated by the sample chart, it's not just a strategy to create gradients. It's also a great way to pick a set of colors that represent discrete things. The result is easier to read for everyone, and it may be particularly critical for a correct interpretation of your graphic for folks with color vision deficiencies.

---

5   Bang Wong, "Color Coding," *Nature Methods,* Vol. 7 (August 2010)

I used a similar process for redesigning the colorful map first presented earlier in this section. Sadly, the characteristic water vapor "tendrils" are not nearly as prominent or dramatic in the redesigned version. But the gradient is truer to the continuous nature of the data. So I simply used other marks (a dotted line and label) to draw reader attention to the areas of particular interest.

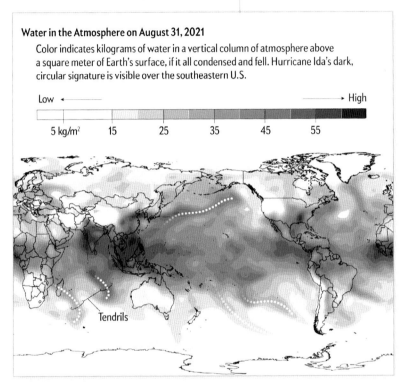

Water in the Atmosphere on August 31, 2021

Color indicates kilograms of water in a vertical column of atmosphere above a square meter of Earth's surface, if it all condensed and fell. Hurricane Ida's dark, circular signature is visible over the southeastern U.S.

Low ← ——————— ——————— → High

5 kg/m²   15   25   35   45   55

Tendrils

It's clear that this is an important issue for data visualizations. But what does all of this mean for illustrated explanatory diagrams that aren't necessarily assigning precise values to colors? If you're relying on color to represent a critical variable, it's wise to somehow double-encode that information, unless your colors pass the grayscale test. For example, when representing different cell types, use different colors *and* different symbol shapes. When representing different star categories, use different colors *and* differently sized dots. Or if your color is being used to define a continuous area or line, consider using a label that directly points to that shape as opposed to defining the meaning of the color in a separate key.

Strategies for Using Color

Color is probably most often thought of as a way to represent something as it appears in real life. Like using yellow for bananas. But color can be a really powerful tool in other ways. Especially when you're illustrating concepts that go beyond basic appearance. Here are three strategies I use when designing science graphics:

- Use color as a tool for problem solving during the planning stages,
- Use color to help a reader track and compartmentalize elements, and
- Use color to help folks more quickly and intuitively grasp new concepts, such as the idea of superposition in quantum mechanics.

In high school I always carried around at least four pens in different colors. I furiously swapped out pens while taking notes in class, or rolled through my notes later, bracketing sections in blue, green, orange, and purple. The habit continues to serve me well, although now it often takes the form of changing the font color of full paragraphs or sections in Google Documents. Chunking up notes into color-coded, thematically related blocks helps me organize information in the early stages of a project. Color-coded blocks of text quickly signal to me what bits of information are closely related to each other. This, in turn, helps identify details that might work well together in illustrated form.

For example, when doing background research for an article about the Ebola virus, I took notes structured according to my leading questions: **what is it?, how does it kill/why is it so deadly?,** and **treatment possibilities.** I used a few highlighters to flag different sections of my hand-written notes. I used those same highlighter colors

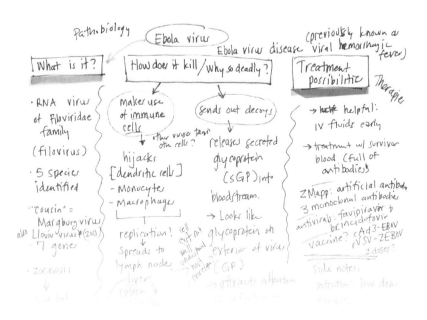

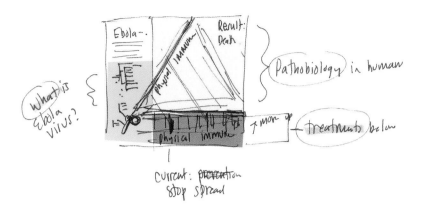

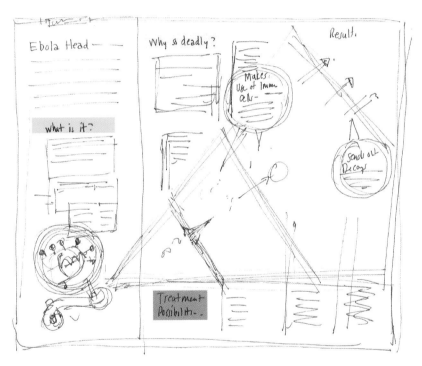

to tag excerpts on digital and printed research papers and other reference material. Those colorized sections informed the basic composition of the graphic. When used in this way, color can function as an organizational and planning tool. The colors shown here were used in the early stages of the process. They weren't incorporated into the final art. (To see more stages of this project, including final art, see pages 216–221.)

In the final image, color can help your reader track parts of a physical object over time, as shown by Kate Francis of Brown Bird Design. In a series of frames that capture a robot's posture as it walks forward, she uses magenta for the right leg and cyan for the left leg. This allows the reader to easily track the changing position of each discrete leg.

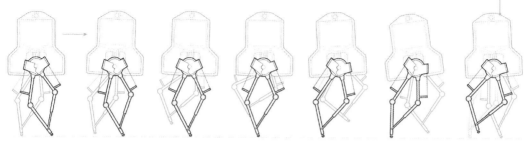

Image Credit: Brown Bird Design, as published in "The Clumsy Quest to Perfect the Walking Robot," by John Pavlus, *Scientific American* (July 2016); Source: "Dynamic multi-domain bipedal walking with atrias through slip based human inspired control," by Ayonga Hereid et al., in *Proceedings of the 17th International Conference on Hybrid Systems: Computation and Control* (April 2014). Reproduced with permission from the artist.

Similarly, color can be used to compartmentalize different parts of a whole. In this schematic of the Genesis probe's trajectory through space, three distinct colors (green, orange, and blue) mark the three distinct phases of the trek. In both of these cases, color does not represent the true color of the object. Instead, color helps the reader isolate and identify key elements of the illustration.

That technique can also be applied to help a reader relate one concept across more than one scenario. Here, artist Matthew Twombly uses color to help the reader make a connection between information they learned in the first part of the graphic, to a more abstract application of that same concept later on. Specifically, he uses red and yellow apples to introduce the idea of superposition, a concept in quantum mechanics that describes a particle as being in two states at the same time. Those two colors are repeated throughout the rest of the otherwise monochromatic graphic, providing a continuous thread as the concept goes from thought experiment (portraying apples), to actual experiment (portraying electrons).

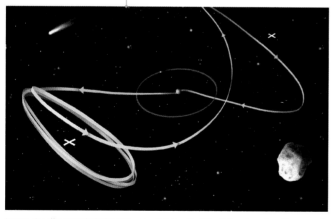

Image Credit: Jen Christiansen, as published in "The Interplanetary Transport Network," by Shane Ross, *American Scientist* (May-June 2006). Reproduced with permission from Sigma Xi, The Scientific Research Society.

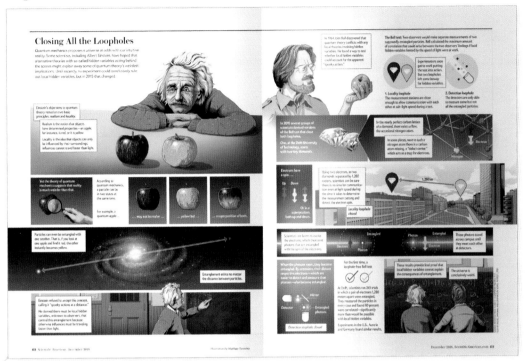

A closer look at two panel strips:

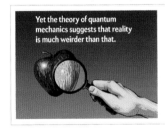

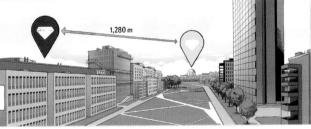

For another article on quantum mechanics, I used color to quickly give the reader a sense of how the material on the page is organized. Three scenarios are examined, through two lenses: quantum (yellow tint) and classical (cyan tint). You could strip out the color, and the information would remain intact, thanks to labels and captions. But, the reader is provided with an intuitive assist when color reinforces the connections.

There are lots of other ways to think about using color in graphics, and no single "correct" solution or palette for any given graphic. Ultimately, my advice is to simply slow down, and think through the options. Before you default to using colors that correspond to object

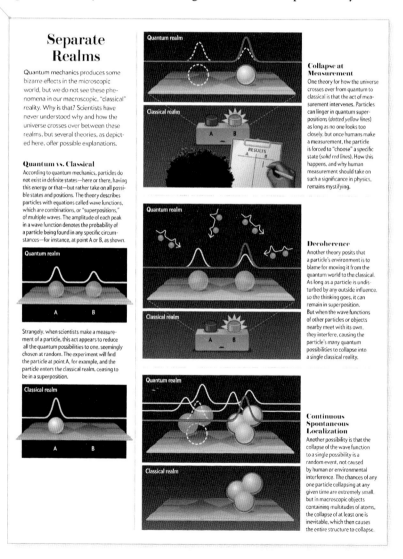

appearance, ask yourself if color could be used to help convey your graphic's take-home message more clearly instead.

Looking for more advice? Eddie Opara and John Cantwell offer up a series of great summary-level suggestions in their book *Color Works*.[6] Some of my favorites are:

- "Understand that various cultures and consumers symbolize colors differently."
- "There is no correct or incorrect way to perceive color; it's an individual, highly personal matter."
- "Keep a record of colors that you have used and like to use."
- "Always look at other examples of how color is used by the likes of painters, fashion designers, and interior designers."

More to Explore

- ***What Is Color?: 50 Questions and Answers on the Science of Color*** by Arielle Eckstut and Joann Eckstut (Abrams, 2020): A breezy and reader-friendly book that addresses the full gamut, from physics to biology.
- **"Visualizing Science: How Color Determines What We See"** by S. Zeller and D. Rogers (*Eos*, May 21, 2020): This article provides a great overview of recent color perception science research as it relates to the changing needs of scientists. *http://eos.org/features/ visualizing-science-how-color-determines-what-we-see*
- **"Elegant Figures—Subtleties of Color"** by Robert Simmon (NASA Earth Observatory, August 5, 2013): This six-part series on color is both comprehensive and concise. *https://earthobservatory. nasa.gov/blogs/elegantfigures/2013/08/05/subtleties-of-color-part-1-of-6/*
- ***Data Stories*, episode 119** (April 27, 2018): Perception researcher Karen Schloss talks with podcast hosts Enrico Bertini and Moritz Stefaner about everything from rainbow colormaps to the association between colors and meaning. *https://datastori.es/119 -color-with-karen-schloss/*
- **Color in Data Vis** blog series by Lisa Charlotte Muth for Datawrapper (accessed March 26, 2022): A companion book is in progress! *https://blog.datawrapper.de/category/color-in-data-vis/*

6   Eddie Opara and John Cantwell, *Color Works: An Essential Guide to Understanding and Applying Color Design Principles* (Rockport Publishers, 2014)

DEMONSTRATION

Color Makeover (part two of three)

This is the second installment of a demonstration that takes part in three stages. Context and content remain steady throughout the makeover. It's a hypothetical graphic destined for a hypothetical academic journal. The redesigned images are all for the same audience and outlet as the original version. The content is completely made up. The initial graphic includes less-than-ideal color palette choices that are not made up. (I've seen a lot of figures that

BEFORE

Figure 1. Pathogenesis of classical cat treat disease and paradoxical cat treat disease. (A) Classical: Protein one, which is produced by the gut upon the ingestion of a treat, forms complexes with protein two. These complexes trigger alpha cells to produce large amounts of protein three. Protein three stimulates beta cells, which releases proteins four and five. Protein four triggers gamma cells to start massing in the gut's lining. Gamma cells then release protein six, pushing gut lining cells into a hypergrowth state, resulting in a grumpy cat. This condition can be confirmed by testing for levels of proteins three, four, and six. (B) Paradoxical: The introduction of drug A successfully blocked classical cat treat disease in most cats, by inhibiting the production of protein four. However, some cats were still grumpy. In 1 to 3 percent of cats, paradoxical cat treat disease may arise due to an increase in production of protein five, a side effect of drug A. The full pathway of paradoxical cat treat disease is not yet understood, but can be confirmed by testing for levels of proteins three and five.

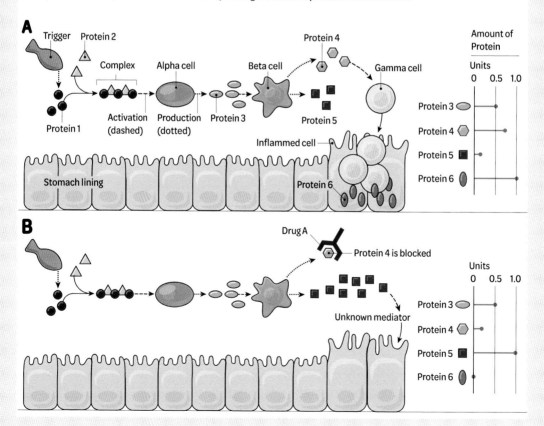

approach color like this, in which color is simply used to distinguish every object from every other object.) The revisions on this spread are limited to changes in color. See pages 88–89 for the initial composition makeover. See pages 124–125 for a typography makeover. Rendering style is the same throughout—and fairly standard—to avoid distracting from the other core design changes with razzle dazzle.

Color changes here are primarily in the service of (1) establishing a hierarchy of information by drawing the readers attention to key players, and (2) facilitating an easy and direct comparison between each scenario.

AFTER

Figure 1. Pathogenesis of classical cat treat disease and paradoxical cat treat disease. (₎ ⁀⁀⁀⁀⁀⁀⁀⁀ ⁀ one, which is produced by the gut upon the ingestion of a treat, forms complexes with protein two. These complexes trigger alpha cells to produce large amounts of protein three. Protein three stimulates beta cells, which releases proteins four and five. Protein four triggers gamma cells to start massing in the gut's lining. Gamma cells then release protein six, pushing gut lining cells into a hypergrowth state, resulting in a grumpy cat. This condition can be confirmed by testing for levels of proteins three, four, and six. (B) Paradoxical: The introduction of drug A successfully blocked classical cat treat disease in most cats, by inhibiting the production of protein four. However, some cats were still grumpy. In 1 to 3 percent of cats, paradoxical cat treat disease may arise due to an increase in production of protein five, a side effect of drug A. The full pathway of paradoxical cat treat disease is not yet understood, but can be confirmed by testing for levels of proteins three and five.

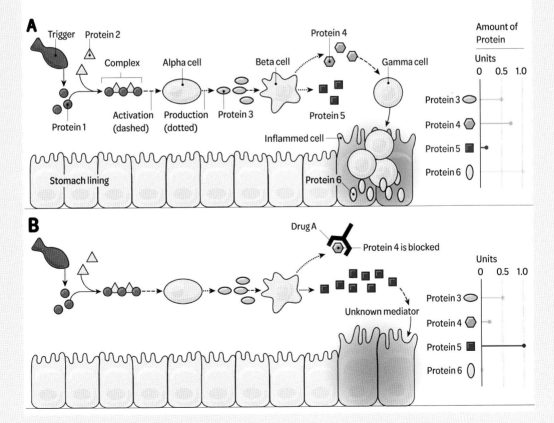

CHAPTER 9

Typography

ONE OF MY OFFICIAL JOB TITLES while on staff at *National Geographic* was "Typographic Designer." No, I didn't design typefaces. (Good thing, too, as that is definitely not my area of expertise.) Rather, I was tasked with ensuring that page layouts designed by senior designers maintained their integrity throughout the editing process, from the moment that place-holding nonsense text was replaced with proper article text, all the way through publication. I focused on aligning text and image boxes (making sure that they adhered to the underlying magazine grid), rebreaking text lines so that the overall shape of a caption or annotation was aesthetically pleasing, and adjusting the amount of space between letters of titles and subheads.

Very little of my time was spent on actually expressively designing with type at that time. Title style decisions and creative use of those typefaces involved choices made by senior layout designers. My job was to mind the smaller, quieter details that impacted a few pretty critical factors: (1) readability, and (2) cues for how to navigate through a space. (This is where hierarchy comes in.) Those two factors are key when it comes to designing science graphics, and are the focus of this section.

Per *Butterick's Practical Typography*, typography refers to the "visual component of the written word."[1] That doesn't just mean the typeface choice. It also includes size, placement, alignment, spacing, color, and a whole host of other considerations. It's not the words themselves, but how those words are presented in visual form. For more typography-related definitions, see "A Closer Look: Typography Jargon, Translated"

---

1   *https://practicaltypography.com/*

on the facing page. And I should note that this section is centered on my experiences—and readings that are focused on—type set in English, for a contemporary audience.

If you think that text and typography isn't in your purview, or that it's something that can be considered and added at the last minute, perhaps findings published by Michelle Borkin and colleagues in 2016 will help change your mind. In an eye-tracking and recall experiment, they found that titles and other text elements in visualizations attracted—and held attention—longer than any other element. And, critically, "the content of a title has a significant impact on what a person will take away from, and later recall, about a visualization."[2]

In a presentation at Eyeo Festival in 2011, Amanda Cox (then a data journalist at *The New York Times*) stated concisely, "The annotation layer is the most important thing we do." You're helping to tell your reader what they should look at, especially if you're trying to show them something that they don't know much about. "Instead of handing someone a chart and saying 'best of luck in this endeavor,' you're holding their hand a little bit and saying 'hey, come with me, this is pretty cool!'"[3] (Annotations are short chunks of text that sit directly on a graphic and address the specific visual details that they're next to. More on annotations is in the Hierarchy section on page 120.)

Many publications and companies have style guides that include type specifications. Guidelines lead to consistency. Typography—like color—is a variable that can be efficiently standardized and imposed across content types. If you have a style guide to refer to, your primary decisions with regards to typography are likely already in-hand, like what fonts to install and what size to use. But that doesn't mean you don't need to think about it further. How these elements might work within specific graphics isn't always prescribed, and should really be considered on a case-by-case basis.

Legibility and Readability

Above all else, text in a graphic should be clear enough to read. Style, size, color, position, and orientation should all be considered with this in mind. Two measures come into play in this regard: legibility and

2   Michelle A. Borkin et al., "Beyond Memorability: Visualization Recognition and Recall," *IEEE Transactions on Visualization and Computer Graphics,* Vol. 22 (January 2016)

3   Amanda Cox, "Shaping Data for News," Eyeo Festival presentation (2011) *https://vimeo.com/29391942*

A CLOSER LOOK ──●

Typography Jargon, Translated

Why do I use the word "typeface" more often than "font" in this chapter? Strictly speaking, "typeface" refers to the letterform design. "Font" is the delivery mechanism, such as a metal cast for printing presses, or the software package used to install a typeface on your computer. Here's a potentially useful analogy: Typeface is to a note as a font is to an email or paper greeting card. The same note (typeface) can be delivered in a few different ways (font). With apologies to purists, I often get sloppy and use them interchangeably.

Broad Terms
This isn't an exhaustive list of type jargon, by any means. Check out the resources listed on page 123 for a much deeper dive.

Type Family • A type family is comprised of all of the styles (Roman, italic, bold, condensed, etc.) of a given typeface.

Type Classifications • There are many type classification systems. The systems generally group typefaces by visual characteristics. Two categories that appear in most typologies: Serif and sans-serif. (Other categories include script, slab serif, etc.) Serifs are slight projections or marks that appear at the end of letter strokes. **Serif** typefaces include them. Sans-serif typefaces don't. This (the typeface Omnes) is sans-serif.

This (the typeface Elena) has serifs.

Intrinsic Characteristics
These variables are inherent to a given font.

Cap height · Ascender · X-height · Baseline · Descender

Flagellum

Extrinsic Characteristics
These variables can be modified, and they relate to decisions you make when using a particular typeface in a graphic.

Tracking refers to universally adjusting the letter spacing across a group of letters.

Not adjusted: Flagellum   Tracked in: Flagellum   Tracked out: Flagellum

Kerning refers to adjusting the spacing between two letters. Digital fonts are designed in such a way that— unless you're designing a bespoke title or other large display type—you probably won't need to manually adjust the space. I reduced the kerning a bit here.

Waveform   Waveform

Leading refers the space between lines. A standard default is 120% of the type size. For this paragraph set at a type size of 8.5 pt, that's a line space of 10.2 pt.

This paragraph has leading that's looser than that. The type size is set at 8.5 pt, and the leading (or line space) is set at 13 pt.

This paragraph has leading that is tighter than the default. The type size is set at 8.5 pt, and the leading (or line space) is set at 7.5 pt.

Alignment is the variable in addition to size, position, and orientation—you're most likely to customize, after choosing a typeface. This block of type is flush left/ragged right.

This block of type, on the other hand, is flush right/jagged left. I use it for the categories in the margin to the left.

This block of type is center-aligned. It has a formal, poetic vibe. It may suit titles or labels, but it can be a bit tricky to make it work for captions in science graphics.

This block of type is justified. The words are forced to extend to each margin. For more on the pros and cons, see page 118.

readability. The words are often used interchangeably, but there are some subtle distinctions.

Legibility refers to how easy it is to distinguish one letter from another. For the most part, this is dependent on the font that you choose. But it's also influenced by variables like size, color, and contrast. Letters are easily distinguished from one another in legible text. Less so in illegible text:

More legible →*Less legible* • More legible →Less legible • **More legible** → Less legible

Readability is a broader descriptor. It refers to how easy it is to read words, sentences, and paragraphs. It's more content-related, and includes things like punctuation and word choice. But design choices play a role here as well. For example, the paragraph you're reading right now is more readable than the paragraph below.

Readability is a broader descriptor. It refers to how easy it is to read words, sentences, and paragraphs. It's more content-related, and includes things like punctuation and word choice. But design choices play a role here as well. For example, the paragraph you're reading right now is less readable than the paragraph above.

It's commonly held that serif type—like the typeface used in this paragraph—is more legible than sans-serif type—like the typeface I'm using in cyan for footnotes and captions in this book. But as summarized by Charles Bigelow, evidence does not strongly support this claim.[4] (Bigelow's paper includes a great overview of research related to many typeface features.) That said, there's a strong tradition—at least in materials typeset for print in English—of using serif type for long stretches of text, and sans-serif type for shorter, supporting text blocks. It's a tradition that I follow in this book.

Interestingly, a 2021 article by Carla Delgado in *Discover* highlights research that indicates that there may be a "desirable difficulty" sweet spot in some cases. She references a few papers that support the counterintuitive idea that, in the case of some hard-to-read styles, "increased demand for mental processing may promote better attention toward the current task and improve the reader's ability to retain information."[5] I should say that I'm a bit wary of this concept when it comes to presenting material that folks aren't *required* to read. (I know that I tend to simply stop reading if I'm having trouble making out the words). And there are caveats. One of the papers cited by Delgado, for example, indicates

---

4   Charles Bigelow, "Typeface Features and Legibility Research," *Vision Research*, Vol. 165 (December 1, 2019)

5   Carla Delgado, "How Fonts Affect Learning and Memory," *Discover Magazine* (October 9, 2021)

that the "difficult to read" styles used were only mildly sub-optimal, and that the study subjects reported disliking the materials that used them, even as they retained more information from those materials.[6]

How do you make text in your graphic as legible and readable as possible? Here's what I recommend: Start by choosing typefaces that are highly legible. Your decisions will likely also be influenced by your intended audience. But in general, when it comes to choosing type for graphics, I recommend avoiding decorative or wildly innovative styles. (Sorry script fans.) In a graphic, you have many opportunities to inject the space with energy. Just as with the other visual variables discussed above, you can use typography to attract attention, and then direct it elsewhere (this is where hierarchy comes in). But if you're using too many of those variables with gusto at once, you may overwhelm your reader.

I don't include a "recommended fonts" list in this book in part because these things are so context-specific. It would be a bit like me prescribing a specific color palette as "the best," when in reality it might work quite well in one situation but fall flat in another. That said, Helvetica is a solid choice for labels and captions. In part because it has a large character set and good symbols for equations. If you're a novice in search of specific names, try searching "legible fonts" or "legible typefaces" online. In general, these characteristics are often associated with typefaces that have a high degree of legibility:

- Tall x-height
- Characters are distinguishable from one another. For example 1, l and L, should be easily distinguishable, as should i and I.
- Adequate letter spacing. Be wary of crashing or v e r y   w i d e l y s p a c e d letters as the default.

Sans-serif faces are a popular choice these days for captions and labels. There are practical reasons for this as well, at least when it comes to print materials. They generally have less variability in stroke weight within each letter. For that reason, they tend to reproduce well when printed over other color tints, or when knocked out as a lighter color within a darker field of color. Sans-serifs are also a much safer bet if you're hoping to use a color other than black on press. (See page 158 for more details about these concepts.) They're also a favorite for websites and slides.

---

6   Daniel Oppenheimer, Connor Diemand-Yauman, and Erikka Vaughan, "Fortune Favors the Bold (and the Italicized): Effects of Disfluency on Educational Outcomes," *Proceedings of the Annual Meeting of the Cognitive Science Society,* Vol. 32 (2010)

Although, as noted above, there's not a large body of research that supports banning serif fonts from these cases, by any means.

Choosing a font is just the first step. There are more decisions to be

made. Line space (also known as "leading"), for example. If too much ver-

tical space is between lines, words that are meant to hang together start

to feel disassociated. Like the top portion of this paragraph. Each line is

perceived as its own unit, and flow between lines is interrupted. But if
there's too little space, or leading, between lines, things feel crowded
and uncomfortable. And readability goes down. As in the last three
lines of this paragraph.

In general, a sweet spot for line space is between 120% and 145%
of the font's point size. Keep line spacing the same for elements that
repeat (like multi-line labels), and avoid the temptation to squeeze the
lines too closely together just so they'll fit in the space you have to
work within.

It's certainly an option to justify your text columns, like I'm doing
with this paragraph. When you justify a text block, space is added between words so that lines extend to the left and right edges of the full
column. It's not inherently bad, by any means. But as the columns become narrower, you increase the odds of creating odd gaps and rivers of
white space that flow down, through the column. This is especially true
if you're not hyphenating text. In general, it's usually safer to default to
left justified text.

Here's an example of that same paragraph, set in narrower columns.
Do you see the awkward long blank spots between some words? That
negative space is a distraction, negatively impacting readability.

It's certainly an option to justify your text columns, like I'm doing with this paragraph. When you justify a text block, space is added between words so that lines extend to the left and right edges of the full column. It's not inherently bad, by any means. But as the columns become narrower, you increase the odds of creating odd gaps and rivers of white space that flow down, through the column. This is especially true if you're not hyphenating text. In general, it's usually safer to default to a left aligned text.

That said, narrow columns of left aligned text are not without their
own downfalls. Take the next paragraph, for example.

If left alone (as in the cyan version of this paragraph), the right side of this left aligned text column creates a shape that draws attention. It's likely that your eye is tracing the right side, trying to enclose the shape as a full unit. It's not quite in balance. In the magenta version of this paragraph (to the right), I've gone in and added soft-returns to force line-breaks. This is pretty picky, but in some cases it can make a real difference.

If left alone (as in the cyan version of this paragraph), the right side of this left aligned text column creates a shape that draws attention. It's likely that your eye is tracing the right side, trying to enclose the shape as a full unit. It's not quite in balance. In the magenta version of this paragraph (to the right), I've gone in and added soft-returns to force line-breaks. This is pretty picky, but in some cases it can make a real difference.

Note that rebreaking this column also resulted in a last line made up of more than one word. That's a good thing! Single words hanging out at the bottom of a paragraph (and short lines at the top of a page) should be avoided, when possible. They make things feel unstable, and unresolved. Without a solid base, the blue column on the left looks like it may topple over.

The preceding examples show what can happen when your columns are narrow. But wide columns can also cause trouble. One, two, or three lines in very wide columns of text can be more or less read without too much trouble, assuming that the reader can shuffle down along the length of the poster, or has the range of motion to physically see the full column width. But if the depth of the text block holds more than three lines, efficiently tracking from the end of one line on the right to the start of the next on the left becomes difficult. Per Matthew Butterick, in *Butterick's Practical Typography*:

> The most useful way to measure line length is by average characters per line. Measuring in inches or centimeters is less useful because the point size of the font affects the number of characters per inch…As line length increases, your eye has to travel farther from the end of one line to the beginning of the next, making it harder to track your progress vertically. Aim for an average line length of 45–90 characters, including spaces. You can check line length using word count.[7]

Finally, three words about distorting text: Don't do it.[8]

---

7   *Butterick's Practical Typography, https://practicaltypography.com* (accessed August 28, 2021). Quote reproduced with permission from Matthew Butterick.

8   Please don't stretch or compress type by distorting the letterforms with percent scale changes. If the font isn't working for you, choose another font. If there's not space to include everything you want to include, edit things down. And yes, I have been known to skew the occasional label, to better align with a surface that I'm labelling. But I don't recommend it. If you're not really careful, it's a really easy way to destroy legibility.

Hierarchy

If you're including more than one text element in your graphic, you'll need to start actively making decisions related to hierarchy. Some levels are self-evident: A title should be the primary text element, and should be styled to attract attention first. Generally—but not always—that means it should be at the top of the graphic, and larger in point size (and/or bolder), than the other text elements. But what about other on-art text blocks? As described by Ellen Lupton in *Thinking with Type*, "Each level of hierarchy should be signaled by one or more cues, applied consistently across a body of text. A cue can be spatial (indent, line spacing, placement) or graphic (size, style, color). Infinite variations are possible."[9]

As a project comes into focus, it's useful to identify the different levels of text elements you may need. Will the graphic need a title and introductory caption? Secondary captions? Annotations or labels? Ultimately, you'll need to create style specifications for each of these categories. (Your publisher or company may already have these specifications described in a style guide.) If your graphic needs several levels of typographic treatments, it can be useful to work with more than one font. (A good rule of thumb on this front is to choose two typefaces that are quite different from each other. For example, by pairing a serif with a sans-serif.) Avoid *too* many distinct styles in a single graphic, though.

Part of the goal is to set up a rubric that signals "like" elements. If there are lots of type elements in your graphic, and each element has a different style, things can appear chaotic. Along those lines, it's generally a good idea to choose an alignment strategy for a category of typography, and stick with it throughout the whole graphic. For example, don't center-align some of your captions, and left-align other captions. The goal is to use variability to signal a change in hierarchy. Like objects should remain as similar as possible.

The following pages contain three graphics, with different levels of text items identified and labelled. One is a piece that I art directed. Actual type specifications are included. The other two are graphics that I didn't work on, labelled out from the point of view of a cold reader. (See pages 122 and 123.)

Always keep your final context in mind. I'll walk you through these

---

9   Ellen Lupton, *Thinking with Type: A Critical Guide for Designers, Writers, Editors, & Students* (Princeton Architectural Press, 2010)

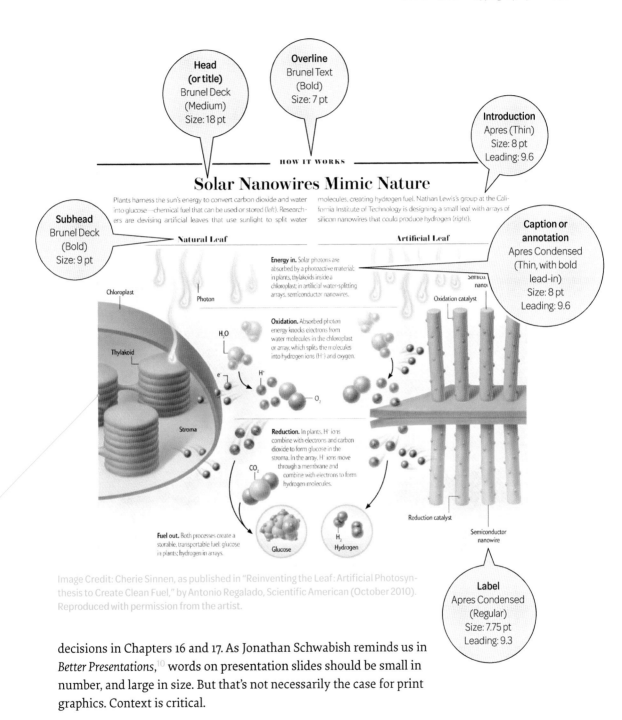

Head
(or title)
Brunel Deck
(Medium)
Size: 18 pt

Overline
Brunel Text
(Bold)
Size: 7 pt

Introduction
Apres (Thin)
Size: 8 pt
Leading: 9.6

Subhead
Brunel Deck
(Bold)
Size: 9 pt

Caption or annotation
Apres Condensed
(Thin, with bold lead-in)
Size: 8 pt
Leading: 9.6

Label
Apres Condensed
(Regular)
Size: 7.75 pt
Leading: 9.3

HOW IT WORKS

Solar Nanowires Mimic Nature

Plants harness the sun's energy to convert carbon dioxide and water into glucose—chemical fuel that can be used or stored (*left*). Researchers are devising artificial leaves that use sunlight to split water molecules, creating hydrogen fuel. Nathan Lewis's group at the California Institute of Technology is designing a small leaf with arrays of silicon nanowires that could produce hydrogen (*right*).

Natural Leaf

Artificial Leaf

Chloroplast

Photon

Thylakoid

H_2O

e^-

H^+

O_2

Stroma

CO_2

Glucose

H_2
Hydrogen

Energy in. Solar photons are absorbed by a photoactive material: in plants, thylakoids inside a chloroplast; in artificial water-splitting arrays, semiconductor nanowires.

Oxidation. Absorbed photon energy knocks electrons from water molecules in the chloroplast or array, which splits the molecules into hydrogen ions (H^+) and oxygen.

Reduction. In plants, H^+ ions combine with electrons and carbon dioxide to form glucose in the stroma. In the array, H^+ ions move through a membrane and combine with electrons to form hydrogen molecules.

Fuel out. Both processes create a storable, transportable fuel: glucose in plants; hydrogen in arrays.

Semicon. nano

Oxidation catalyst

Reduction catalyst

Semiconductor nanowire

Image Credit: Cherie Sinnen, as published in "Reinventing the Leaf: Artificial Photosynthesis to Create Clean Fuel," by Antonio Regalado, *Scientific American* (October 2010). Reproduced with permission from the artist.

decisions in Chapters 16 and 17. As Jonathan Schwabish reminds us in *Better Presentations*,[10] words on presentation slides should be small in number, and large in size. But that's not necessarily the case for print graphics. Context is critical.

10   Jonathan Schwabish, *Better Presentations: A Guide for Scholars, Researchers, and Wonks* (Columbia University Press, 2016)

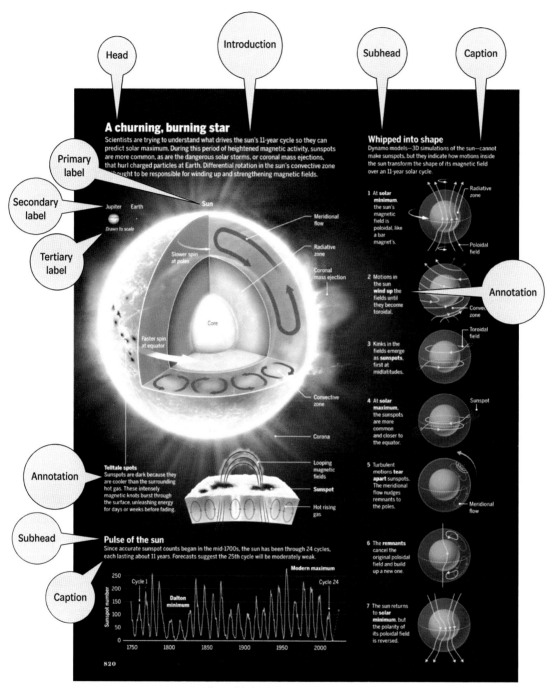

Image Credit: C. Bickel/*Science*; From "The Calm before the Storms," by Sarah Scoles, *Science* Vol. 364, No. 6443 (May 31, 2019). Reproduced with permission from AAAS.

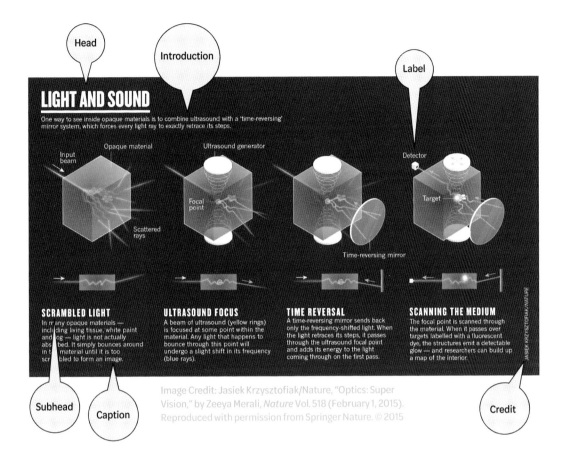

Image Credit: Jasiek Krzysztofiak/Nature, "Optics: Super Vision," by Zeeya Merali, *Nature* Vol. 518 (February 1, 2015). Reproduced with permission from Springer Nature. © 2015

More to Explore

- *Thinking with Type: A Critical Guide for Designers, Writers, Editors, & Students,* by Ellen Lupton (Princeton Architectural Press, 2010)
- *The Non-Designer's Design Book,* 4th edition, by Robin Williams (Peachpit Press, 2014): The section on designing with type is particularly helpful for novices.
- *Butterick's Practical Typography,* by Matthew Butterick, *https://practicaltypography.com/*
- **"Readable, Serious, Traditional: Investigating Scholarly Perceptions of the Visual Design and Reading Experiences of Academic Journals,"** by Jessica Barness and Amy Papaelias, *She Ji: The Journal of Design, Economics, and Innovation,* Vol. 7 (December 1, 2021)

Typography Makeover (part three of three)

This is the third installment of a demonstration that takes part in three stages. Context and content remain steady throughout the makeover: It's is a hypothetical graphic destined for a hypothetical academic journal. See pages 88–89 and 110–111 for the first two revision rounds—composition and color. The revisions on this spread are limited to changes in type. Many academic publications request minimal on-art text, and ask that most of the words be provided

BEFORE

Figure 1. Pathogenesis of classical cat treat disease and paradoxical cat treat disease. (A) Classical: Protein one, which is produced by the gut upon the ingestion of a treat, forms complexes with protein two. These complexes trigger alpha cells to produce large amounts of protein three. Protein three stimulates beta cells, which releases proteins four and five. Protein four triggers gamma cells to start massing in the gut's lining. Gamma cells then release protein six, pushing gut lining cells into a hypergrowth state, resulting in a grumpy cat. This condition can be confirmed by testing for levels of proteins three, four, and six. (B) Paradoxical: The introduction of drug A successfully blocked classical cat treat disease in most cats, by inhibiting the production of protein four. However, some cats were still grumpy. In 1 to 3 percent of cats, paradoxical cat treat disease may arise due to an increase in production of protein five, a side effect of drug A. The full pathway of paradoxical cat treat disease is not yet understood, but can be confirmed by testing for levels of proteins three and five.

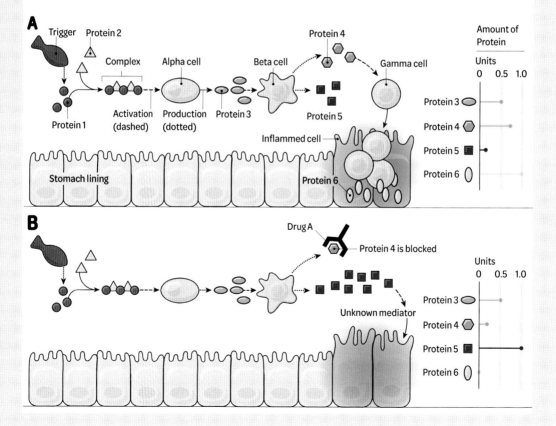

in a separate main caption. (Likely due to workflow and production related reasons.) Although I don't think that's optimal, working within constraints is one of the fun parts about designing. I've largely honored that here. (Although I have taken the liberty of adjusting the caption styles in this demo, which wouldn't be an option for an author submitting a figure.) Normally, I'd recommend a smaller introductory caption, supplemented with on-art annotations.

Typography changes here are primarily in the service of (1) legibility and readability, and (2) establishing a hierarchy and clear two-part grouping.

AFTER

Figure 1: **Pathogenesis of classical cat treat disease and paradoxical cat treat disease**

CLASSICAL: Protein one, which is produced by the gut upon the ingestion of a treat, forms complexes with protein two. These complexes trigger alpha cells to produce large amounts of protein three. Protein three stimulates beta cells, which releases proteins four and five. Protein four triggers gamma cells to start massing in the gut's lining. Gamma cells then release protein six, pushing gut lining cells into a hypergrowth state, resulting in a grumpy cat. This condition can be confirmed by testing for levels of proteins three, four, and six.

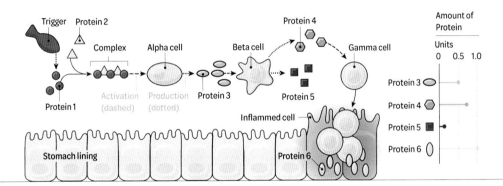

PARADOXICAL: The introduction of drug A successfully blocked classical cat treat disease in most cats, by inhibiting the production of protein four. However, some cats were still grumpy. In 1 to 3 percent of cats, paradoxical cat treat disease may arise due to an increase in production of protein five, a side effect of drug A. The full pathway of paradoxical cat treat disease is not yet understood, but can be confirmed by testing for levels of proteins three and five.

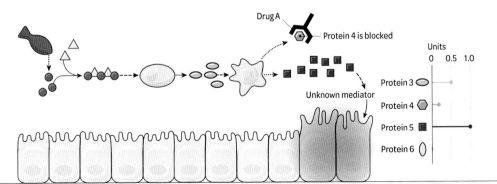

CHAPTER 10

Visual Style

I ENTERED THE SCIENCE PUBLISHING SCENE just as desktop publishing surged. Pen and ink, airbrush, watercolors, gouache, and other paints gave way to vector and pixel-based art. With the shift in tools came a shift in rendering styles and color palettes, which then shifted yet again as user-friendly 3D digital programs became more widely available. My personal drawing style, and the style of many of the artists I worked with, evolved, as did the aesthetic tone of entire publications.

The rapid adoption of new tools certainly made an impact on graphic design and illustration, but that moment isn't unique in history. Steady and slow shifts in aesthetic trends across space and time have long been punctuated by the impact of new technologies related to the tools of the trade, such as the printing press and photography.

The phrase "visual style" is a loaded term in some academic circles. It's often used to describe broad art movements or time periods, such as Cubism or Pop Art. And as art historian Matthias Bruhn notes, categorizing these styles in art history is complicated, in that it sometimes offers up an *explanation* for visual phenomena, as opposed to a *description* of them. That said, he maintains that it's a useful term in the realm of scientific visualization, in part because it invites a conversation about how one tool (like a camera) can be wielded in different ways, resulting in "entirely different depictions, depending upon the handling, the choice of position, and other accidental factors."[1]

Visual style in science graphics goes much deeper than how drawings are influenced by new tools, and fashionable color palettes and

1   Matthias Bruhn, "Beyond the Icons of Knowledge: Artistic Styles and the Art History of Scientific Imagery," in *The Technical Image: A History of Styles in Scientific Imagery*, ed. Horst Bredekamp, Vera Dünkel, and Brigit Schneider (University of Chicago Press, 2015)

Selection of drawings from Series I: Splash of a drop of mercury that has fallen onto glass.

Selection of engravings from Series XIII: Splash of a drop of milk that has fallen onto glass.

flourishes of the time and place. At its core, it also reflects an underlying tension between the concepts of objectivity and subjectivity.

In *Objectivity*, Lorraine Daston and Peter Galison explore this idea in detail, rooted in a deep knowledge of the practice of science in Europe and North America, from the 18th century to the mid-20th century. Specifically, their book describes three "epistemic virtues," during this interval—truth-to-nature, objectivity, and trained judgment—and how those concepts influenced the making of scientific images.

How does a shift in philosophy impact imagery? One example from Daston and Galison describes physicist Arthur Worthington's quest to record the stages of a drop of liquid impacting a horizontal glass plate. His drawings of mercury drops originally published in 1877—based on direct observation with the aid of light flashes—are symmetrical, confident, and clean. Nearly 20 years later he was able to catch the sequence with photographs, revealing a much more irregular splashdown pattern. (It's important to note that he recorded many irregular splashdown patterns in his earlier sketches of the process. He consciously dismissed them, focused on capturing an "ideal splash.") In the words of Daston and Galison,

> For two decades, Worthington had seen the symmetrical, perfected forms of nature as an essential feature of his morphology of drops. All those asymmetrical images had stayed in the laboratory—not one appeared in his many scientific publications. In this choice he was anything but alone—over the long course of making systematic study of myriad scientific domains, the choice of the perfect over the imperfect had become profoundly entrenched. From anatomical structures to zoophysiological crystals, idealization had long been the governing order ... But after his 1894 shock, Worthington instead began to ask himself—and again he was not alone—how he and others for so long could have only had eyes for a perfection that wasn't there.[2]

I'm a practitioner, not a historian. And you are presumably reading this handbook in search of actionable strategies to help guide your personal drawing style choices as you build graphics at this moment. The rest of this section aims to do that. But I encourage you to keep the history and context described above in mind.

When I refer to "style," I'm referring to design and rendering deci-

2   Lorraine Daston and Peter Galison, *Objectivity* (New York: Zone Books, 2007) p.15. Quote reproduced with permission from Zone Books.

sions that are related to the task at hand. Should the objects be drawn in a realistic or abstract manner? Should the linework be sketchy and expressive or precise and controlled? Should the imagery be playful or subdued? How much detail is appropriate? Your decisions should be informed by practical forces in play (more on this in Chapter 12), including your ultimate audience, scale of final imagery, and tools available. Keep the ultimate goal of your graphic in mind when considering style and tone.

I find the way that Alberto Cairo discusses these ideas in *The Functional Art* quite useful. He writes that "a good graphic realizes two basic goals: It **presents** information, and it allows readers to **explore** that information."[3] With that foundation in mind, he warns against styles or flourishes that explicitly distract from the point of the graphic, or impede exploration. But that doesn't mean that all graphics need to adhere to a minimalist design philosophy. He shifts the focus away from the idea that style is the key element to a graphic's success. Rather, making thoughtful decisions with regards to content and composition is the critical part. Then just make sure that your stylistic choices don't actively get in the way.

As I wrote in a paper for the Communicating Complexity conference in 2013,[4] before you can even begin to communicate a complex topic, you must first engage an audience. **Minimalist and abstract iconography might be the most efficient way to communicate findings within a research community. But that design approach may be off-putting to a non-specialist audience.** I argue that if a graphic does not incorporate immediately-visible context, a familiar visual vocabulary, or a welcoming gesture for the non-specialist reader, it may simply confirm a preconception that the content itself is abstract and unrelatable—thereby shutting down the opportunity to convey that information to a new audience.

How this translates into practice depends upon your audience. I should note that I haven't tested these strategies experimentally. And it seems that the research literature is a little thin on this topic when it comes to illustrated graphics, less so with data visualization.[5]

3   Alberto Cairo, *The Functional Art* (New Riders, 2013)

4   Jen Christiansen, "A Defense of Artistic License in Illustrating Scientific Concepts," *Communicating Complexity, 2013 Conference Proceedings*, edited by Nicolò Ceccarelli (Edizioni Nuova Cultura, 2013)

5   Andy J. King and Allison J. Lazard, "Advancing Visual Health Communication Research to Improve Infodemic Response," *Health Communication,* Vol. 35 (December 5, 2020)

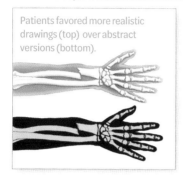

Patients favored more realistic drawings (top) over abstract versions (bottom).

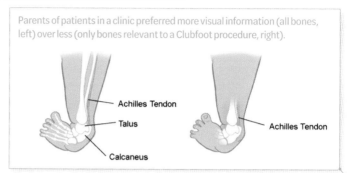

Parents of patients in a clinic preferred more visual information (all bones, left) over less (only bones relevant to a Clubfoot procedure, right).

Achilles Tendon

Talus

Achilles Tendon

Calcaneus

That said, some studies provide support for the general concepts. For example, over the course of a collaborative design and research project conducted at a hospital in New Zealand, Emma Scheltema, Stephen Reay, and Greg Piper found that both medical professionals and patients preferred realistic, detailed, and dimensional illustrations over streamlined and abstract drawings. *Understanding* of the subject matter was not tested or otherwise evaluated. "Patient participants tended to associate 'realistic' (colour-tonal rendered) representations with both a greater quantity of information, and a more credible source of information." Interestingly, "patients often favoured illustrations that depicted a greater amount of information than professionals suggested was necessary." [6]

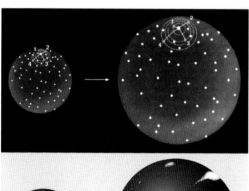

Image Credits: Jon Lomberg/SCIENCE PHOTO LIBRARY (top); Jen Christiansen (bottom)

Immediately Visible Context

The image on the top in the pair shown here is a schematic that shows expansion of some sort. But without a title, caption, labels, or other additional context, it is not terribly clear that it's a graphic about the universe.

6   Emma Scheltema, Stephen Reay, and Greg Piper, "Visual Representation of Medical Information: The Importance of Considering the End-User in the Design of Medical Illustrations," *Journal of Visual Communication in Medicine,* Vol. 41 (January 2, 2018)

The image on the bottom addresses the same topic, but visible figurative context is added. The casual reader now has a better sense of place—this is a graphic about the cosmos. There's something intellectually and aesthetically appealing about the top version. But the immediately-visible context in the bottom panel—in the form of tiny galaxy illustrations— helps set the scene. Readers can picture themselves on a planet in one of those tiny galaxies in an expanding universe.

Familiar Visual Vocabulary

To spark recognition and prime the reader for a less familiar concept, a graphic can lead in with a comfortable and familiar visual vocabulary. This graphic by Cherie Sinnen is from an article on artificial photosynthesis. The goal was to invite the readers in with a warm and welcoming aesthetic, keep them engaged with some basic primer information about photosynthesis that would likely feel a bit familiar (on the left), then have them build on that more familiar content by showing how the new technology works (on the right).

This approach is probably not the best solution for a research paper

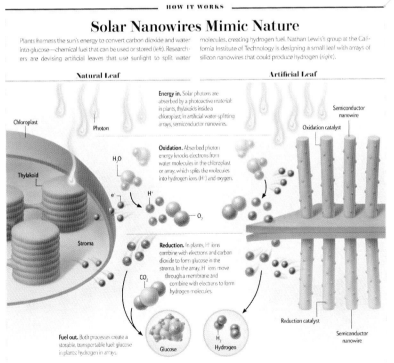

Image Credit: Cherie Sinnen, as published in "Reinventing the Leaf: Artificial Photosynthesis to Create Clean Fuel," by Antonio Regalado, *Scientific American* (October 2010). Reproduced with permission from the artist.

with an expert audience. But for a consumer magazine with a more generalist audience, we have the freedom to be playful with the rendering style, and a responsibility to provide the tools and information that a generalist reader needs in order to really understand the new science being presented.

Welcoming Gesture

Illustrative details can help make an abstract topic more relatable. For example, a small drawing of an object (the subject matter of the graphic) or the use of a visual metaphor can provide immediate context when used next to a less figurative chart. Or, as in the case of "The Swiss Cheese Respiratory Virus Pandemic Defence," by Ian M. Mackay, the metaphor can be the central conceit. It helps make an abstract concept tangible, by representing the information using familiar objects.[7]

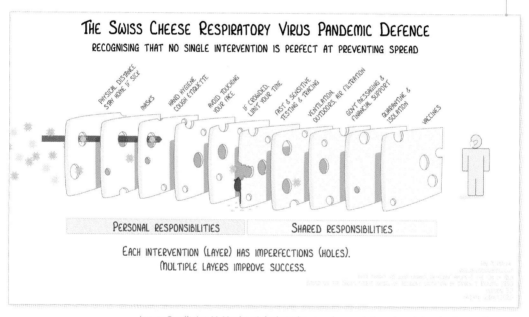

---

7   For more on the research that this illustration was based on, as well as nods to other folks that were using the Swiss cheese model in the context of COVID at the same time, see Mackay's blog post "The Swiss Cheese Infographic That Went Viral," Virology Down Under (December 26, 2020) *https://virologydownunder.com/the-swiss-cheese-info-graphic-that-went-viral/*

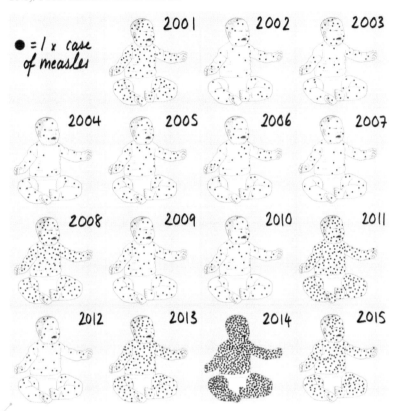

In some contexts, as demonstrated by data journalist Mona Chalabi, offbeat humor and a distinct personal style can also go a long way in engaging people. Designer Nigel Holmes (see page 134) has made a career out of it.[8]

In general, be wary of proclamations that make sweeping statements about "correct" rendering styles for science graphics. Yes, certain styles are more at home in certain contexts. And not all stylistic flourishes will be appropriate for all contexts. But that doesn't mean that one style solution fits all. If you're new to building graphics and you're developing an image for an outlet that embraces a specific vibe or aesthetic, make note of the hallmarks of the work they've published before, and make your design decisions accordingly.

8   Nigel Holmes, *Joyful Infographics : A Friendly, Human Approach to Data* (A K Peters/ CRC Press, forthcoming)

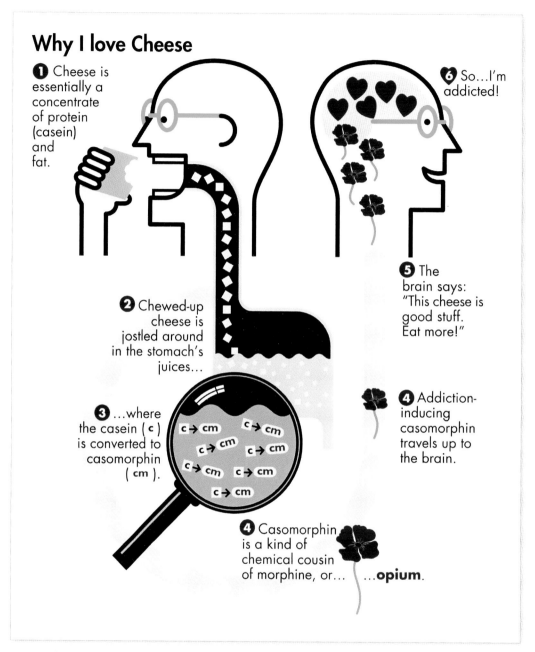

Why I love Cheese

1 Cheese is essentially a concentrate of protein (casein) and fat.

2 Chewed-up cheese is jostled around in the stomach's juices...

3 ...where the casein (c) is converted to casomorphin (cm).

c → cm   c → cm
c → cm   c → cm
c → cm   c → cm
c → cm

4 Casomorphin is a kid of chemical cousin of morphine, or...   ...**opium**.

4 Addiction-inducing casomorphin travels up to the brain.

5 The brain says: "This cheese is good stuff. Eat more!"

6 So...I'm addicted!

A CLOSER LOOK ———————————————————————————————•

From Figurative to Abstract

Sometimes, the object being illustrated is more or less observable. And theoretically could be drawn—more or less—as it exists. Although the illustration on the left is a cleaned up and idealized version of the cardiovascular system, it functions to show the position of things. But what if, instead of showing the shape of it, you wanted to get across the idea that the cardiovascular system is a closed loop, in which blood continuously circulates? That idea is shown more clearly in the illustration on the right, in a more streamlined rendition of the subject matter. Although the tools, color palette, line quality, overall aesthetic, and vibe are consistent across both examples, the content is shown in a more figurative manner on the left, and a more abstract manner on the right.

Image Credit:
© Mesa Schumacher

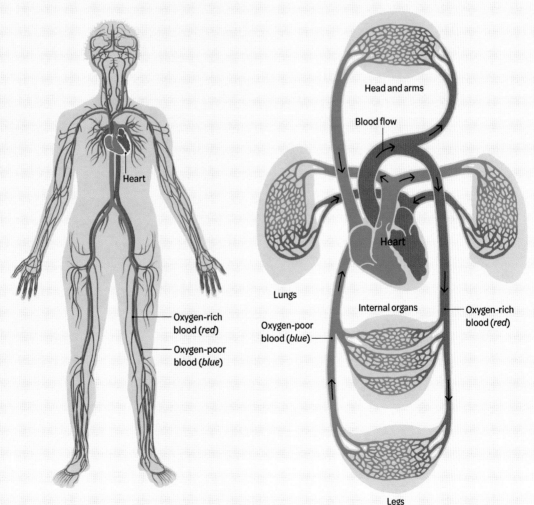

CHAPTER 11

Storytelling Strategies

MUCH OF MY WORK IS EXPOSITORY in nature, and I think it's fair to say that most information graphics lean toward that end of the spectrum, as opposed to embracing true narrative storytelling. Often graphics and data displays are used to explain and illuminate (hallmarks of expository stories), not necessarily to engage a reader's emotions or take them on a journey (hallmarks of narrative stories). But the graphics field more broadly is shifting toward personal and creative approaches that are more aligned with the strengths of narrative storytelling. Science communicators are also embracing narrative storytelling, as discussed in Chapter 3 (see pages 35–36).

First, I should articulate more clearly the difference between expository and narrative storytelling. Simply put, narrative non-fiction tells a story, and expository non-fiction informs and explains. Narratives often include characters, scenes, and conflict. Expository works are generally pretty linear, logical, and direct in structure.[1]

Now, let's get into how I think graphics—both data visualizations and illustrated explanatory diagrams—can serve narrative stories. Specifically,

- how graphics can encapsulate full stories as the primary medium,
- how graphics can support text-driven narratives as the secondary medium, and
- how graphics can be principal characters in and of themselves— especially in the case of science journalism.

1   Raymond A. Mar et al., "Memory and Comprehension of Narrative versus Expository Texts: A Meta-Analysis," *Psychonomic Bulletin & Review*, Vol. 28 (June 1, 2021)

Graphics as the Primary Medium

How can things flip more overtly from expository to narrative when encapsulating a full story with graphics? To my mind, capturing the reader's imagination is the crux. When that's done really well, a graphic is poised to step more fully into the world of narrative storytelling. Although I tend to emphasize rendering style and the idea of evoking empathy here,[2] the structure and framing of graphical stories also play a big role.[3]

STRATEGY 1: Use an immediately recognizable narrative form, like comics • For a graphic about the origin of life on earth, artist Matthew Twombly uses a sequence of panels of varying sizes and scales, signalling to the readers that they're about to walk through a step-by-step story in the form of a comic. There are no anthropomorphic characters in this series. The form creates drama nonetheless, zooming from views of the universe, to a volcanic landscape on earth, to the microscopic ingredients for life. The reader is engaged, in part, by imagining the space between frames.

Twombly's success in signaling that this graphic portrays a narrative story is particularly evident when compared to another graphic on the same subject matter. This example by artist Andrew Swift addresses earlier findings on the same basic topic, but doesn't go as far in setting the scene. It's an expository graphic. The graphic on the bottom walks me through a process, step by step. But the graphic on the top primes me for a story about that process.

STRATEGY 2: Introduce characters • For an article on two early waves of humans into what is now commonly known as North and South America, artist Tyler Jacobson's painted vignettes give a face to the folks

---

2   For more on empathy in data visualization, see Kim Bui's post "Designing Data Visualisations with Empathy," (June 11, 2019) *https://datajournalism.com/read/longreads/data-visualisations-with-empathy* and Giorgia Lupi's article "Data Humanism: The Revolutionary Future of Data Visualization," *PRINT* Magazine (January 30, 2017) *https://www.printmag.com/article/data-humanism-future-of-data-visualization/.*

3   In addition to the references focused on comics listed on page 149, you can read more about the anatomy and framing of visual stories in these papers: E. Segel and J. Heer, "Narrative Visualization: Telling Stories with Data," *IEEE Transactions on Visualization and Computer Graphics,* Vol. 16 (January 2011); and Jessica Hullman and Nicholas Diakopoulos, "Visualization Rhetoric: Framing Effects in Narrative Visualization," *IEEE Transactions on Visualization and Computer Graphics,* Vol. 17 (December 2011).

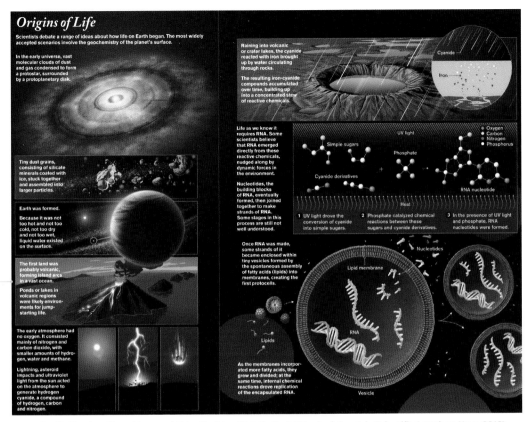

Image Credit: Matthew Twombly, as published in "How Did Life Begin?" by Jack Szostak, *Scientific American* (June 2018). Reproduced with permission. © 2018 Scientific American, a Division of Springer Nature America, Inc. All rights reserved.

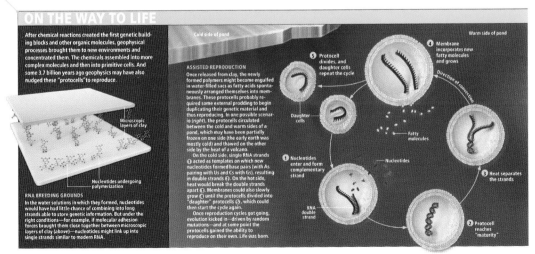

Image Credit: Andrew Swift, as published in "The Origin of Life on Earth" by Alonso Ricardo and Jack W. Szostak, *Scientific American* (September 2009). Reproduced with permission from the artist.

behind the trail of new archaeological evidence. Fast-moving overland travelers that pre-date earlier estimates by about 2,000 years, to even earlier explorers from East Asia, and their coastal journey. The charts and map by XNR Productions suggest change and movement over time, albeit in a less narrative-forward way than the earlier example of life on earth. Critically, artist Tyler Jacobson fleshes out the individuals making the trek, giving the reader characters to identify with.

The strength of that tactic is particularly evident when compared to another graphic on the same topic. This 2015 example from the journal *Nature* shows possible travel routes. But it doesn't provide a sense of the people undertaking the voyage. It's an expository graphic on the topic.

Calvert Island
— 13,200 years ago

The Manis mastodon site
13,800 years ago

Cooper's Ferry
13,200 years ago

**Buttermilk Creek and
Debra L. Friedkin sites**
15,500 years ago

Paisley Caves
14,100 years ago

WELCOME TO AMERICA
Humans could not have walked into the heart of North America until a corridor opened between the continental ice sheets: 14,000 years ago at the earliest, and possibly not until 12,500 years ago. However, a number of New World archaeological sites date from before then (yellow dots), so researchers are exploring whether humans colonized the Americas by boat.

····· Land migration route
···· Coastal migration route

Monte Verde
15,300 years ago

STRATEGY 3: Include a narrator • For an article on how climate change writ large has resulted in more local extreme weather events, author Jennifer Francis set forth a clear sequence of events in the text, supported by a series of maps and data visualizations as reference material. But simply presenting one map and chart after another felt like it would do a disservice to the very personal and urgent tone of the manuscript. And we've presented images like this over and over again to our readers. I was worried about jetstream and warming ocean map fatigue on the reader's behalf. So, I enlisted artist Matthew Twombly again, to fold those jetstream and ocean temperature maps into a visual story. This time, we introduced a narrator, Jennifer Francis. She's not only the author of the story, but also a scientist at the Woodwell Climate Research Center. She experienced the extreme weather event described in this graphic first-hand. So Twombly was able to authentically represent that here.

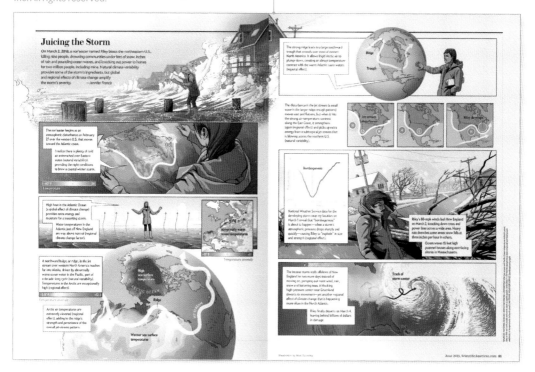

The strength of that tactic is particularly evident when compared to another graphic on the same topic. For an article on climate change's impact on the jetstream and its connection to extreme weather events, the team at 5W Infographic developed a series of globes to help show cause and effect. This particular story was focused more on the physics of the jetstream. It relied less on first-person accounts of the impact, on the ground. So I think that this was the correct solution for this particular article. Although I find the globe series in that graphic intellectually interesting—and quite appropriate for its context—the approach by Mathew Twombly on the previous page brings things down to a very human level, flipping them over from expository to narrative.

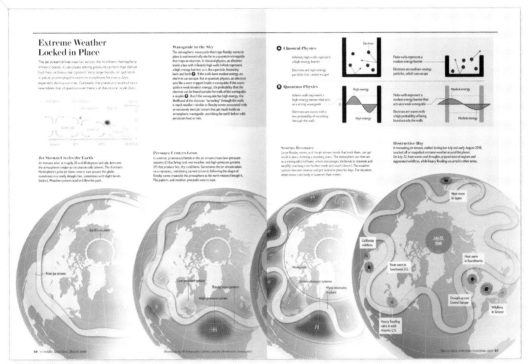

Graphics as the Secondary Medium

In the magazine world, graphics are often used to support text-driven narratives as the secondary medium. This approach works quite well when the imagery is part of a larger package, including text or other elements.

STRATEGY 1: Show, don't tell (pull dense explanatory information out of the main text narrative) • Graphics can present background information so that the flow of the narrative is not loaded down with details that not all of your readers may need. For example, for an article on neutrinos, it was useful to present the technical information in a contained graphical spread.

A neutrino is an oddball and still mysterious type of sub-atomic particle—a pretty esoteric subject matter that we can't assume that our readers are up-to-speed about. That said, we know that some of our readers are quite well-versed in the topic. A visual primer on the topic provided a built-in reference guide and visual glossary for folks who are new to it, or for those who could use a refresher. This freed up the text to address the latest efforts to study it, and the scientists who believe that they are on the cusp of a major revolution in particle physics. Basic background information on the neutrino is available in visual form to readers who need it, without intruding on the flow of the narrative of the text.

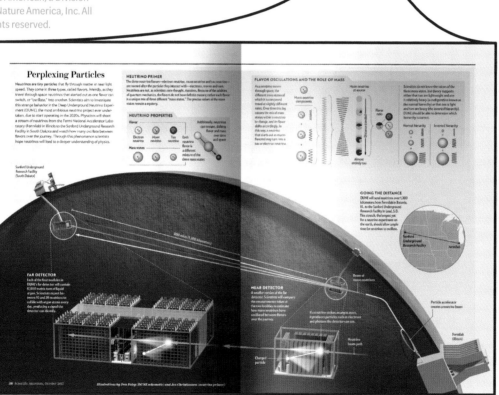

STRATEGY 2: Use graphics to present a more complete story • I like to think of it as team storytelling. Graphics can often more fully nod to the complexity of the bigger picture, providing context for the written story. In this case, I'm not referring to a few basic background concepts served up to the reader in the form of visual primers. In this case, I'm referring to diving headfirst into all the complexities of the topic.

For example, in a special report on the Arctic, articles written by Mark Fischetti and Kathrin Stephen explored the global struggle over the resources in the region. The conflicts exist in part because the claims of land ownership overlap. Many countries are playing by a version of the rules that serves their interests best. But with many rules in play—as well as the rapidly changing ecology of the area due to climate change—things get really convoluted really quickly. A series of maps and graphics developed by Katie Peek allowed us to represent those complexities. This type of content can be described in a limited way via text. Graphics allowed us to *show* the full story.

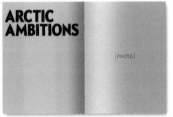

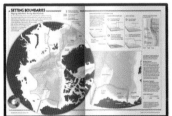

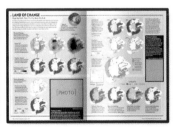

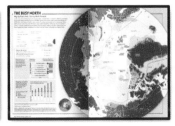

STRATEGY 3: Use graphics to pull a reader through the story •
Graphics can also support written narratives by acting as connective tissue. As my text editing colleague Clara Moskowitz put it when writing about an article on orbiting bodies for a competition entry-form,

> *Mathematics is not meant to be communicated through words alone. Its purest language, equations, also falls short if the audience is the lay public. Art, therefore, is sometimes the best tool available. Rather than sequester the art in separate boxes, in this piece we integrated illustrations throughout the text so that art keeps pace with the story, arriving to explicate concepts right when readers need it. A color-coding system with lead lines explicitly links graphics to the associated blocks of text, making it easy to find the correct illustration and adding a sense of movement and energy to the page. The colorful art draws readers in and keeps them reading, reassuring them that the article, though complex, will be accessible and enjoyable. It offers a visual payoff for every new section and concept...Ultimately, the design was essential for telling the story we wanted to tell: a first-person account of mathematical research.*[4]

That fall I traveled to Spain to meet with Simó, who had a reputation as one of the most inventive and careful numerical analysts working in celestial mechanics. He is also a direct man who does not waste time or mince words. My first afternoon in his office, after I had explained my question, he looked at me with piercing eyes and asked, "Richard, why do you care?"

The answer goes back to the origins of the three-body problem. Isaac Newton originally posed and solved the two-body problem when he published his *Principia* in 1687. He asked: "How will two masses move in space if the only force on them is their mutual gravitational attraction?" Newton framed the question as a problem of solving a system of differential equa-

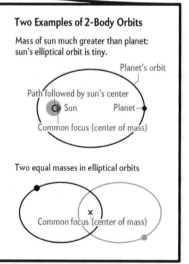

Two Examples of 2-Body Orbits

Mass of sun much greater than planet: sun's elliptical orbit is tiny.

Planet's orbit
Path followed by sun's center
Sun   Planet
Common focus (center of mass)

Two equal masses in elliptical orbits

Common focus (center of mass)

---

4   Quote reproduced with permission from Clara Moskowitz

Graphics as the Principal Character

Particularly in the case of science journalism, graphics can be principal characters in and of themselves. Many first-person accounts written by scientists for general audiences include a moment early in the story arc in which the author is faced with surprising data, often in the form of a visualization. A blip in a curve or an unexpected pattern catches their eye during data analysis. Charts that trigger follow-up research can be featured as a character in the story, published with an annotation or two that point out the details that caused researchers to scratch their heads, or shout "eureka!"

Other graphics have become icons them-selves. Take the chart that became known simply as the hockey stick graph. After initial publication by Michael Mann, Raymond Bradley, and Malcolm Hughes in a 1998 issue of the journal *Nature*, it took on a life of its own, triggering a smear campaign by climate change deniers. The chart traces Northern Hemisphere mean temperature over time. Relatively small fluctuations from 1400 to 1900 then give way to a sharp rise, remini-cent of the upturned blade of a hockey stick. (Subsequent versions of the chart show that line continuing to rise over time, adding to the hockey stick effect.) It supports the assertion that human activity is impacting climate: Hu-mans are warming the globe. Climate change deniers tried to undermine the chart, pointing out natural fluctuations in the earlier years, and questioning the models used for recon-structed temperature data. Ultimately, they conducted professional and personal attacks on the authors that initially published it. But the graph has held up. Subsequent studies by other authors—using different methodologies—resoundly support its message.

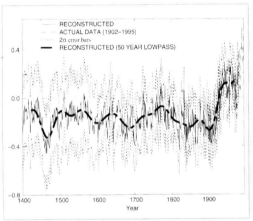

Original Caption: "Time reconstructions (solid lines) along with raw data (dashed lines)...for Northern Hemisphere mean temperature (NH) in °C. ...the zero line corresponds to the 1902–80 calibration mean of the quantity. ...raw data are shown up to 1995 and positive and negative 2[sigmaTK] uncertainty limits are shown by the light dotted lines surrounding the solid reconstruction...." Image Credit: as published in Michael E. Mann, Raymond S. Bradley, and Malcolm K. Hughes, "Global-Scale Temperature Patterns and Climate Forcing over the Past Six Centuries," *Nature*, Vol. 392 (April 1998). Reproduced with permission from Springer Nature. © 1998

And finally, an obligatory recognition of my favorite data visual-ization character of all time, a pulsar chart that made its way from a student dissertation in 1970 to an album cover in 1979. As I wrote for *Scientific American* in 2015,

Drop this image on someone's desk and chances are they'll reflexively blurt, 'Joy Division.' The band's 1979 Unknown Pleasures album cover leaned entirely on a small mysterious data display, printed in white on black. No band name, album title or other identifiers. An interesting move [by designer Peter Saville] for a debut studio album. Even as knowledge spread about the band's inspiration point—a preexisting pulsar data visualization ...the true origin of that visualization continued to be a bit of a riddle. Somewhere along the way, I became obsessed with the narratives behind pulsar discovery and stacked plots, along with a growing desire to learn all that I could about the image and the research it was connected to. What follows is an abridged story borne of that obsession, starting with a video screened at a data visualization conference and ending with an interview with Harold (Hal) Craft, the radio astronomer who created the plot from data collected at the Arecibo Radio Observatory.[5]

Image Credits: Photograph by Jen Christiansen, featuring Joy Division's *Unknown Pleasures* album cover designed by Peter Saville, and Figure 5.37 in "Radio Observations of the Pulse Profiles and Dispersion Measures of Twelve Pulsars," by Harold D. Craft, Jr. (Cornell University; September 1970)

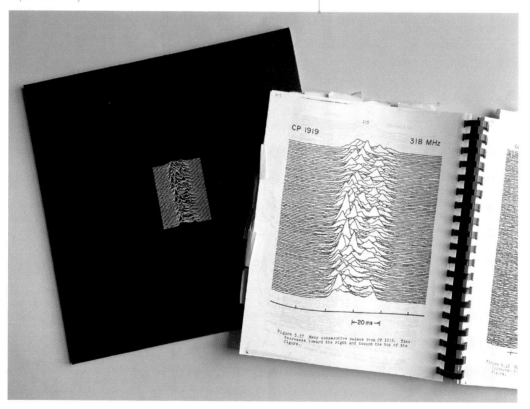

5   Jen Christiansen, "Pop Culture Pulsar: Origin Story of Joy Division's *Unknown Pleasures* Album Cover," SA Visual (blog), *Scientific American* (February 18, 2015). For more, check out "Pop Culture Pulsar: The Science Behind Joy Division's *Unknown Pleasures* Album Cover," SA Visual (blog), *Scientific American* (October 13, 2015).

More to Explore

Some artists and graphical forms (including comics) have been telling stories with imagery for a very long time. And there's a whole field of study—visual narrative theory—dedicated to understanding it. For a much deeper dive, including historical context, research findings, and practical applications, I recommend these resources:

- *The Visual Narrative Reader,* edited by Neil Cohn (Bloomsbury, 2016): This book provides a broad look at the topic—from structure and cognition to culture and social contexts—in a selection of articles by academics.
- *Understanding Comics,* by Scott McCloud (William Morrow Paperbacks, 1994); and *Making Comics,* by Scott McCloud (William Morrow Paperbacks, 2006): These two long-form comics by Scott McCloud are classics on the topic of sequential art.
- *Data-Driven Storytelling,* edited by Nathalie Henry Riche, Christophe Hurter, Nicholas Diakopoulos, and Sheelagh Carpendale (A K Peters/CRC Press, 2018): This compilation includes contributions from both researchers and practitioners. It explores how and why data-visualization-centric storytelling can make data understandable to the general public.
- **"The Potential of Comics in Science Communication,"** by Matteo Farinella, *Journal of Science Communication*, Vol. 17 (January 23, 2018): This is a relatively short, but mighty, academic paper. Although Farinella concludes that many questions remain unanswered in the field, he cites a large number of key studies and references on the topic of comics, and visual narratives in the service of science communication.

CHAPTER 12

Practicalities

ONE OF MY FAVORITE THEMES when talking with scientists about graphics is the dynamic between content and context. Content is usually top-of-mind when a person sits down to build a graphic. It's the information to be visualized. Context is equally important, but it's too often neglected at the start of a project. What tools will be used to make the graphic, where will it appear, who is the audience (and what's the designer's relationship to that audience), and when does it need to be completed? All of these factors shape decisions related to what pieces of the content are critical to include, and how it should be presented. These variables—a selection of practical forces related to context[1]—are the focus of this chapter.

Some of these practical forces are more regimented than others. For example, the destination for your graphic might dictate the size and format. A journal may provide you with very clear dimensions and file type instructions. Other variables—like the intended audience and accessibility measures—are more complex and less prescriptive. **My hope is that the sections below will help you make informed decisions that result in graphics that honor both**
- **the spaces they'll be presented in, and**
- **the people that you're designing them for.**

What does honoring the "presentation space" of a graphic mean? It refers to being aware of—and making design decisions informed by—the

---

1   My thoughts on practical forces are directly influenced by Jacob Bronowski's essay, "The Shape of Things," as published in *The Visionary Eye: Essays in the Arts, Literature, and Science* (MIT Press, 1978).

ultimate destination. Destination can refer to a variety of things. Broadly speaking, it refers to how the image will be displayed. Will people be looking at the graphic on a mobile phone, a printed page, or a large presentation screen in a conference setting? Each of those scenarios comes with different recommended specifications for image size, resolution, and color settings. Destination can also refer to how that physical or digital thing is situated. Is the graphic printed and presented within the pages of a scientific journal, an organization's annual report, or a magazine? Each of those scenarios comes with different audiences and expectations.

There are levels even within what might be thought of as a single destination. Take the journal *Nature*. As creative director Kelly Krause explains, there are three discrete types of content within each issue:

1. Original research articles with peer-reviewed visuals created by external authors,
2. Surveys of the literature (i.e., reviews) with non-peer-reviewed visuals co-created by *Nature* staff and external authors, and
3. News items with non-peer-reviewed visuals by *Nature* staff

The answers to these two questions guide the process:

1. Is the intended audience technical (specialists) or non-specialists?
2. Who has creative ownership (external authors, shared internal/external, or internal only)?

Per Krause, "the 'audience' question guides content creation, such as how much detail to provide in a visual or its editorial style. The 'ownership' question guides the publishing process, helping us place the design of each visual in a clear framework, with predetermined levels of design intervention for each." [2]

The range of combined possibilities outside of a specific outlet is endless. Even if I just focus on the broader issue of how the image will be displayed, it's not practical—or even possible—to try to describe the ideal specifications for every destination. The graphics-building guides in Chapters 16 and 17 prompt you to think through these variables as they relate to your specific project. In the meantime, here's more context.

Tools

The preferred implements and programs used to draw and design vary between disciplines and individuals. Here are some basics.

2   Kelly Krause, "A Framework for Visual Communication at *Nature*," *Public Understanding of Science,* Vol. 26 (January 1, 2017)

ANALOG • This classification is also sometimes referred to as "traditional" art media. Analog tools, materials, and surfaces are age-old technologies that exist outside of the digital space. Think pen/ink/paper, brush/paint/canvas, and chalk/board. One analog tool in particular is indispensable, regardless your final output type. The humble pencil.

There's something freeing about taking a pencil to paper and simply scribbling out ideas. I know it prevents me from feeling too precious about any particular idea. After all, I'm just doodling, right? When thinking through ideas and experimenting with how elements might fit together, a quick series of small rough cartoons can be informative. Pencil sketches are fast, foster an exploratory mentality, and are low risk. As written by Bang Wong and Rikke Schmidt Kjærgaard in a *Nature Methods* column:

> Making quick sketches or doodles as a way to rationalize information can expose gaps in our thinking and lead to alternative conclusions and new ideas. ...Pencil and paper provide an immediacy that is unmatched. ...There is no learning curve with pencil and paper as there often is with software designed for generating graphics. The typical input devices for computers (that is, keyboard and mouse) are woefully inadequate for supporting the kinds of expressiveness and fluidity that is required to engage the mind. The practical aspects of the digital medium often interfere with the cognitive process because we frequently need to stop and think about 'how' to do something. [3]

Most of my projects start like this:

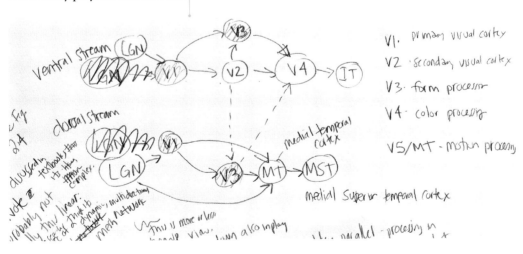

3   Bang Wong and Rikke Schmidt Kjærgaard, "Pencil and Paper," *Nature Methods*, Vol. 9 (November 2012). Quote reproduced with permission from Springer Nature. © 2012

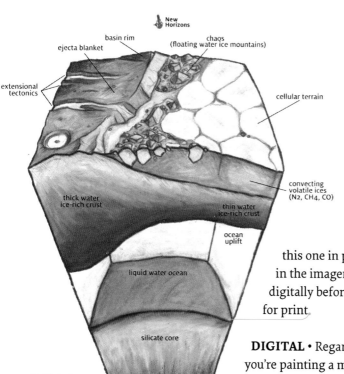

New Horizons

basin rim

ejecta blanket

chaos
(floating water ice mountains)

extensional
tectonics

cellular terrain

convecting
volatile ices
(N2, CH4, CO)

thick water
ice-rich crust

thin water
ice-rich crust

ocean
uplift

liquid water ocean

silicate core

The interior
structure of
Pluto. Image
Credit: © James
Tuttle Keane

I'm not alone. Many examples of preliminary pencil sketches for information design projects are presented in the book *Raw Data: Infographic Designers' Sketchbooks*.[4]

Although I think it's fair to say that most science graphics will ultimately be digitized before being shared with others, it's completely possible to remain in the analog world right up to the end. For example, planetary scientist James Tuttle Keane develops images like this one in pen and colored pencil, scanning in the imagery, then editing and adding labels digitally before sharing online or with a publisher for print.

DIGITAL • Regardless of your starting point, unless you're painting a mural or creating a limited edition series of art prints or the like, your graphic will ultimately need to be digitized for distribution. This can be as straightforward as taking a digital photo with a smartphone (may be suitable for social media sharing without additional work), or scanning and possibly editing the digital file using a program like Photoshop (to optimize contrast, clean up the background, etc.). Or, you can build the graphic from start to finish digitally.

I often take a photo of my pencil sketch and use it as a temporary virtual layer. This helps me speed past the first obstacle. Making the initial mark on the blank slate on my computer screen often takes more energy than it warrants. For me, starting with a messy virtual layer helps take the pressure off.

There are a variety of digital drawing and design program options available. The default in the print publishing world today is the Adobe Creative Suite, which includes vector drawing capabilities (optimized in Illustrator), raster drawing capabilities (optimized in Photoshop),

4   Rick Landers and Steven Heller, *Raw Data: Infographic Designers' Sketchbooks* (Thames Hudson, 2014)

and design capabilities (optimized in InDesign, in which text and images can be imported and composed into page layouts). More on the difference between vector and raster images are in the "File Settings" section (see page 157).

I hesitate to dive too far into a discussion of software here, as this book isn't meant to be an instructional guide for how to use different programs. But, I think it's important to note that there are other options for two-dimensional work, including Affinity Designer (combines raster and vector tools), Affinity Photo (optimized for raster files), and Affinity Publisher (for layout design); as well as Google Drawings and Inkscape (free Web-based vector drawing tools that accomodate placed raster images). Procreate is another raster option, for folks looking for a digital approximation of analog painting tools.

I think it's fair to say that computer languages such as R and Python as well as Processing software and the D3.js JavaScript library are more routinely used for data visualization than for explanatory graphics. But they may be useful for outputting imagery to be used within explanatory graphics related to concepts based in mathematics.

There are also lots of three-dimensional modelling programs available, with a wide range of output file types. For the purposes of creating static graphics, you'll likely be saving out a two-dimensional scene, and then adding labels using another program.

In general, I advise against using presentation tools like Powerpoint, Keynote, and Google Slides as your platform for *creating* graphics, as the drawing tools within those programs are rigid and limited. But if they are your only options, you can totally make it work.

DNA helix illustrations employing a variety of image programs: a vector file created with Illustrator (left), a raster file created with Photoshop (middle), and a raster file created with Maxon Cinema4D using the ePMV (embedded Python Molecular Viewer) plugin and Adobe Photoshop (right). The terms don't refer to the visual style. For example, vector programs—best known for crisp linework and clean shapes—can also be used to create complicated shading patterns. And raster programs—best known for an airbrush-like aesthetic—can also be used for clean linework. So don't be fooled by style when trying to deduce file type. Image Credits: Jen Christiansen (left, middle), © Falconieri Visuals (right).

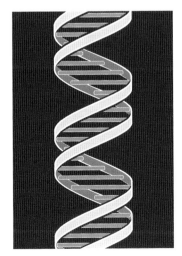
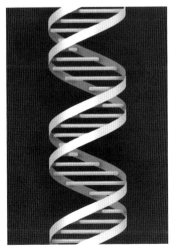
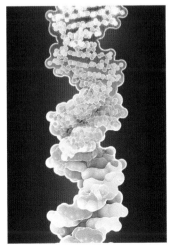

GUIDES AND WORKSHEETS • These aren't implements, per se, but I think they're useful guides that encourage the practice of thinking through, and honoring, the context of your graphic, at the all-important concept stage:

- **Five Design-Sheets: Creative Design and Sketching for Computing and Visualisation,** by Jonathan Roberts, Chris Headleand, and Panagiotis Ritsos: The step-by-step guides presented in Chapters 16 and 17 specific to science graphics in this book were inspired by a paper Roberts, Headleand, and Ritsos presented at a IEEE meeting in 2015.[5] The authors of that paper (and the book to follow[6]), set forth a problem-solving process rooted in sketching for developers, data scientists, and visualization educators. A discussion of the process—from brainstorming to initial designs to realization—and downloadable worksheets are also currently available here: *http://fds.design*

- **MapCI Cards,** by Sheila Pontis: MapCI is short for "Mapping Complex Information." This deck of cards includes a series of 40 questions in five different categories: problem, audience, content, boundaries, and layout. Each question is a prompt for thinking through solutions during the concept-stage of any information design project. Some examples are: "What is the 3-level hierarchy: critical, important, and nice-to-have content?" and "What would be a clear way to visually establish a focal point or center of attention?"[7]

- **Critical Alphabet,** by Lesley-Ann Noel: Available in the form of a physical set of cards and as a digital app, the project introduces critical theories and concepts, from A to Z. Each card (physical or digital) poses questions. The goal is to prompt people to make a connection between the critical theory on the card and their design practice. An example is: "Marginalization is the process where something or someone is pushed to the edge of a group and is treated as insignificant or peripheral. How does your design disrupt the marginalization of people? If you work with marginalized or un-

5   Jonathan C. Roberts, Chris Headleand, and Panagiotis D. Ritsos, "Sketching Designs Using the Five Design-Sheet Methodology," *IEEE Transactions on Visualization and Computer Graphics,* Vol. 22 (January 2016)

6   Jonathan C. Roberts, Christopher J. Headleand, and Panagiotis D. Ritsos, *Five Design-Sheets: Creative Design and Sketching for Computing and Visualisation,* (Springer, 2017)

7   *MapCI Cards,* by Shelia Pontis, accessed September 3, 2021, *http://www.mapcidesign. com/cards/*

derserved groups, how will you ensure that the work is developed from their perspective and not your own?" [8]

File Settings

What do fairly dry and mundane details like file size have to do with something as lofty-sounding as honoring your intended space? Sloppy—or uninformed—use of color settings and resolution can result in files that reproduce poorly, or load too slowly. For example, an image that looks sharp when you view it at one size on your monitor may look blurry or pixelated when reproduced at another size. And those gorgeous and glowing fluorescent colors visible on screen can completely fall flat on paper unless you've taken some steps to prepare your file correctly for print.

If you take the steps of thinking through the settings that will lead to the best-possible version of your final graphic in its ultimate viewing space, you're helping to honor that viewing space and the people viewing it. Here's a succinct guide to often-used topics and terms, to help you navigate the options.

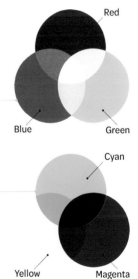

COLOR • I'll stick to practical and succinct color descriptions here, as they pertain to setting up digital files. For more on how color can be *used*, see Chapter 8. The two dominant color models in publishing are RGB and CMYK.

RGB—an acronym for Red, Green, and Blue--is an additive color model: A wide range of colors can be created with light when the wavelengths of those three main colors are combined. As you might expect, files with RGB settings are optimized for being reproduced in light. Think computer monitors and projection screens.

CMYK—an acronym for Cyan, Magenta, Yellow, and Key [9] --is a subtractive color model: A wide range of colors can be created with ink when the pigments of those colors are combined. (Painters will be quite familiar with another subtractive color model: RYB—an acronym for Red, Yellow, and Blue.) Some light wavelengths are absorbed, or subtracted, by the pigment. The wavelengths perceived are reflected

8   *Critical Alphabet*, by Lesley-Ann Noel, accessed September 3, 2021, *https://criticalalphabet.com/*

9   "Key" in printing refers to the "key plate." It's typically associated with black. So much so that "K" in drawing programs is shorthand for black. But strictly speaking, it refers to the key ink color that provides the most detail and contrast. For example, in a two-color printing job in which neither color is black, the darker color may be assigned "key" status.

back at the viewer from the surface that they are printed on, as opposed to being projected from the image itself. As you might expect, files with CMYK settings are optimized for being reproduced on paper. A four-color printing press uses cyan, magenta, yellow, and black inks in combination to create a wider range of colors.

What does this mean in practical terms? If you build images digitally, you have access to a range of colors that can be reproduced elsewhere faithfully (more or less) using projected light. You have options for virtual color-tuning control systems to employ, in which precise values can be input for different variables. Some popular color spaces are HSV (hue–saturation–value), HLS (hue–lightness–saturation), and HCL (hue–chroma–luminance). But if you're using a color space that is rooted in an RGB color model, that color might look dramatically different when reproduced with ink on paper. Any scientist who uses fluorescent tagging dyes in their research knows this all too well. Screen-friendly glowing greens print disappointingly dull unless you have access to special inks.

What to do? Always keep your original image and all of its original data and color specifications intact (especially in the case of scientific images that are captured using a digital camera). Then prepare a copy of that image for your final destination. Follow guidelines, if available, from the organization you'll be handing the files over to. If those guidelines don't exist, I recommend, if possible, creating a version of that original image for each intended use.

If you know the image is going to be reproduced using a four-color printing press, confirm that your file's color settings (including embedded elements) are CMYK. If not, convert them. Then adjust the brightness, saturation, and contrast to maximize legibility. To optimize your odds of a cleanly printed end-product, confirm that black lines and text are set for black (typically "K") ink only. When you convert from RGB to CMYK, that won't automatically be the case. Thin lines that are composed of more than one ink color are less likely to print sharply than lines comprised of one ink color. And neutral gray tones that are composed of more than one color (as opposed to a percent coverage of black ink only) may behave unpredictably on press, unintentionally resulting in a warm or cool gray, or a shape that shifts in hue.

If you know that your image is going to be shared digitally, confirm that your file's color settings are RGB. If not, convert it. Then adjust the brightness, saturation, and contrast to maximize legibility. This step is mostly about seeing an approximation of how things will reproduce in a controlled way before it's too late to make adjustments.

This is an exaggerated and enlarged simulation of a letter printed in black ink.

This is the same letter printed with cyan, magenta, and yellow (to appear as black, without using black ink).

I've offset the ink color channels just a bit, as printing presses lay down each ink color as dots in separate passes. If the registration—or alignment—isn't precise, very thin lines made up of more than one color of ink can easily become blurry. For example, the horizontal bar in the "e" letterform in the three-color version is losing its integrity.

FILE TYPE • Most files you'll be working with are either raster or vector. Some files can include elements of both. Rasterized (also known as bitmapped) images are composed of a grid of individually colored pixels. The file includes data for the color of every pixel in the grid. Vector images are rooted in algorithms as opposed to pixels. The file includes coordinates for endpoints and equations for the lines that connect those points, as well as border and fill color data. Each file type has pros and cons. See the box below for more details.

A CLOSER LOOK

File Type Overview

The two primary digital image file formats are raster and vector. (Although some files include elements of both. For example, a raster image can be embedded in a vector file. Although the file type suffix may suggest that the whole file is vector, a raster image embedded in a vector file does not magically take on vector characteristics.) Here are pros, cons, and common file types for each.

Raster (also known as bitmapped)

Detail of a raster image at 300% of its rendered production size.

Raster images are grids of dots. Each dot (or pixel) is assigned a color. Digital photographs, screenshots, and the output from virtual painting programs are raster files.

Pros • Great for complex gradients and textures, as well as for drawing in painterly and photorealistic styles.

Cons • Resolution is fixed. Enlarging a bitmapped image may result in a pixelated appearance, with jagged or fuzzy edges. Individual objects or shapes can't be selected and moved independently of other objects, unless the original file is set up with the ability to do so, with discrete layers.

Examples • JPG, GIF, PNG, TIFF, RAW, PSD, and some EPS files

Vector

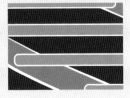

Detail of a vector image at 300% of its rendered production size.

Vector images are comprised of points, lines and curves (not dots). Equations describe the coordinates. Each feature described by an equation can be assigned a color, stroke, and/or fill. (Note that dropshadow and glow effects created in some vector drawing programs may be raster, and may not scale as cleanly as the linework. One workaround: in Illustrator, use "Blend" as opposed to "Drop Shadow" to create true vector shadows.)

Pros • Great for type, logos, and icons. It suits projects with flat and bold styles, although gradients and textures are certainy possible. Resolution is not fixed. Enlarging a vector image does not result in a degraded image. Individual objects or shapes can be selected and moved independently of other objects, even if the file is not set up with discrete layers.

Cons • Drawing with vector programs may not be as intuitive as raster programs for novices. Images with lots of detail and shapes may not be particularly large in file size, but may still be glitchy and/or take time to render as a preview on screen.

Examples • PDF, AI, SVG, and some EPS files

IMAGE RESOLUTION AND SIZE • If the resolution of a raster image is higher than it needs to be, the file size (in terms of memory) is larger than it needs to be, making it less manageable for sharing with others. If your file resolution is lower than it needs to be, fine details may be lost and the image will appear pixelated or blurry.

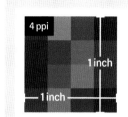 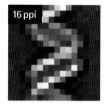 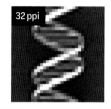 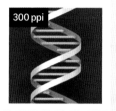

Resolution is measured in points (or dots) per inch, and expressed as ppi or dpi. In general, for print, a resolution of 300 ppi is standard. But—this part is critical—the file should be 300 ppi when sized at 100% of the ultimate print size. If your digital image file is scaled at 1×1 inch, a resolution of 300 ppi is not sufficient when that image is enlarged to 2×2 inches in a layout program for print.

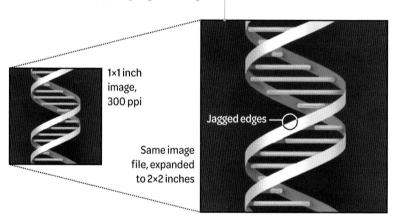

Some programs and filters can fudge things a bit and help you approximate detail when you force a resolution change by typing in larger settings. But in this case, the software adds in pixels based on the neighboring pixels. This is known as upsampling or artificial enlargement. In the case of images captured by camera in the lab, it's important to note that those pixels are not reflecting real data. It's best to capture images in high resolution from the start, then save out and downsize copies of that file for specific purposes.

For images that will appear only on screen, it's best to think in terms of pixel dimensions. Pixel dimensions are written as width × height. For example, 1200 × 628 means the width is 1200 pixels and the height is 628 pixels. Larger pixel dimensions equate to larger file size in terms of memory. Social media platforms and other Web-based applications generally include guidelines for optimal pixel dimensions. If you're preparing images to hand over to a publisher, ask for their preferred dimensions.

Don't be lulled into a sense that image size and resolution for vector images isn't really something that needs much attention, since the file type can be scaled up and down without becoming jagged or blurry. As a graphics editor who works with lots of different artists, failure to think about the final destination for vector files is the most-often file-type sin that I encounter. I've seen many seasoned artists pack way too much detail into the space available, including both data visualizers who code solutions as scalable vector graphics (SVGs) and medical illustrators who use Illustrator. Much of the detail and linework is simply not printable, much less legible in final form. If the digital canvas size is scaled appropriately for print while the image is being built, decisions with regards to the appropriate level of detail can be made from an informed point of view. At the very least, I recommend taking your near-final vector file, and pasting it into a template that matches the dimensions and resolution of the final print destination, as a reality check. Why does this matter? If you don't consider the amount of detail that is legible and appropriate for the image as it will be reproduced, you're failing to honor the final destination.

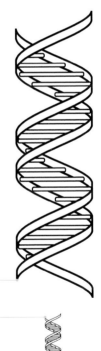

Here's an example. If you're creating a vector line drawing of DNA that will be reproduced at about 1 inch wide, this level of detail works really well. But if that vector object is to be incorporated into a larger graphic, and is reduced to reproduce at less than one-quarter inch wide, the detail is muddled. The key identifying form—the double helix—is lost amidst unnecessary linework. And that linework may even get broken up in the printing process. If the stroke weights are too thin, the printing press may not be able to define the line clearly, resulting in a blurry end-product even if your vector lines are beautifully sharp on screen. Less detail is a better match for tiny objects. Omit secondary details that muddle the main form, and make the linework bold enough to hold up on press.

If you're creating the graphic on a huge vector canvas, then you may not see the problem of too much detail until it's too late. Keep your final destination in mind, and better yet, build your graphic at the correct scale from the start. Even if it's vector. Also, keep in mind that high-end processing for print can sometimes stall when a vector file is loaded with too many small areas of blends. PDFs can also take forever to redraw an illustration on screen. Limiting the use of blends (or rasterizing blend elements) will help make file processing more efficient.

Things get counterintuitive when it comes to presentation software, like Powerpoint, Keynote and Google Slides. The images are destined for a screen, right? So you'd expect pixel dimensions for slide size. And yet, the page setup details are often listed as inches. Screen and projector resolutions vary, so the number of pixels that fit into those inch dimensions varies depending upon what you're using to build and project slides with. In general, I error on the large size in terms of resolution. If your images look blurry or pixelated on your screen when you're previewing your presentation, chances are that they'll be blurry or pixelated for others as well, unless they're viewing on a screen significantly smaller than yours, like a phone.

If you're developing (or reformatting) a graphic for a known destination—such as a specific journal—ask for their preferred specifications or guidelines for reproducing graphics! Some organizations may even provide you with a style guide, complete with color palettes and font recommendations.[10] In general, it's useful to know the ideal file size in terms of dimensions and resolution, as well as color space and file type preferences.

Audience

Audience informs content, composition, and style. As demonstrated here, a coloring book for kids may exclude some technical details and jargon, and be rendered in a more playful style than a graphic on the same topic for adults. (More examples and discussion of designing science graphics with different audiences in mind are in Chapter 10.)

Outlet often predicates who your audience is. For example, a

---

10 I'm heartened by evidence of folks pushing graphics style guides beyond default chart styles, color palette, and font specifications. For example, style guide authors at the Urban Institute are investigating including standards for thoughtful and intentional use of things like icons and labels through the lens of diversity, equity, and inclusion. See "Applying Racial Equity Awareness in Data Visualization" (*OSF Preprints,* August 27, 2020) by Jonathan Schwabish and Alice Feng.

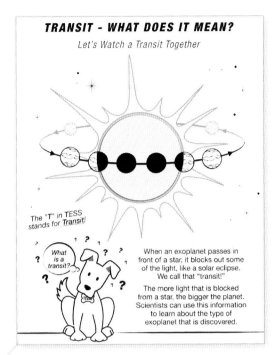

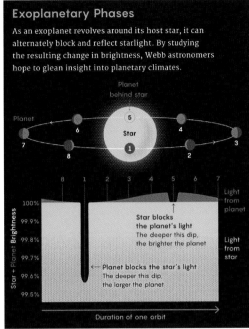

graphic destined for a peer-reviewed journal is generally destined for an audience of scientist peers. Jargon is appropriate in this context and the designer of the graphic can assume a particular level of familiarity of the topic from their readers. But it's often more nuanced than that. With an eye to expanding your audience and making things as accessible as possible, it's important to think critically and deeply about who you're building the graphics for and why.

In the book *Design Justice*, Sasha Costanza-Chock writes—and demonstrates—that "designers tend to unconsciously default to imagined users whose experiences are similar to their own." This results in artifacts and systems that serve the needs and preferences of the folks designing those artifacts and systems. Potential audiences that don't align with the designer's perspective are, thus, marginalized. Their needs aren't met, and they aren't engaged. Or they are actively disengaged.[11]

As a designer of static graphics rooted in science, it's tempting to excuse myself from the conversation. After all, my goal is to simply translate evidence-based information into a visual form, right? Not the high-stakes and high-impact world of designing a digital platform, a

Similar content designed for an audience of kids (left) and adults (right). Image Credits: A page from *Exoplanet Coloring Book*, NASA, *http://tess.gsfc.nasa.gov/* (left); Samuel Velasco/Quanta Magazine (Source: NASA), as published in "The Webb Space Telescope Will Rewrite Cosmic History. If It Works," by Natalie Wolchover, *Quanta Magazine* (December 3, 2021). Reproduced with permission from *Quanta Magazine.*

---

11   Sasha Costanza-Chock, *Design Justice: Community-Led Practices to Build the Worlds We Need* (The MIT Press, 2020)

physical space, or an imagined future. Yet, it's becoming clear that no designer should step back from the conversation. Every design decision has an impact. And the worlds of science and journalism are not immune to bias.

Much of my work has been shaped by thinking about developing graphics **for** a defined audience. Some decisions with regards to level of appropriate detail, visual vocabulary, style, and framing are fairly intuitive. If I'm starting with a graphic from a research journal (an audience of specialists), and redesigning it in a way that will be meaningful to a broader, non-specialist audience, some things are clear: Jargon should be removed, and some context should be added.

However, there are limitations. As an experienced designer I have instincts on what might best suit a particular audience. But the intuition of designers and subject-matter expert consultants don't always align with audience preferences. Remember that example from page 130? In a study about the visual representation of medical information, researchers Emma Scheltema and her collaborators found that patients generally preferred complex representations over simplified schematics. The audience (patients) preferred illustrations that depicted more information than the content-experts (clinicians) deemed necessary—or advisable—for patient education.[12]

Many researchers are putting the emphasis on developing graphics **with** a defined audience. In general, the concept is that your audience is an expert with regards to their needs. (This is in line with the inclusion-centric science communication framework described on page 33.) Tapping into that point of view makes a lot of sense if you're trying to engage with those needs directly. But how does that translate to practice? Where does one start when it comes to developing graphics with your audience? How does one even truly co-design a science graphic for news on deadline? I don't have the answers. But some people and writings have prompted me to start and try to figure out how to be better.

(Folks interested in exploring these ideas as they relate to journalism should check out the *The View from Somewhere* podcast. In the episode "The End of Extractive Journalism," host Lewis Raven Wallace chats with several guests about moving away from the extractive practice of reporting on communities without input or accountability,

---

12 Emma Scheltema, Stephen Reay, and Greg Piper, "Visual Representation of Medical Information: The Importance of Considering the End-User in the Design of Medical Illustrations," *Journal of Visual Communication in Medicine*, Vol. 41 (January 2, 2018)

and toward community-driven journalism.[13] For a rich and deep discussion of these ideas as they relate to data science and data visualization, I recommend the book *Data Feminism* by Catherine D'Ignazio and Lauren F. Klein.[14])

Developing graphics with a defined audience doesn't necessarily mean that someone from your target audience should look over your shoulder and provide recommendations on how to move elements around or use a particular color. Relatedly, Costanza-Chock wrote this in an answer to the question of whether or not the practice of design justice requires design by committee:

> The answer is simple: it does not. On the contrary, in a well-functioning design process, the design team recognizes and values the unique skillsets and experiences of each participant. ... There is nothing about design justice as a framework that necessarily implies that particular talents or skills must be devalued or subordinated to an abstract 'collective will.'[15]

Rather, you're relying on different people within the co-design group to lend their specific expertise. As stated by the Design Justice Network: **"We believe that everyone is an expert based on their own lived experience, and that we all have unique and brilliant contributions to bring to a design process."**[16] Many folks that design science graphics are used to some level of this already. It's not unusual to collaborate with scientists to make sure that the content being depicted is accurate.

In *Making Sense of Field Research: A Practical Guide for Information Designers*, Sheila Pontis argues that it behooves everyone to routinely fold in members of the ultimate audience as well. She does this with field research; a set of qualitative, contextual research methods that aim to provide a holistic understanding of the behaviors, attitudes, and needs of people. Her framework addresses soliciting feedback at three points in time (concept stage, prototype stage, and the essentially final information design), across four dimensions (satisfaction, usability, behavior change, and action).[17] Candidly, I've yet to fold this into my routine, but

13   Lewis Raven Wallace and Ramona Martinez, "The End of Extractive Journalism," *The View from Somewhere* podcast, episode 13 (June 9, 2020) *https://www.lewispants.com*

14   Catherine D'Ignazio and Lauren F. Klein, *Data Feminism* (The MIT Press, 2020)

15   Sasha Costanza-Chock, *Design Justice: Community-Led Practices to Build the Worlds We Need* (The MIT Press, 2020)

16   Design Justice Network Principle #6: *https://designjustice.org/read-the-principles*

17   Sheila Pontis, *Making Sense of Field Research: A Practical Guide for Information Designers* (Routledge, 2018)

I'm keen to figure out how to make room for it in my production process for magazine graphics. More thoughts on how are in Part 3.

Accessibility

Accessibility in the context of graphic design is a very broad topic. In general, I use it here to refer to the practice of ensuring that the information within a graphic is designed—or supplemented—in a manner that makes it accessible to as many people as possible. Below are a handful of practical guidelines that are particularly relevant to static science graphics. I should be clear, though—there is so much more to the subject.

If you're looking for an entry point for a richer understanding, I recommend Josh A. Halstead's contributions to the book *Extra Bold*.[18] Lots of people have a life long disability, many more will move in and out of having them over the years, and everyone situationally benefits from accessible design. For example, if your vision is otherwise sound, has a screen glare ever compromised your ability to see what's on your phone clearly, or have you had to puzzle over a color-coding system in a black and white copy of what was originally designed as a full-color graphic?

PRINT • *AccessAbility 2: A Practical Handbook on Accessible Graphic Design*[19] identifies 11 primary items in the accessible designers toolbox for print, specifically, grid, hierarchy, printing surface (avoid glare), color, as well as the shape/weight, scale, style, dimension, spacing, and alignment of type. The idea is to use those tools to make your design as *clear and easy-to-read* as possible.

Intentional and thoughtful use of a grid system—combined with a clear hierarchy of things like section heads, body text, and labels, and a logical flow of information—provides signposts and consistency for folks who may struggle to read a jumbled or complex presentation. Remember, text legibility and readability isn't just about font size. Font style choices and text spacing are critical, too.

Considerate use of color goes beyond avoiding red-green pairings for readers with red-green colorblindness. Although that's a great place to start! (On that topic, as someone who goes back and forth

18   Ellen Lupton et al., *Extra Bold: A Feminist, Inclusive, Anti-Racist, Nonbinary Field Guide for Graphic Designers* (Princeton Architectural Press, 2021)

19   *AccessAbility 2: A Practical Handbook on Accessible Graphic Design* (Association of Registered Graphic Designers), accessed September 6, 2021, *https://www.rgd.ca/resources/accessibility/access*

between CMYK and RGB color models, I appreciate Adobe's online accessible color tool because it allows the user to create custom five-color palettes with both CMYK and RGB color mix breakdowns.[20])

Also aim for high contrast between details (or type) and the background tone, to boost legibility. Consider double encoding critical information with color-independent visual signals too, like a change in icon shape to reinforce a difference that is also marked in color.

See Chapters 7 through 9 for color and typography tips, and more information about using a grid system to help organize your content in a clean and clear manner.

ONLINE • All of the variables referenced in the print section apply to digital environments as well. But the Web also provides the opportunity—and responsibility—to take things even further. The resources at the bottom of this section provide really detailed information and guidelines for how to strive for universal access to information and functionality online.

The most commonly employed tactic for static raster imagery is the use of "alt text." Alt text is a short description that provides a textual alternative to imagery. It can be read by screen readers and search engines and may be displayed in place of the image in browsers if images are suppressed for any reason. Good alt text succinctly describes the imagery in a useful manner. And keep in mind that some screen readers cut things off at 125 characters. Explanatory diagrams are often tricky to describe succinctly. The same challenge is true for data visualization. So perhaps it's no surprise that one of my favorite guides on the topic is written by a data visualization designer. In a post for *Nightingale*,[21] Amy Cesal suggests following this model:

alt = "[***Chart type***] of [***type of data***] where [***reason for including chart***]."

Wherein "chart type" provides context, and is helpful for folks with partial sight, "type of data" provides content clues, and "reason for including chart" prompts you to describe what is meaningful about the display. Cesal also suggests including a link to the data source,

High contrast, like this example of dark type on a light backgound, is good.

Low contrast, like this example of dark type on a dark background, should be avoided.

Avoid juxtaposing colors that inhabit the same (or a similar) tonal range. The blue type and olive background color in this box are way too similar in visual weight. Much more contrast is needed.

Avoid juxtaposing colors that inhabit the same (or a similar) tonal range. The blue type and olive background color in this bottom box are way too similar in visual weight. Much more contrast is needed.

20 "Accessible Color Palette Generator | Adobe Color," (accessed September 7, 2021) *https://color.adobe.com/create/color-accessibility*

21 Amy Cesal, "Writing Alt Text for Data Visualization," *Nightingale: Journal of the Data Visualization Society* (July 23, 2020) *https://nightingaledvs.com/writing-alt-text-for-data-visualization/*

when possible, associated with the image, but not in the alt text itself.

When I'm pondering alt text, I often return to my original goal statement (as discussed in Chapter 15) as a starting point. For example, here's my goal statement for the image below→ Goal: demonstrate that image quality deteriorates when a 1×1 inch 300 ppi raster image is enlarged to 2×2 inches.

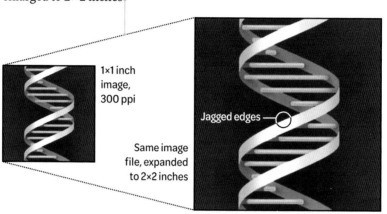

1×1 inch image, 300 ppi

Same image file, expanded to 2×2 inches

Jagged edges

Here's my alt text for that image: "Two DNA drawings. One is a raster image with smooth lines. The other is the same image printed at 200%, now with jagged lines." (I excluded the resolution and size specifics from the alt text to reduce character count. Those details are provided in the text immediately before the image in the original context, so it's not critical information to include again.)

For more in-depth information on how to write effective alt text for a wide range of educational graphics types, check out the Poet Training Tool site.[22] Their recommendations are really comprehensive and aren't limited to the 125-character succinct style preferred for general websites.

Vector images, in the form of SVGs—an extensible markup language (XML) for describing two-dimensional graphics—are more flexible in that they are defined by code. As such, more information about the imagery itself can be articulated in words to folks, or screen readers, in the image's source code. Also, as described in the file settings section above, vector graphics can be enlarged without becoming pixelated or blurry. This allows your audience to scale the image up as needed, without loss of detail.

---

22 Poet Training Tool: a Benetech Initiative Developed by The DIAGRAM Center (accessed September 8, 2021) *https://poet.diagramcenter.org/*

More to Explore (Accessibility)

These resources are useful in helping to identify areas for improvement, along with guidelines and suggestions for doing better.

- **AccessAbility 2: A Practical Handbook on Accessible Graphic Design**[23] • This document, presented by the Association of Registered Graphic Designers of Ontario, is a concise guide for both print and digital design.
- **Chartability** • Chartability is a methodology created by Frank Elavsky (and staged online) for improving accessibility for data visualizations in a way that honors enjoyment (not just compliance): *https://chartability.fizz.studio/*
- **The 18F Accessibility Guide** and **W3C's Web Accessibility Initiative** • Although these online guides are more broadly focused on websites in general, they include a wide range of resource links and tips related to imagery in particular: *https://accessibility.18f.gov/* and *https://www.w3.org/WAI/*
- **Poet Training Tool** • This site, presented by the DIAGRAM Center, provides guidelines for—and prompts for practicing—writing alt text for complex and information-rich images. Lots of science graphics are included as examples, and there are discrete sections addressing chemistry and math: *https://poet.diagramcenter.org/*
- *Extra Bold: A Feminist, Inclusive, Anti-Racist, Nonbinary Field Guide for Graphic Designers* (Princeton Architectural Press, 2021)

Timeline

A practical force that doesn't budge is time. I recommend scaling your expectations for the graphic you hope to achieve with an eye to the amount of time you have to create it. If time is short, it may be wise to pare down your project to something less epic. That could mean editing down the amount of content you hope to cover, or reducing the complexity of the rendering style. In all cases, I suggest that you chunk up your project and create incremental deadlines. A model for how to break down your project into discrete stages is in Chapter 15. If your time is short, and you have a budget, you can also consider hiring a collaborator. More on this is in Chapter 18.

---

23 *AccessAbility 2: A Practical Handbook on Accessible Graphic Design* (Association of Registered Graphic Designers), accessed September 6, 2021, *https://www.rgd.ca/resources/accessibility/access*

CHAPTER 13

Special Considerations for Science Graphics

WHY DO SCIENCE GRAPHICS MERIT SPECIAL CONSIDERATIONS?
They're kind of an odd beast. From a design point of view, they're be-holden to the same best practices as other types of graphics. But the content they convey is often rooted in a process that a lot of people aren't familiar with. Building bodies of scientific knowledge is a slow, incremental, collective, and self-correcting enterprise. Conclusions are rooted in evidence, but those interpretations may shift as additional evidence is collected, or when the same evidence is re-analyzed from a different perspective.

It's no surprise that folks can get frustrated with science news coverage. It can be confusing to be told one month that you should focus on washing your hands and not worry about wearing a mask as COVID-19 prevention measures. Only to be told the next month that wearing a mask is one of the best ways to avoid contracting the virus. How can we expect people to "trust the science," if the "science" appears to flip-flop, or when graphics from just a year ago are no longer considered accurate? (In actuality, public health recommendations shifted in the first months of the pandemic as scientists learned more about the virus.) It doesn't help when the source material is often cloaked in a highly specialized language or locked behind paywalls.

In the *KSJ Science Editing Handbook*, journalist Apoorva Mandavilli encourages folks covering science to remain cognizant of the "deliberate and incremental nature," of scientific discovery. She reminds us that "the best scientists are careful and methodical, moving from hypothesis to confirmation step by deliberate step. ... That can make reporting on science challenging—first to discern where in the research process a particular study falls and then to engage audiences and clearly explain why that single step matters." [1]

These challenges are also a factor when it comes to illustrating science. It's important to sort out what background or context your audience needs. And it's important in many cases to honor the fact that the findings that you're presenting are both the product of a rigorous study that builds upon past studies, and that interpretations may eventually shift a bit as future research sheds more light on the topic.

This chapter provides you with some strategies for addressing those challenges. In particular, four overarching themes that are particularly pertinent to science graphics: honoring complexity, providing context, avoiding misinformation pitfalls, and visualizing uncertainty.

Honoring Complexity

More often than not, scientific content is complex. And the research papers that describe it can be dense. If you try to strip away that complexity, you're at risk of producing either an oversimplified primer graphic that doesn't really present the latest findings, or graphic that shows the latest discovery without proper context for folks new to the topic. As discussed in Chapter 6, I think it's incredibly useful to think in terms of clarifying the information for visual presentation, as opposed to simplifying it.

With an eye to clarity, you become a translator, or a guide. The focus shifts away from watering the information down, and turns toward knocking down barriers of entry, and beckoning the reader in. The goal is to make complex and specialized information accessible to your audience. This is particularly critical when developing a graphic for a broad audience. But it's also a helpful mindset when creating graphics for content-area experts, as it can prevent you from falling back on too many assumptions with regards to your shared language.

For example, for a *Scientific American* article on gene expression in the brain by scientists Ed Lein and Michael Hawrylycz, I started with two complex charts provided by the authors that were similar to the one shown here. These charts portray how gene expression varies between individuals. Color indicates the extent of variability. It's a brain map style that allows for easy cross-comparison of brain structures (within a chart) and between different scenarios (across more than one chart). (The example shown here shows variability between two human

---

1   *The KSJ Science Editing Handbook*, a project of the Knight Science Journalism Fellowship at MIT, supported by the Kavli Foundation and the Howard Hughes Medical Institute's Department of Science Education. *https://ksjhandbook.org*

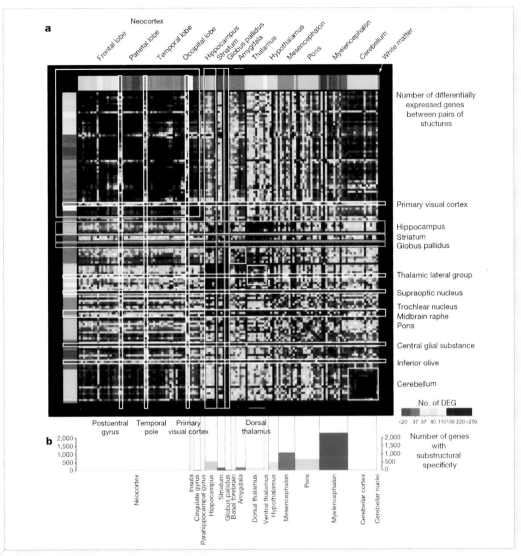

Image Credit: As published in Michael J. Hawrylycz et al., "An Anatomically Comprehensive Atlas of the Adult Human Brain Transcriptome," *Nature*, Vol. 489 (September 2012). Reprinted with permission from Springer Nature, © 2012

brains. The reference material for our article included a chart on human variability and a chart on mouse variability, both with more than two subjects each.) The original charts were designed to communicate results within a peer group—an audience of other neuroscientists highly motivated to read and understand the images. They lean on a visual vocabulary of symbols and colors that would be familiar to other neuroscientists. I like to think of it as using "visual jargon."

Jargon can be incredibly useful. Words and imagery that carry a highly specific meaning within a specific context can be a really

efficient way to present complex information to others within a community. But jargon—in both written and drawn forms—can act as a brick wall to folks who are not fluent in that language. (Or perhaps even worse, those highly specialized words and images can take on a very different meaning when the material is removed from its original specialized context.[2])

For the gene expression graphic makeover, I ultimately collaborated with data designer Jan Willem Tulp to develop something more broadly accessible. In this case, that didn't mean a different chart form. Instead, we stripped away the barriers of entry, and added welcoming gestures. We started with the source material, then slowly walked through it, translating one detail at a time into a more broadly understood written and visual language, adding in layers of context for folks new to the topic. The full dataset remained intact. Tulp simply removed insider conventions (such as the rainbow color palette), replacing it with a more intuitive and aesthetically pleasing tonal scale; we included a few

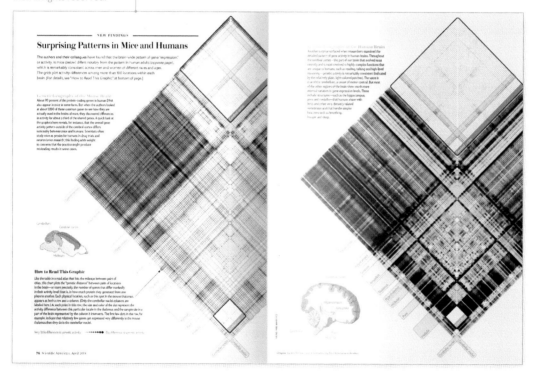

2   Anna Nellis B. Smith and Bethann Garramon Merkle, "Meaning-Making in Science Communication: A Case for Precision in Word Choice," *The Bulletin of the Ecological Society of America,* Vol. 102 (2021)

brain illustrations to make abstract brain region terms tangible and relatable; explained how to read the graphic in plain language, with a leader line pointing directly to the referenced spot in the chart; and energized the layout by turning the charts 45 degrees and cropping off some of the redundant portions of each plot.

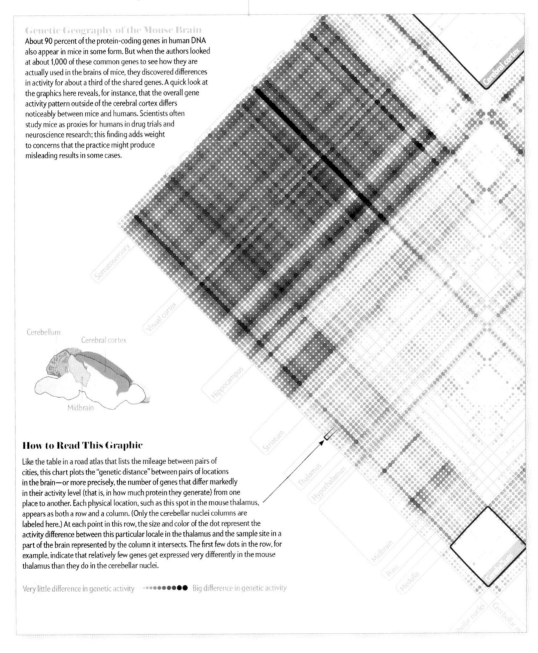

Genetic Geography of the Mouse Brain

About 90 percent of the protein-coding genes in human DNA also appear in mice in some form. But when the authors looked at about 1,000 of these common genes to see how they are actually used in the brains of mice, they discovered differences in activity for about a third of the shared genes. A quick look at the graphics here reveals, for instance, that the overall gene activity pattern outside of the cerebral cortex differs noticeably between mice and humans. Scientists often study mice as proxies for humans in drug trials and neuroscience research; this finding adds weight to concerns that the practice might produce misleading results in some cases.

Cerebellum

Cerebral cortex

Midbrain

How to Read This Graphic

Like the table in a road atlas that lists the mileage between pairs of cities, this chart plots the "genetic distance" between pairs of locations in the brain—or more precisely, the number of genes that differ markedly in their activity level (that is, in how much protein they generate) from one place to another. Each physical location, such as this spot in the mouse thalamus, appears as both a row and a column. (Only the cerebellar nuclei columns are labeled here.) At each point in this row, the size and color of the dot represent the activity difference between this particular locale in the thalamus and the sample site in a part of the brain represented by the column it intersects. The first few dots in the row, for example, indicate that relatively few genes get expressed very differently in the mouse thalamus than they do in the cerebellar nuclei.

Very little difference in genetic activity ·········●●●● Big difference in genetic activity

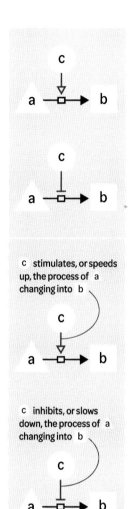

Figures in scientific papers generally rely on visual jargon a lot. If you're a scientist working up a graphic about your work, pause and think about your audience. You may need to decode some of the visual elements that you use as shorthand. At the very least, I recommend making sure that you define the specialized symbols that you use. For example, arrowheads and bars are often used in biology to represent activation and inhibition. It's a useful shorthand for others fluent in that visual language. But I don't recommend leaning back on them for broader audiences. The addition of a simple label or annotation can help clarify the meaning.

The same goes for abbreviations. They're often suitable shorthand for communicating with your inner circle of research peers, but remember that even in a conference setting among other researchers, you may be presenting your work in poster or slide form to folks that don't use those abbreviations on a regular basis. Writing out the full terms—or even translating those terms into plain language—can help ease comprehension for a cold reader.

Decoding jargon is just one step in helping your audience parse complex information. As written by Fabiola Cristina Rodríguez Estrada and Lloyd Spencer Davis, "the popularization of science should not be regarded as a simplification or a 'translation' but as a recontextualization of the scientific discourse into another domain."[3] Some of the strategies that follow are modest steps towards making complex information more accessible across domains, such as adding explanatory labels. Others are more ambitious, such as folding in background information.[4]

Providing Context

Newsworthy scientific discoveries generally stand on a foundation of lots of incremental research findings. Although it's often tempting to dive right into showing the latest results, your audience may not be primed to understand or appreciate the breakthrough without back-

3   Fabiola Cristina Rodríguez Estrada and Lloyd Spencer Davis, "Improving Visual Communication of Science Through the Incorporation of Graphic Design Theories and Practices Into Science Communication," *Science Communication,* Vol. 37 (February 1, 2015)

4   Many of these suggestions were first published in a chapter I wrote for *The KSJ Science Editing Handbook,* a project of the Knight Science Journalism Fellowship at MIT, supported by the Kavli Foundation and the Howard Hughes Medical Institute's Department of Science Education. *https://ksjhandbook.org/illustrating-complex-science-stories/*

ground information. Here are three strategies for providing non-specialist readers with the context they need in order to better understand the latest development.

STRATEGY 1: ANNOTATE THE PRIMARY SOURCE MATERIAL DIRECTLY, IN PLAIN LANGUAGE • Press releases and academic publications often include key visualizations that highlight the latest development. For example, you may remember these abstract images that circulated widely in July 2012 related to the Higgs Boson. Many news outlets ran the pickup images as-is. But how many non-specialists could really understand what they were looking at?

Image Credit: © 2012 CERN

Image Credit: © 2012 CERN

A few labels can go a long way in helping with reader comprehension, and helping folks better understand the image's significance. If you choose to present an academic chart to a non-specialist audience, think about how annotations and labels can help a reader focus on the critical take-away points.

─────────────── FINDINGS ───────────────

The Delicate, Rare Fingerprints of the Higgs

The Higgs boson is an extremely unstable particle that quickly decays via a number of different processes, or "modes." Unfortunately, many decay modes are indistinguishable from the thunderous din of ordinary background events that result from 500 million proton-proton collisions every second. The ATLAS and CMS experiments are designed to spot the occasional interesting events that might come from the Higgs decay and throw much of the rest away. The drawings below show four of the most important decay modes that experiments use to search for the Higgs, along with images of actual Higgs-like signals that CMS observed in the 2011 and 2012 runs. (Because the discovery is statistical in nature, no single event can be used as definitive proof.)

Photons

Each detector includes multiple calorimeters, devices for measuring the energy of particles. The innermost calorimeter is particularly alert for photons. These are absorbed in the calorimeter and create tiny electrical signals. If a Higgs decays into two photons, the detector can measure their total energy at extremely high accuracy, which helps to precisely reconstruct the mass of the newly found particle.

Z Bosons

The Higgs may decay into a pair of Z bosons, each of which can decay into an electron paired with an oppositely charged antielectron or two muons. An inner tracker and calorimeter measure the electrons, while muons fly out, leaving footprintlike tracks as they go. High magnetic fields bend the path of electrons and muons during their trip, allowing for a high-resolution measurement of their energy and the original Higgs mass.

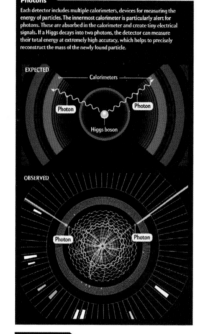

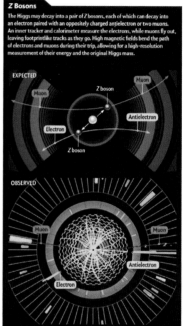

Bottom Quarks

The Higgs can also decay to a bottom quark and its antiparticle, each of which decays into a tight "jet" of secondary particles called hadrons (composite particles made of quarks). These hadrons fly through the detector's inner layers and deposit their energy in the outer calorimeters. Unfortunately, many ordinary collisions also generate jets of hadrons from bottom quarks, which makes it difficult to separate these Higgs events out from the background.

W Bosons

The Higgs can also decay to two W bosons, each of which can decay into an electron, antielectron or muon, plus a neutrino or antineutrino. Neutrinos are nearly impossible to detect—they fly out of the detector as if they were never there, taking with them some of the event's energy. Researchers use this missing energy to infer their presence, but the missing energy also prevents them from accurately reconstructing the mass of the original Higgs boson.

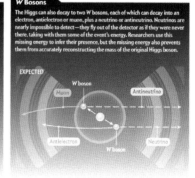

STRATEGY 2: FOLD BACKGROUND INFORMATION INTO THE MAIN GRAPHIC • Sometimes a few explanatory annotations aren't enough, and companion schematics are needed. You may be familiar with Boyajian's star, also known as Tabby's star after the astronomer Tabetha Boyajian, who first noted the odd fluctuations in its apparent brightness when viewed from Earth. The star usually makes the news whenever it starts dimming again, as scientists try to shake out what's causing the dimming, and headlines capitalize on hypotheses that revolve around ideas of alien superstructures in orbit around the star. For an article in which Kimberly Cartier and Jason T. Wright explored some of the different hypotheses in play, we relied on data visualization to tell one piece of the story: Why is the light-dimming pattern perplexing? Presenting a graph of perceived light intensity from Tabby's star was a start. Tiffany Farrant-Gonzalez plotted out data provided by the scientists, styled it to match the magazine's style, replaced axis label jargon with plain language, and added a few on-art labels to point out critical details. The key addition was a companion chart for context. Specifically, a representation of a more ubiquitous star-dimming situation—a pattern of regular dips caused by a planet passing in front of the star in a fixed orbit. Armed with that information, the reader can then see why the irregular pattern exhibited by Tabby's star is so odd.

STRATEGY 3: INCLUDE A PRIMER BOX • Torn between the need to provide background material, and the desire to get-right-to-it with information on the latest discovery? Consider breaking things down into two independent graphics. A primer box can introduce basic concepts to readers who may need more context. Readers more familiar with the topic can jump straight to the new stuff.

OBSERVATIONS

Enigmatic Light Patterns

To astronomers, there is usually no mystery behind a star fading in the sky. Starspots as well as the shadows of planets or debris disks routinely dim the otherwise steady light from mature stars. But none of these explanations seems to apply for one mercurial middle-aged sun known as KIC 8462852—also called Boyajian's star.

Typical Light Curve

A dimming star can be studied by its light curve—its brightness plotted over time. A planet or disk "transiting" across a star causes a dip in the curve; for planets, this dip recurs every orbital period. Starspots create patterns in light curves based on a star's rotation rate and activity cycle.

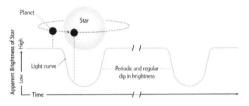

Not So Typical: Boyajian's Star

The light curve of Boyajian's star is wildly variable. Some dips last for days, and others persist for months; some scarcely dim the star's light, and others reduce it by 20 percent. Besides these dips, Boyajian's star also is steadily dimming and may have darkened by more than 15 percent during the past century. Transiting planets, debris disks and starspots cannot explain these phenomena, leading astronomers to look for exotic solutions—including the idea that the star's light is blocked by swarms of satellites built by an advanced alien civilization.

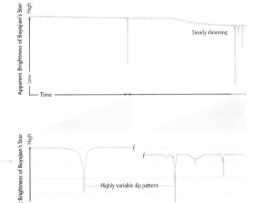

Combating Misinformation

My default position is to simply not honor disinformation and misinformation with a graphic. It's too easy for folks to remove the graphic from the context of the article or caption, and disseminate on social media. Nuance and explanation are easily stripped away from visuals, leaving a core bit of shareable falsehood, regardless of the original intent or new framing. Nevertheless, gray areas exist, particularly when a graphic was created in good faith but, as a result of unintentional mistakes or revised data, proves to be erroneous.

Occasionally I find that representing the old (mistaken) and new (corrected) views side-by-side can help readers understand how the errors led to a faulty analysis, and why the newer interpretation is more solid. But in those cases, I move forward with an eye to how the graphic could be used by folks with ill intent. My goal is to make it as hard as possible for someone to isolate and amplify what we know to be incorrect. For example, for a *Scientific American* article by Melinda Wenner Moyer on guns and public health, we wanted to address some oft-cited gun-control studies directly. Subsequent analysis revealed serious errors in some classic papers that are often referenced by the pro-gun lobby: The data actually show that more firearms do not keep people safe.

Rather than brush aside the earlier studies that implied otherwise, we decided to go ahead and show the original analysis with a critique baked into the visual presentation. Annotations addressed the statistical errors that influenced the initial interpretations, along with companion charts on the same topic with updated information. The annotations were placed in bold inset circles that were dropped directly onto the charts, making it a bit more difficult to crop and share out of context.

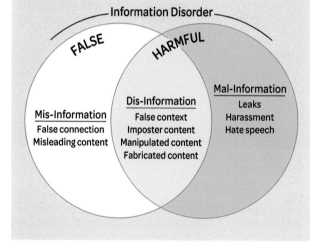

What is misinformation? According to Claire Wardle and Hossein Derakhshan as published in a report on information disorder by the Council of Europe in 2017, "Mis-information is when false information is shared, but no harm is meant; Dis-information is when false information is knowingly shared to cause harm; and Mal-information is when genuine information is shared to cause harm, often by moving information designed to stay private into the public sphere."

Information Disorder

FALSE   HARMFUL

Mis-Information
False connection
Misleading content

Dis-Information
False context
Imposter content
Manipulated content
Fabricated content

Mal-Information
Leaks
Harassment
Hate speech

Image Credit: Restyled from *Information Disorder: Toward an Interdisciplinary Framework for Research and Policy Making*, by Claire Wardle, PhD and Hossein Derakhshan, with research support from Anne Burns and Nic Dias. © Council of Europe (October 2017)

Communicating Uncertainty and Unknowns

Uncertainty is a particularly important concept as it relates to major stories like climate change and global pandemics. Yet I think it's fair to say that until relatively recently, visual journalists—including my-self—defaulted to sweeping the very notion of uncertainty under the rug when presenting scientific information to the broader public. How many of us have chosen to ignore error ranges when preparing a chart for publication?

Academics and research scientists, on the other hand, regularly include uncertainty indicators such as error bars. But as it turns out, many of those visual techniques might not be terribly effective at communicating uncertainty, even within a peer group.[5] Why does it matter? There are consequences. As Barauch Fischhoff and Alex L. Davis wrote in "Communicating Scientific Uncertainty:" "All science has uncertainty. Unless that uncertainty is communicated effectively, decision makers may put too much or too little faith in it."[6]

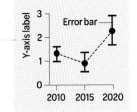

In 2015, at the Gordon Research Conference for Visualization in Science and Education, geographer Diana Sinton[7] caused me to think about how I depict uncertainty more critically. We kicked off a collaboration, with support by a mini visionary grant funded by NASA. Many of the thoughts that follow lean heavily on ideas that emerged over the course of our conversations.

Scientific illustrations, diagrams, charts, and maps show what is known—and, sometimes, how it is known. Less attention is paid to representing what is not known.[8] And as Sinton points out, the categories of "known" and "unknown" aren't as binary as the words suggest. There's an uncertain space between those endpoints. The extent to which something is known is a function of what question was asked

5   Sarah Belia et al., "Researchers Misunderstand Confidence Intervals and Standard Error Bars," *Psychological Methods,* Vol. 10 (December 2005)

6   Baruch Fischhoff and Alex L. Davis, "Communicating Scientific Uncertainty," *Proceedings of the National Academy of Sciences*, Vol. 111 (September 16, 2014)

7   Diana Sinton is Senior Research Fellow at the University Consortium for Geographic Information Science (UCGIS), and an adjunct associate professor at Cornell University.

8   See Mimi Ọnụọha's work and writings for a compelling discussion of missing data. Here's one of my favorite excerpts from her article "What is Missing is Still There," *Nichons-Nous Dans L'Internet* (April 2018): "Datasets are the end products of classification systems, the clean outputs of intentional orderings...datasets point to their own contrasts—specifically the things that we haven't collected. And if it is true that we make sense of the world through exclusion, then perhaps there is a special type of meaning to be found in the things that we leave out."

and how it was answered. The measurement devices, choices about model parameters, and unknown effects of changing conditions are only some of the factors that will affect the result. Ambiguous or unclear answers may be just as common as definitive results at the end of a scientific experiment or survey.

Perception researchers including Lace Padilla, Matthew Kay, and Jessica Hullman have been chipping away at sorting out which techniques are most effective in communicating uncertainty in data visualizations.[9] But how does this translate to explanatory diagrams? Can we learn something about uncertainty by evaluating how it is represented across different domains and phenomena? In particular, perhaps we can glean useful information from the realm of quantum mechanics, a field in which the concept of uncertainty is pretty pervasive.

As written by David Deutsch and Artur Ekert in a 2013 article in *Scientific American*, "The famous Heisenberg uncertainty principle limits the precision of certain measurements. If you pin down the position of a particle exactly, it will start moving with a range of different velocities simultaneously; if you measure its velocity exactly, you likewise force its position to spread out uncontrollably."[10][11]

Position:
Sharply defined

Velocity:
Not sharply defined

Already—within one example—we're encountering a few different types of uncertainty. There are unknowns with regards to both position and velocity. I've used the same illustration technique, fuzzy edges, to convey both.

Position:
Not sharply defined

Velocity:
Sharply defined

But does one solution work for all cases? Sinton and I were keen to see how other cartographers, designers, and illustrators solved the problem for a wide range of uncertainty types. First, though, we

---

9   For a great summary of the current state of knowledge, see Lace Padilla, Matthew Kay, and Jessica Hullman's chapter "Uncertainty Visualization," in *Wiley StatsRef: Statistics Reference Online* (John Wiley & Sons, Ltd, 2021); and the Multiple Views: Visualization Research Explained blog post "Uncertainty + Visualization, Explained," by the MU Collective (June 5, 2019).

10 David Deutsch and Artur Ekert, "Beyond the Quantum Horizon," *Scientific American*, (May 2013)

11 It's worth underscoring that the uncertainty principle describes quantum behavior and uncertainty at the particle level. It isn't a perfect analogy for uncertainty at the macro or classical physics level. For instance, although we cannot simultaneously pinpoint the position and velocity of a particle with precision, we can pinpoint the position and velocity of a baseball flying through the air with a pretty high level of certainty. But I'm more concerned with how we illustrate the uncertainty associated with the idea, so I think that studying figures that depict quantum mechanics can still be really useful beyond the quantum world.

needed some general classifications, to help guide our search. Here are the six general categories of uncertainty we delineated, along with examples that show how different visualizers addressed the challenge.

MEASUREMENTS AND SCALE • Measuring and recording things —such as the total number of objects, size of features, frequency of events, time elapsed, etc.—is a pretty critical part of the scientific process. The scale of the thing being measured relative to the granularity of the instrument being used to measure it can lead to different levels of precision. For example, the measurement in the top vignette here can be reported with a higher level of precision—and lower level of uncertainty—than the measurement in the lower vignette. Uncertainty can be masked—or introduced—by modifying the scale, or by adjusting the resolution of how the information is represented.

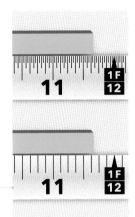

LOCATION • If you want to communicate uncertainty about the location or position of an item, what are your options? One way is to avoid ascribing precision to a location. For example, this brain illustration published in 1846 is vague with regards to defining the geography of the brain. The edges of the labelled regions are not all defined.

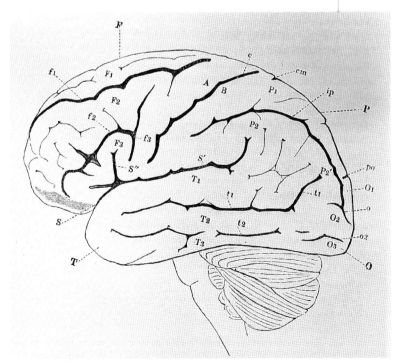

Image Credit: As published in *The Functions of the Brain*, by David Ferrier (Smith, Elder & Co., 1876). File accessed from the Wellcome Collection, November 30, 2021. *https:// wellcomecollection.org/ works/ev7wzbvc*

As advances in imaging and related technologies have allowed neuroscientists to have much greater confidence in declaring the locations of different functions of the brain—brain maps have shifted toward more concrete representations of those regions, as shown here, by Jill Gregory. But for some regions (such as the prefrontal cortex), fuzzy edges of the tinted areas still convey a level of uncertainty or variability.

Image Credit: Jill K. Gregory, CMI; printed with permission from ©Mount Sinai Health System.

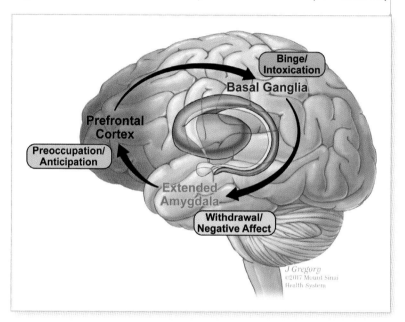

To address the future location of an object, models or statistical probabilities can be used to suggest likely—or unlikely—places that could be correct at a particular moment in time. For example, a "cone of uncertainty" is a conventional approach in representing hurricane forecasts. The cone defines an area that includes the projected storm center path with a 60-70 percent level of certainty. (As Alberto Cairo clarifies, that also means that "one out of three times we experience a storm like this, its center will be outside the boundaries of the cone"[12] at some point in the following five days.) But research has confirmed that these cones of uncertainty are not ideal. Lots of people read the cone as a representation of projected storm size, or the area under threat.[13]

12   Alberto Cairo and Tala Schlossberg, "Those Hurricane Maps Don't Mean What You Think They Mean," *The New York Times*, Opinion section (August 29, 2019)

13   Ian T. Ruginski et al., "Non-Expert Interpretations of Hurricane Forecast Uncertainty Visualizations," *Spatial Cognition & Computation*, Vol. 16 (April 2, 2016)

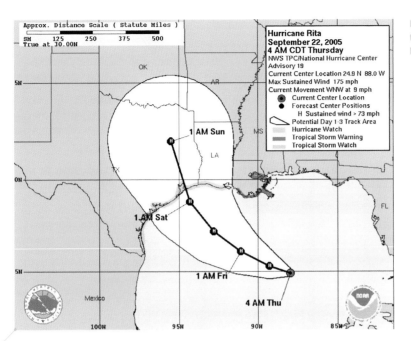

Le Liu, Lace Padilla, Sarah H. Creem-Regehr, and Donald H. House have investigated alternatives, including an approach that shows a selection of different path possibilities, color coded with possible intensities and punctuated with projected storm sizes.

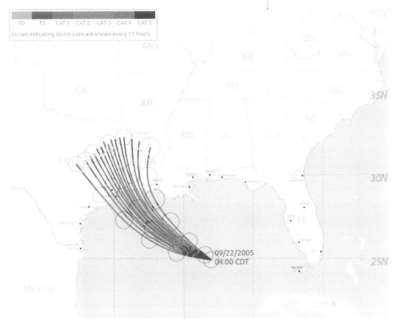

That hurricane visualization style is called an ensemble plot. Each path plotted is an "ensemble member." It outperforms the cone of uncertainty by some measures, but it's not a perfect solution. As Lace Padilla and collaborators have observed, "people overreact when they see one ensemble member impacting their point of interest, such as their town. The same people do not overreact when an ensemble member barely misses their point of interest."[14]

People need more context. Yes, we should aim to represent uncertainty as clearly as possible in visual representations, and continue to explore better ways to do it. But your audience will likely need supporting information in order to ensure that they're interpreting things correctly. Particularly in the case of uncertainty projections that are directly tied to risk evaluation and decision-making. (This may take the form of clearly written guides on how to read the graphic, and/or some clear and basic information about the probabilities at play.)

RELATIONSHIPS AND CONNECTIONS • The practice of science is often an organized approach to documenting the existence of things and the relationships and connections between those things. Visual representations of that knowledge—like elements organized in a periodic table and family trees—help viewers see those relationships. When there is an unknown item in the sequence, or an unconfirmed connection, my favorite refreshingly honest solution is to use a symbol that is universally understood to represent uncertainty: the question mark. In this hominid family tree example, dashed and dotted lines are used along with question marks to indicate tentative relationships among species. Solid symbols and darker colors often suggest greater certainty than ones that are broken or lighter colored.

This same strategy is often used in animal reconstructions: The "knowns" (i.e., recovered bones) may be drawn in darker ink, or in greater detail, or in full color. The unknowns (i.e., presumed missing bones, based on what's already known about the species or close relatives) might then be added with lighter ink or less detail for full context. These unknowns are generally rooted in knowledge from other specimens, or represent a best guess based on available information at the time. They're included in order to provide an educated guess at the full form, without implying that every single piece of information is certain.

14   Lace Padilla, Matthew Kay, and Jessica Hullman, "Uncertainty Visualization," in *Wiley StatsRef: Statistics Reference Online* (John Wiley & Sons, Ltd, 2021)

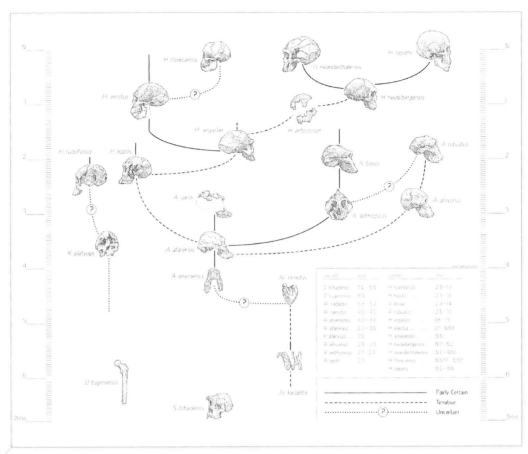

Or, the unrecovered bones may be left out entirely, with a silhouette of the full critter drawn in to complete the picture, as in the case of this prosauropod embryo reconstruction, in which dark gaps are left where bones presumably exist. As indicated in the original caption, the total length of the tail could not be determined: Cropping it off avoids making an unnecessary judgment call.

Image Credit: Michael Hagelberg, as published in *Lucy's Legacy*, by Donald C. Johanson and Kate Wong (Three Rivers Press, 2009). Reprinted with permission from the artist.

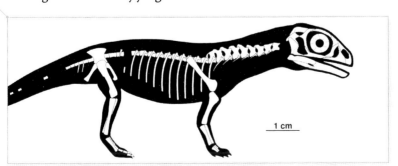

1 cm

Image Credit: From Robert R. Reisz et al., "Embryos of an Early Jurassic Prosauropod Dinosaur and Their Evolutionary Significance," *Science*, Vol. 309 (July 29, 2005). Reprinted with permission from AAAS.

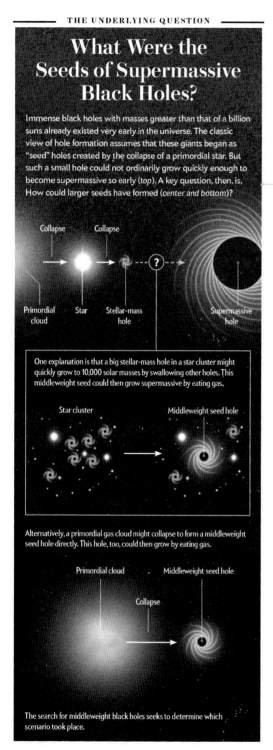

Image Credit: Gavin Potenza, as published in "Middleweight Black Holes: Clues to the Universe's Evolution" by Jenny E. Greene, *Scientific American* (January 2012). Reproduced with permission from the artist.

PROCESSES • Sometimes scientists are prepared to document their understanding of the actors and conditions at two points in time, but what happens in between? Being uncertain about the processes taking place in the middle doesn't need to stop you from sharing what *is* known. A clear gap or question mark placed within the sequence is a simple and honest option.

PAST AND FUTURE • Extrapolating forward or backward in time might include one well-defined slice: the present. In cosmology, a standard way of representing the uncertain deep past and future is to show competing hypotheses side-by-side. The center frame—the present—is consistent across possible scenarios.

DECISION MAKING • Visualizations can provide a sense of relative risk, to aid decision-makers in managing the unknown. When different projections representing different defined variables are included, a quantitative visualization can suggest that there's some control over the range of uncertainty.

The key, to my mind, is to be aware of—and critical of—the uncertainties that exist within the process that you're illustrating. In practice, I've started by embracing uncertainty as an element to be addressed head-on. For example, for an article on calculating the expansion rate of the cosmos, author Richard Panek wrote about a few different measuring techniques. Initial calculations in-

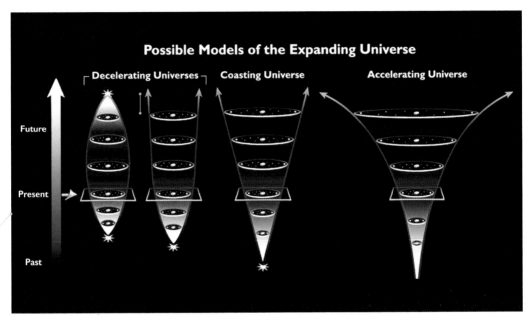

Image Credit: NASA, ESA and STScI (formatting modified slightly in this version from the original May 25, 1999 press release).

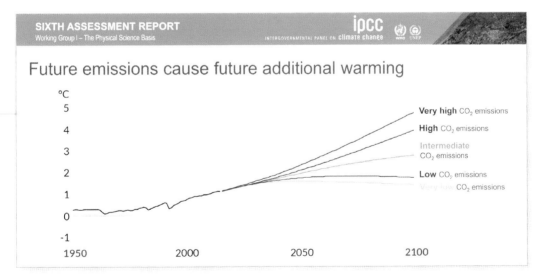

Image Credit: Intergovernmental Panel on Climate Change, August 9, 2021 press conference slides, slide number 12. (Accessed on November 30, 2021, *https://www.ipcc.ch/report/ar6/wg1/downloads/outreach/IPCC_AR6_WGI_Press_Conference_Slides.pdf*). Slide image derived from page 22 of IPCC, 2021: Summary for Policymakers. In: *Climate Change 2021: The Physical Science Basis.*

Contribution of Working Group I to the Sixth Assessment Report of the Intergovernmental Panel on Climate Change [MassonDelmotte, V., P. Zhai, A. Pirani, S.L. Connors, C. Péan, S. Berger, N. Caud, Y. Chen, L. Goldfarb, M.I. Gomis, M. Huang, K. Leitzell, E. Lonnoy, J.B.R. Matthews, T.K. Maycock, T. Waterfield, O. Yelekçi, R. Yu, and B. Zhou (eds.)]. Cambridge University Press. In Press.

DIVERGING RESULTS

The CMB-based, early universe value for H_0 is 67 (in units of kilometers per second per 3.26 million light-years). The Cepheid-based, late universe value is 74. A new alternative to Cepheids—red giant stars that flare with a known intrinsic brightness—only complicated the tension. They indicated an H_0 of about 70—a value that is midway between the other two, with no overlap of error ranges.

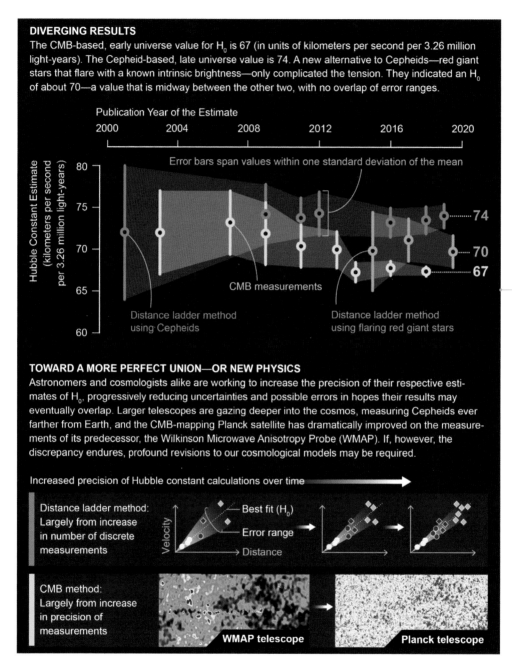

TOWARD A MORE PERFECT UNION—OR NEW PHYSICS

Astronomers and cosmologists alike are working to increase the precision of their respective estimates of H_0, progressively reducing uncertainties and possible errors in hopes their results may eventually overlap. Larger telescopes are gazing deeper into the cosmos, measuring Cepheids ever farther from Earth, and the CMB-mapping Planck satellite has dramatically improved on the measurements of its predecessor, the Wilkinson Microwave Anisotropy Probe (WMAP). If, however, the discrepancy endures, profound revisions to our cosmological models may be required.

Image Credits: Jen Christiansen (schematics); ESA and PLANCK Collaboration (Planck CMB); NASA and WMAP Science Team (WMAP CMB detail); as published in "A Cosmic Crisis," by Richard Panek, *Scientific American* (March 2020); Data Source: "The Carnegie-Chicago Hubble Program. VIII. An Independent Determination of the Hubble Constant Based on the Tip of the Red Giant Branch," By Wendy L. Freedman et al., in *Astrophysical Journal*, Vol. 882 (August 29, 2019). Reproduced with permission. © 2020 Scientific American, a Division of Springer Nature America, Inc. All rights reserved.

cluded large, overlapping error bars. It was presumed that the different measuring techniques would eventually hone in on the same singular answer, or end point. But over time, as the error bars shrunk, it became clear that expansion rate estimates were diverging, not converging.

Like many other media outlets covering the same topic, we opted to include a chart plotting the measurements over time for each method, including error bars. But in order to help our readers more fully understand why the error bars changed in size over time, I also included an explanatory diagram on precision. For one method, the error bar reduction was largely due to an increase in the number of discrete measurements. For the other method, it was largely due to an increase in the resolution of each discrete measurement, thanks to more powerful telescopes. A visual explainer allowed us to acknowledge why uncertainty exists in projects of this nature, and some of the ways in which uncertainty can be reduced over time.

Artist Kathryn Killackey does a super job of representing a range of possibilities in the graphic on the following page, for a paper on the Early Natufian site of Shubayqa 1 in northeastern Jordan. Leading interpretations—based on on a combination of experimental archaeology, botanical remains, and stone artifacts—are slightly larger, and rendered in full contrast (such as post-roast grinding). Less favored interpretations are smaller and faded slightly (such as post-roast pounding). Connecting flow lines help the reader track a variety of possibilities without losing sight of the progression from harvest (top) to prepared tubers (bottom).

These two examples provide context, helping folks understand what parts of the puzzle are well established, and what parts are still missing. By shedding light directly on the uncertainties, reasons behind those uncertainties, and/or a variety of leading explanations, the reader is set up to better understand why some things are well known, and other things are less well known at this moment.

If some degree of uncertainty is inherent in all scientific endeavors, is it ever okay to downplay it? Sure. For example, if the graphic portrays a basic process that's pretty well established, I don't think it is necessary to dramatically point out the spots that are still a bit fuzzy. Unless the context warrants it. It really all hinges on the goal of your graphic. (More on this is in Part 3.)

Harvesting

Season

method

tuber
development

Processing

Stem removal

Scale-leaves, roots,
and rhizome removal

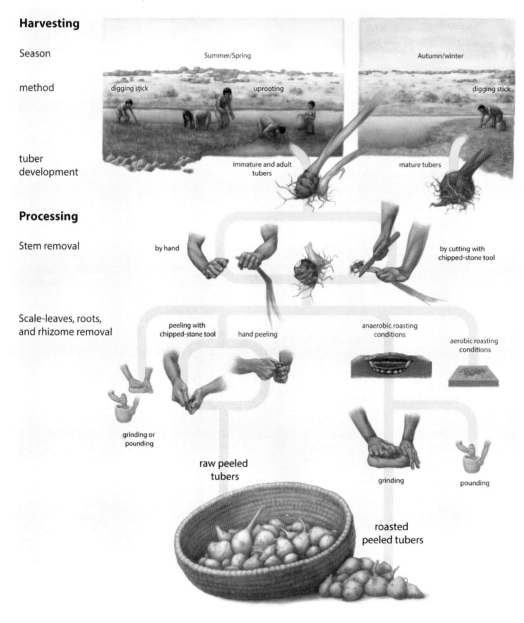

More to Explore

- ***The KSJ Science Editing Handbook:*** This is a super—and free—resource that includes sections on how to read science papers and press releases, fact checking basics, covering controversial science, and more. From the Knight Science Journalism Program at MIT, (Massachusetts Institute of Technology, 2020) *https://ksjhandbook.org.* Full disclosure: I wrote the "Illustrating Complex Science Stories" chapter.

- ***The Craft of Science Writing: Selections from* The Open Notebook,** edited by Siri Carpenter (The Open Notebook, 2020): This collection is centered on writing, but the lessons and guides within are relevant to designers of science graphics as well. *https://www.theopennotebook.com/the-craft-of-science-writing/*

- **"Advocating for Your Reader":** A presentation by Lucy Reading-Ikkanda for SciVizNYC 2018, in which she discusses developing science graphics for a lay audience. *https://www.youtube.com/watch?v=y_HKSAb3jkM*

- ***Style.org:*** A collection of posts and talks by Jonathan Corum, an information designer and science-graphics editor at *The New York Times.* Start with "Design for an Audience," *http://style.org/ku/* (April 25, 2018)

- **Data Stories, episode 59: Behind the Scenes of "What's Really Warming The World?" with the Bloomberg Team:** Hosts Moritz Stefaner and Enrico Bertini chat with journalists Blacki Migliozzi and Eric Roston about how they developed the climate explainer, including interactions with the scientists behind the model, and the challenge of translating complex information into something accessible to a broad audience. *https://datastori.es/* (August 21, 2015)

- ***Nature Collections: Visual Strategies for Biological Data****,* by Bang Wong et al.: This e-book is comprised of the "Points of View" columns published in *Nature Methods* through February 2015, providing practical advice on effective strategies for visualizing biological data to researchers in the biological sciences. (Nature Collections, March 2015)

- **"Uncertainty Visualization"** by Lace Padilla, Matthew Kay, and Jessica Hullman, in *Wiley StatsRef: Statistics Reference Online* (John Wiley & Sons, Ltd, 2021). Also see Hullman's article **"Confronting Unknowns,"** *Scientific American* (September 2019)

CHAPTER 14

Types of Science Graphics

TAXONOMIES HAVE THEIR PROS AND CONS. On one hand, classification systems can be a useful way to organize ideas. On the other hand, placing things in boxes or categories can be limiting and artificially reduces complexity. That said, I find some diagram classification systems helpful when I need some structure to help organize my thoughts when I start sketching, or if I get stuck. And I think that they can be a useful starting point for folks who are new to designing graphics.

Taxonomies that are organized according to the *shape* of the graphic are one option: Sub-divisions in this sort of approach may include cyclical diagrams, flowcharts, and network diagrams, for example. Those sorts of classifications provide a shared vocabulary with which to talk with others about graphics. It's really handy to be able to say to a collaborator, "I plan to execute this graphic in the form of a network diagram." But at the start of a project, I find that they tend to shift focus too far away from the goal of the image. It's a bit akin to selecting a website template or a desk drawer organizer insert before thinking about the things that will be placed within it. When it comes to building science graphics, I prefer classification strategies that reflect the *function* of the graphic.

There are many ways of delineating science graphics types by function. In *The Scientific Image*, Harry Robin breaks science images into six categories: observation ("I looked, and this is what I saw"); induction ("I looked, and this is what I thought"); methodology ("this is how I think it works"); self-illustrating phenomena (such as x-ray imagery); classification ("think of it this way"); and conceptualiza-

Cyclical diagram

Flowchart

Network diagram

1   Harry Robin, *The Scientific Image: From Cave to Computer* (Harry N Abrams Inc, 1992)

tion (thought experiments). Robin uses these categories to make sense of historic imagery, and it's pretty linked to the idea of the scientist as scribe.

I find the breakdown academically interesting, but not incredibly useful as a tool for thinking about how to build new science graphics for communication. Rather, the focus is more on images as a tool for recording and problem-solving, and the framing skews toward image as a sense-making tool for the scientist/designer, as part of the practice of doing science.

In *Visual Strategies*,[2] Felice C. Frankel and Angela H. DePace approach things from a more practical and audience-centered point of view. They describe three types of science graphics: "those that illustrate form and structure; those that illustrate processes over space and time; and those that encourage readers to compare and contrast." (They also note that some graphics may tick more than one of those boxes.) Their categories describe common themes in science communication, and they directly point to possible visual solutions. For example, if the goal of your graphic is to illustrate the form and structure of an object, then it could very well make sense to visually organize your information around that central object. I find Frankel and DePace's framework—and the suggestions that they include in their book on how to execute those types of graphics—really useful. But I often work on graphics that don't fit into their schema.

So, I developed my own taxonomy. This chapter describes seven primary science graphics types. It's a framework rooted in function that helps me remain focused on the goal of the graphic when I start a project. It's not wildly innovative. You'll see that some categories echo the ones described above. It's a variation on other schemas that I find useful when working on a wide range of topics in science.

Descriptive Imagery

The goal of descriptive imagery is to show how something looks, and/or to define its components. This includes classic figurative scientific illustration (such as dinosaur reconstructions and specimen drawings), as well as cutaways, exploded and x-ray views, and abstract

---

2   Felice C. Frankel and Angela H. DePace, *Visual Strategies: A Practical Guide to Graphics for Scientists and Engineers* (Yale University Press, 2012)

renditions that are centered on the physical form of an environment or object(s). The composition of these sorts of science graphics is dependent on the thing being described. The primary object is generally the compositional anchor. For example, Veronica Falconieri Hays depicts the components of a SARS-CoV-2 virion in this dimensional cutaway view (according to molecular research as of April 2020). She includes spike proteins (orange), the lipid envelope (pink), envelope proteins (yellow), membrane proteins (purple), nucleoprotein (blue), and RNA (red). Here's a more symbolic descriptive image of the same subject matter, also published in 2020, demonstrating that the rendering itself doesn't need to feel dimensional or realistic to fit within this category.

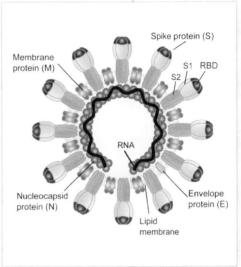

Image Credits: Falconieri Visuals. Republished with permission from the artist (left); Franz X. Heinz and Karin Stiasny, as published in "Profile of SARS-CoV-2," *Wiener Klinische Wochenschrift,* Vol. 132 (November 1, 2020). Image detail of original Figure 3a republished here without modification in accordance with the Creative Commons Attribution 4.0 International License. *https://creativecommons.org/licenses/by/4.0/* (right).

Process Diagrams

Process diagrams show: (a) How something physically works, or (b) How something conceptually works. There are many composition solutions, including a series of step-by-step panels, numbered captions that walk the reader through a composite scenario, or annotations that highlight a path of action through a scene. In this example, Mica Duran illustrates the process by which old or damaged bone is replaced by new bone. In a single vignette, five stages of the process are represented—from detection of damage (left), to resorption of damaged area, and bone formation (right).

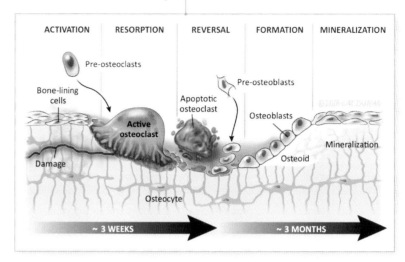

Conceptual process diagrams are similar in spirit but take a metaphorical approach. For example, this graphic demonstrates how gravitational lensing works. It relies on a classic spacetime visual metaphor: a warped grid is depicted, pulled in by the yellow sphere near the center of the frame, representing stronger gravitational forces near that object. Neither the warped grid nor the orange sheets are objects in space. They are depicted to help explain the process visually, making forces visible.

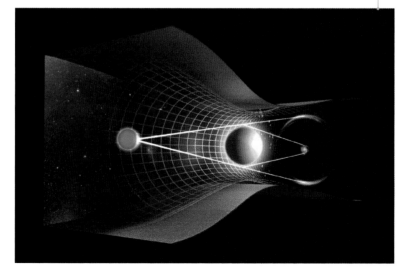

Instructional Guides

Instructional guides represent a methodology—or recipe—in visual form. They're pretty similar to process diagrams in that a step-by-step approach is often used, but the goal is slightly different. They don't explain how something works. Rather, they show how to do something, such as construct an object, conduct an experiment, or practice safety or health protocols.

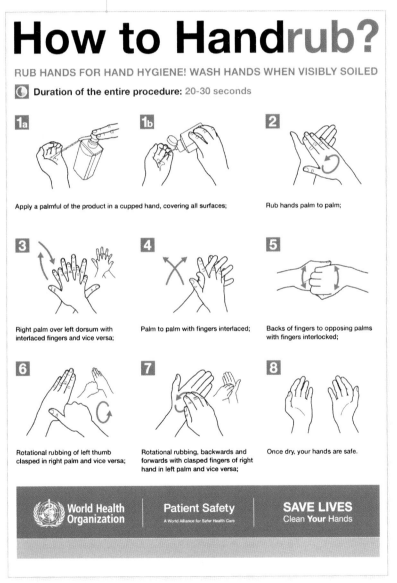

Image Credit: World Health Organization. (WHO acknowledges the Hôpitaux Universitaires de Genève (HUG), in particular the members of the Infection Control Programme, for their active participation in developing this material) © 2009

Organizational Charts

Organizational charts depict classifications or relationships between things or ideas. Family trees, cladograms and venn diagrams are all examples of chart forms that define relationships between entries. But not all forms are predefined. Some involve bespoke solutions—customized charts that are very specific to a specific dataset—like the periodic table of elements.

Image Credit: National Center for Biotechnology Information. "PubChem Periodic Table of Elements" PubChem, https://pubchem.ncbi.nlm.nih.gov/periodic-table/ (Accessed December 7, 2021)

Thought Experiment Vignettes

Thought experiment vignettes portray imagined scenarios that are conducted as a way to intellectually test scientific concepts. As described by Dan Falk in *Aeon*, "There are—allegedly[3]—occasions

3   With the use of "allegedly" here, Falk nods to the idea that some philosophers describe them as arguments or mental models, not experiments that result in new forms of knowledge. See his full essay for a deep dive.

when we come to understand something about the world via a peculiar kind of experiment that takes place only in the mind." The scenario is considered intellectually, not physically. In deducing the consequences, "we seem to learn something about the laws of nature."[4] It's important to note that empirical evidence is not collected in these mental exercises. But they can provide a theoretical foundation that can be tested at a later date.

Famous examples include Galileo's proposition that all objects (regardless of their mass) fall at the same rate, and aspects of Einstein's special theory of relativity.

Image Credit: Samuel Velasco/5W Infographic, originally produced for *MIT Technology Review*. Sources: *Relativity: the Special and the General Theory*, by A. Einstein, and *Relativity Simply Explained*, by Martin Gardner. Republished with permission from the artist.

SPECIAL THEORY OF RELATIVITY

Based in a basic asumption: the speed of light is always the same regardless of the speed of the light source or observer. This fact has unexpected and astonishing ramifications.

RELATIVITY OF TIME

Light source

Mirror

1 A man is riding on a moving train. He is timing a ray of light that travels from a source in the ceiling to a mirror in the floor and back to the ceiling. From his point of view the light source and the mirror are stationary, so the light travels directly down and up in perfectly vertical rays.

2 From the point of view of a stationary observer standing outside the train, the light source and the mirror are moving, so the light follows a path in the shape of a V. This path is longer than the one observed by the man on the train. Since light travels at the same speed for any observer, from the stationary point of view the ray takes longer than from the perspective of the man on the train. Or, in other words, time passes slower for the man in the train than for the stationary observer. **So, there is no meaning to the concept of absolute time. Time is relative to the observer.**

Stationary observer

Comparisons

Comparisons present two or more items in a way that encourages readers to explore similarities and differences. This type of graphic is helpful when portraying before and after views, competing hypotheses, and baseline versus diseased states. It's often useful to present information in a symmetrical composition, so that the reader can

4   "Do Thought Experiments Really Uncover New Scientific Truths?" by Dan Falk, *Aeon* (December 20, 2017)

An organ under attack

In one scenario for a severe form of kidney disease, a blood-borne molecule called soluble urokinase plasminogen activator receptor (suPAR) disrupts the organ's filtration units, or glomeruli, which remove waste and fluid from the bloodstream. Other molecules may intensify this attack.

Neutrophil · Monocyte · Immature myeloid cell · suPAR · Bone marrow · Kidney

A dangerous immune response
Animal models suggest immature immune cells in the bone marrow release more suPAR when an organism is under attack. The molecule, an all-purpose marker of ill health, may be directly toxic to the kidney.

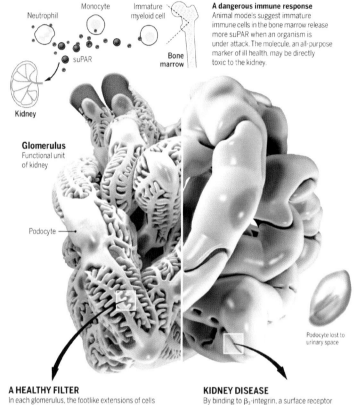

Glomerulus
Functional unit of kidney

Podocyte

Podocyte lost to urinary space

A HEALTHY FILTER

In each glomerulus, the footlike extensions of cells called podocytes wrap around capillaries, fitting together tightly to create narrow "slit diaphragms." The slits form a fine mesh that allows only small molecules to escape from the bloodstream into the urine.

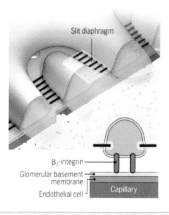

Slit diaphragm

β_3-integrin

Glomerular basement membrane

Endothelial cell

Capillary

KIDNEY DISEASE

By binding to β_3-integrin, a surface receptor on the podocyte feet, suPAR is thought to change their shape, disrupting the kidney's filter. That allows large proteins such as albumin to leak into the urine—a sign of kidney disease.

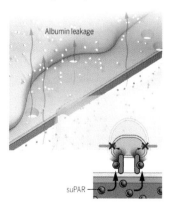

Albumin leakage

suPAR

efficiently spot meaningful differences and similarities between states, as in this graphic by Valerie Altounian.

Summary—or Multi-Part—Graphics

Summary graphics present a comprehensive visual outline of a full concept, project, or the graphic's accompanying text. They can be compact, in the form of a visual abstract. Or they can be large and epic, like a magazine spread or poster that aims to summarize the current state of knowledge about a particular subject matter. These sorts of multi-part graphics include two or more of the graphics types above folded into a single—sometimes modular—composition.

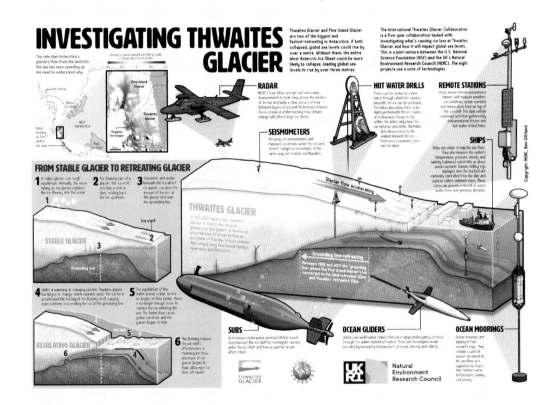

•   •   •

IN THE FOLLOWING CHAPTERS, I'll speak more directly to the process of building science graphics, starting with establishing its goal. The classification system presented in this chapter is designed to work within that framework. That said—like most classification systems—it's not definitive. It's just a tool. Many graphics will tick more than one box or fall someplace in between categories.

More to Explore

- *Visual Strategies: A Practical Guide to Graphics for Scientists and Engineers,* by Felice C. Frankel and Angela H. DePace (Yale University Press, 2012)
- *The Scientific Image: From Cave to Computer,* by Harry Robin (Harry N Abrams Inc, 1992)
- *Visual Cultures of Science: Rethinking Representational Practices in Knowledge Building and Science Communication,* edited by Luc Pauwels (Dartmouth College Press, 2006)
- *The Technical Image: A History of Styles in Scientific Imagery,* edited by Horst Bredekamp, Vera Dünkel, and Birgit Schneider (The University of Chicago Press, 2015)
- *Design for Information,* by Isabel Meirelles (Rockport Publishers, 2013)

Data visualization is out of the scope of this book, but I can't help recommending a few further readings on the topic here. There are numerous visualization taxonomies, chart choosers, and resources that describe them, and a range of opinions on their usefulness.

- **"Pros and Cons of Chart Taxonomies"** (Nightingale post), by Amanda Makulec (September 17, 2019) *https://nightingaledvs.com/pros-and-cons-of-chart-taxonomies/*
- **"Data Visualization Has a Taxonomy Problem"** (Noteable post), by Elijah Meeks (September 27, 2021) *https://medium.com/noteableio/data-visualization-has-a-taxonomy-problem-f3f8954f577e*
- *Effective Data Visualization: The Right Chart for the Right Data,* by Stephanie D. H. Evergreen (SAGE Publications, 2016)

- ***Better Data Visualizations: A Guide for Scholars, Researchers, and Wonks,*** by Jonathan Schwabish (Columbia University Press, 2021), as well as the companion video series "One Chart at a Time." *https://policyviz.com/2021/01/11/one-chart-at-a-time-video-series/*
- ***Data Visualisation: A Handbook for Data Driven Design,*** by Andy Kirk (SAGE Publications Ltd, 2019)
- **Visual Vocabulary,** from the *Financial Times*, by Alan Smith, Chris Campbell, Ian Bott, Liz Faunce, Graham Parrish, Billy Ehrenberg-Shannon, Paul McCallum, and Martin Stabe (accessed December 8, 2021) *ft.com/vocabulary*
- **The Graphic Continuum,** by Jonathan Schwabish and Severino Ribecca (2014) *https://policyviz.com/2014/11/11/graphic-continuum-desktop-version/*

PART 3 — D.I.Y. (Do It Yourself)

CHAPTER 15

The Process of Building Graphics

SOMETIMES, DECISIONS ABOUT WHAT SHOULD BE ILLUSTRATED,
and the process to be followed when developing an image plan, are
made for you. That's often the case for me when I'm wearing my scientific illustrator hat. Lots of gigs come with a project brief, deadline
schedule, reference material, and a point person that's acting as the
project manager. But what if your team doesn't include anyone with art
directing or graphics editing experience, or *you* are the project manager? In that case, you'll need to make decisions about what should be
illustrated, and how to best use your time and resources.

When I stepped into an art director role early in my career, I got
a crash course in how to set up projects and artists for success. Over
time, I've formalized an approach that works for me. An idealized version of my process for developing science graphics for non-specialist
audiences on a deadline is described in this chapter. It works particularly well for text-led projects, in which the graphics will ultimately
support a larger story being told with words. But the process can be
morphed to work for other contexts as well.

The process described here is the framework I default to when I'm
building the graphic myself. It is malleable. The stages reflect my personal approach, for pieces that I design from start to finish. When I'm
art directing another designer, that collaborator has freedom within
this framework to apply their own philosophy for developing sketches.
And occasionally a project will circumvent a step due to the deadline
schedule or scope of the project.

**The key is to remember that building graphics is a process,
with stages. You can't expect graphics to emerge fully formed at
the last minute, in a single go.** With some forethought and structure,

you can set up your graphics-building process to dovetail with the stages of your larger project, so that the graphics can be properly reviewed by others in context. See Chapter 16 for a step-by-step guide based on this approach that centers your specific project.

At the start of the project, ask yourself—and your collaborators, if you're working on a team—if a graphic would be *useful* in conveying any of the information at-hand. To my mind, a graphic may be useful if

- an image can tell the story—or a piece of the story—more efficiently, effectively, or completely than words. (For example, a visual that pictorially represents an abstract formula, like a Feynman diagram that portrays interactions between subatomic particles),
- the narrative involves complex and intertwining relationships or processes, and an image map can help the reader track connections. (For example, a diagram that explains the intricacies of photosynthesis),
- the reader might benefit from seeing and exploring trends and patterns of the complete dataset, as opposed to being served up a few key numbers in the text, or
- a direct and immediate visual comparison is useful in highlighting change, or differences between states, such as competing hypotheses, or before-and-after views.

Note that the bullet points above are centered on the **content** to be communicated. I'm not a fan of deciding to build a graphic because there's room or money to spare and folks like the idea of filling it with a snazzy visual to engage people. Engagement is an honorable goal. But if that's your sole goal, I'd encourage you to consider if a representative illustration (like a straight-up drawing of an object), an editorial illustration (a metaphorical piece of art that is evocative in nature), or a photograph might be a more fitting solution. If the project also ticks one or more of the boxes above, then a graphic may be the way to go.

This preliminary phase can also benefit from folding in feedback from members of your intended audience. Unsure if a graphic would be useful for your audience? Consider asking them directly. See page 231 for an interview with Sheila Pontis on why this is a good idea (and tips on how to get started), and page 304 for an interview with Angela Morelli on the topic of co-design.

STAGE 1: ESTABLISH THE GOAL OF THE GRAPHIC • Once it's determined that a graphic would be useful, I articulate the goal of the graphic. The goal statement takes two things into consideration;

- content (what is the point of the graphic?), and
- context (who is the audience and what is the outlet?)

That stated goal is my touchstone. I keep coming back to it, and make design decisions that honor it. It's also a handy statement to have when communicating with collaborators about the project, to help ensure that intentions are aligned. I find it useful to set up a working digital document with that goal written at the top, along with projected deadline schedules (dates pinned to each stage below) and collaborator contact information. That document then grows with notes and placed images as the stages below unfold.

STAGE 2: CONTENT RESEARCH • Whenever possible, I begin with the primary source: ideally the key journal paper that describes the latest research. Then I expand out from there, starting with papers that catch my eye in the primary paper's citations, and basic searches on the lead scientist and their collaborators. Then I move on to the bigger picture: How does this latest finding fit into other research in this area?

More often than not, I need to do some basic searches on core concepts, to make sure that I'm not wildly misinterpreting things, and that I have a basic understanding of the terminology. Keyword-driven Google image searches help me quickly sort out what other graphics have already been produced on the topic, and often help me identify weaknesses or holes in the broader coverage—focusing my line of thought on how I can add something new to the conversation.

Are you new to conducting research, or could you use a refresher? Here are some great references on the topic of finding—and evaluating—credible sources:

- *Navigating Digital Information* video series hosted by John Green on Crash Course (in partnership with MediaWise, The Poynter Institute, and The Stanford History Education Group) *https://thecrashcourse.com/topic/navigatingdigitalinfo/*
- **"Sources and Experts: Where to Find Them and How to Vet Them,"** By Melinda Wenner Moyer, in *The KSJ Science Editing Handbook* (a project of the Knight Science Journalism Fellowship at MIT, supported by the Kavli Foundation and the Howard Hughes Medical Institute's Department of Science Education) *https://ksjhandbook.org*

If you're new to reading research papers, I recommend these resources:

- **"How to Read a Scientific Paper,"** by Alexandra Witze, The Open Notebook (November 6, 2018) *https://www.theopennotebook.com/2018/11/06/how-to-read-a-scientific-paper/*
- **"How to Read and Understand a Scientific Paper: A Guide for Non-Scientists,"** by Jennifer Raff, LSE Impact Blog (May 9, 2016) *https://blogs.lse.ac.uk/impactofsocialsciences/2016/05/09/how-to-read-and-understand-a-scientific-paper-a-guide-for-non-scientists/*
- **"Ten Simple Rules for Reading a Scientific Paper,"** by Maureen A. Carey, Kevin L. Steiner, and William A. Petri Jr, *PLOS Computational Biology*, Vol. 16 (July 30, 2020)

As I'm reading, I'll dash off notes in a sketchbook alongside cartoons/doodles that help me make sense of things. I'll also copy and paste article excerpts into a single long digital document, along with screenshots of reference figures or photos of my pencil sketches and any potentially useful handwritten notes. **Keeping track of your information sources (like urls or article citations) alongside your preliminary notes can save a lot of time later in the process. It's likely that you won't need all of the information as the project progresses, but you'll be so grateful to your past self for recording things as you go.**

It's much more efficient to simply copy and paste a url or a paper title into a "scratchpad" brainstorming document when you first encounter potentially useful information, as opposed to backtracking and trying to piece together where you saw something useful from several weeks ago. These notes are also critical for projects that include a formal fact check stage, or as you go back and confirm that you're showing things accurately as the project wraps up. Organize your material in a way that works best for you. I'm a huge fan of color-coding by sub-section for multi-part projects (either with highlighters or by changing the font color in digital documents), as it allows me to quickly scan through material and ultimately move content into theme-driven sections with a quick copy-and-paste.

STAGE 3: CONCEPT SKETCH DEVELOPMENT (GESTURAL PENCIL SKETCH EQUIVALENT) • Now it's time to put that research to use and translate my written notes and doodles into a cohesive sketch. I begin with re-examining what, exactly, the graphic aims to explain, starting with the wide view. Am I comparing and contrasting competing hypotheses? Two panels side-by-side might make sense. Showing change over time? A linear or cyclical step-by-step approach may be useful. Showing how something works? The physicality of the subject may help inform the layout.

Once I've spent some time thinking through the basic form, I develop a rough layout. These sorts of illustrations don't live within a vacuum. They exist on a page or screen, with titles, captions, and labels. I find that thinking through all of those pieces from the very start really helps to streamline the whole process and forces clarity of intention. I'll even draft straightforward and descriptive headlines and subheads, so that I can better communicate my intentions to the editor and author. All the while, I'm thinking in terms of:

- centering the new research finding,
- supporting that new information with broader context,
- considering what additional details might help engage a reader who is initially unfamiliar with the broader topic,
- shaking out label jargon (by using plain language), and
- shaking out visual jargon (by avoiding icons only familiar to scientists from a specific discipline).

STAGE 4: CONCEPT SKETCH REVIEW • Once I'm happy with the concept sketch, I seek feedback from colleagues to make sure that preliminary plans for the text and graphic are still cohesive and complementary. Then the concept sketch gets sent out to an expert consultant (the author or another research scientist) for an accuracy review. If my initial interpretations don't pass muster with the content experts, I'll need to loop back around to Stage 3. In this case, I'll ask the content expert for more reference material, to help guide the revised plan.

This review stage, as well as review Stages 6 and 8, presents a great opportunity for a round of feedback from members of your intended audience. For more guidance on how to do this, see page 231.

STAGE 5: TIGHT SKETCH DEVELOPMENT (DETAILED PENCIL DRAWING, ROUGH 3D RENDER, OR EQUIVALENT) • If the concept sketch is approved by collaborators and content experts, the next stage is all about folding specific notes and edit requests into a tight sketch. At this point, I sharpen the illustrative details and flesh out the labels, and the text editor starts in on preliminary captions. As I'm refining the plan, I'm also thinking through how the composition will be adjusted for multiple platforms (print, mobile phone screens, and desktop Web viewing).

STAGE 6: TIGHT SKETCH REVIEW • Once I'm happy with the tight sketch, I send it out for another round of reviews. Feedback loops that focus on specific details of the illustration are fine at this stage, but the composition and overall plan should be locked in at this point. If there was a fundamental problem with the content—and therefore fundamental problem with the composition—it should have been flagged at Stage 4. I've found that really thinking things through completely at the start of the project saves a lot of time and energy later on. Looping back to Stage 3 should be avoided. Looping back around to Stage 5 to refine specific details of the graphic is fine.

STAGE 7: FINAL GRAPHIC • Once the technical details are all in place, focus shifts to the final rendering.

STAGE 8: FINAL GRAPHIC REVIEW • The final rendering is sent around for a last look by collaborators (including a copyeditor and fact checker) to ensure that no errors were introduced in the final rendering stage, and that the details are sound.

By working through these stages, with concept sketches that start as broad-stroke composition guides that are deeply rooted in the concept being explained, I find that I'm forced to really think through the content before getting distracted by drawing details. **If the organization of the graphic is solid, then the illustrative details can develop organically within that framework. In the spirit of an anatomical artist, I strive to get the bones organized properly before fleshing things out.** If the final illustration is complex or time-consuming to execute (like complicated 3D renderings or traditional paintings), organization clarity early on is also a really important time and money saver. Here are a few concrete examples, from start to end.

Case Study: Ebola

On the heels of a major Ebola outbreak in West Africa, journalist Helen Branswell wrote about a few emerging experimental treatments and potential vaccines, and how the scale of the outbreak made those advances possible. I read the preliminary manuscript of the text, conferred with my colleagues at *Scientific American*, and established that a graphic would be a useful supplement to the text. Specifically, in helping to explain how the virus impacts the human immune system.

We established an ambitious goal for the graphic.

- Content: Answer these questions, in visual form→ What is the Ebola virus, why is it so deadly, and what are some of the emerging treatment possibilities?
- Context: Print magazine→ science-savvy but non-specialist audience

Since the goal was multi-pronged, I dissected it into more manageable chunks using the color-coding strategy discussed on page 104: **What is the Ebola virus,** why is it so deadly, and **what are some of the emerging treatment possibilities?**

Branswell provided some references that she found useful when writing the text. I supplemented with additional scientific research papers and review papers that provided information directly related to the specific goals of the graphic. (Research papers generally cover very focused and narrow original research findings. Review papers summarize the current state of knowledge about a particular topic, and can be really helpful if you're looking for an overview from a technical and authoritative source.) I also collected graphics from news sites to see how others covered the topic for non-specialist audiences, largely to see if there were any details that most outlets often gloss over that we could step up and help explain in more depth.

I color-coded references and my written notes to help organize my thoughts, then started to translate those notes into a visual language, like this:

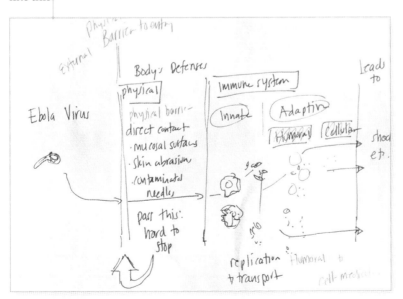

This still represented note-taking and research mode. I wasn't thinking of these notes as prototypes for the final graphic. I simply shifted away from thinking in sentences, and toward thinking in terms of systems and relationships. Some of the nouns became icons, and categories became lists organized by time (not space). After I established a reasonable level of comfort with the content, and had started to think about that content in a visual way, I advanced to Stage 3.

I started with low-stakes mini versions of the general space I planned to work within. Here's one in a series of tiny doodle-esque possibilities.

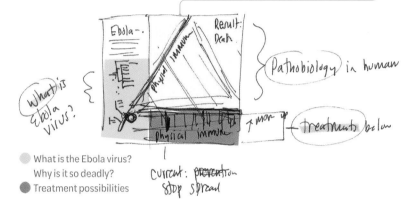

⬤ What is the Ebola virus?
  Why is it so deadly?
⬤ Treatment possibilities

Then I mapped out a slightly larger version, introducing more detail.

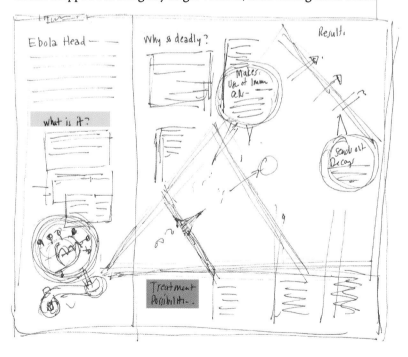

Then I moved on to an actual-size template. These sketches were for my eyes only. I wasn't sharing these stages with anyone else on the project team, so there was no pressure for them to be intelligible to anyone else. I was still very much in problem-solving mode, not presentation mode.

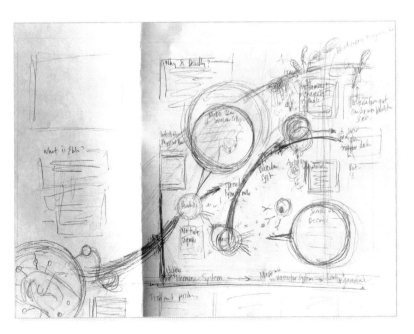

Once I was feeling good about the core plan, I shifted over to digital drawing tools, so I could introduce properly styled text blocks and more easily refine the position of elements. I shared a concept sketch with collaborators, to make sure that (1) we were all still aligned in terms of the goal of the story and the graphic, and (2) that I was representing the information accurately.

Image Credit: Jen Christiansen, sketches for "New Hope for Ebola?," by Helen Branswell, *Scientific American* (March 2015)

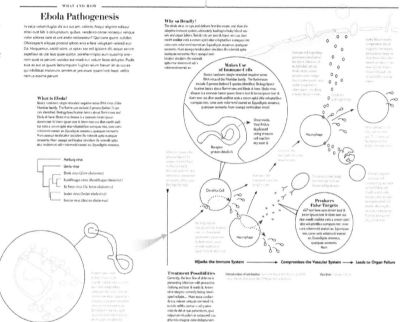

If memory serves right, in this case I didn't send the concept sketch out to a research scientist, in part because the final rendering style was going to be straightforward (and easy to edit), but also because it made sense to address some minor author and editor comments first. I made corrections and added a few more details, then I sent that tight sketch out for expert review in the form of a pdf. The expert consultant annotated the pdf with general notes and answers to specific questions. I coordinated with the text editor (Christine Gorman) to address the comments, then introduced tints of color and refined the style, leading to the final version that was reviewed by a fact checker and ultimately published.

In the final graphic, introductory text, a family tree, and a straightforward illustration of the virus sets the scene. Then readers dive into the microscopic world of a human infected with Ebola, to see how the virus is thought to hijack the immune system and compromise the

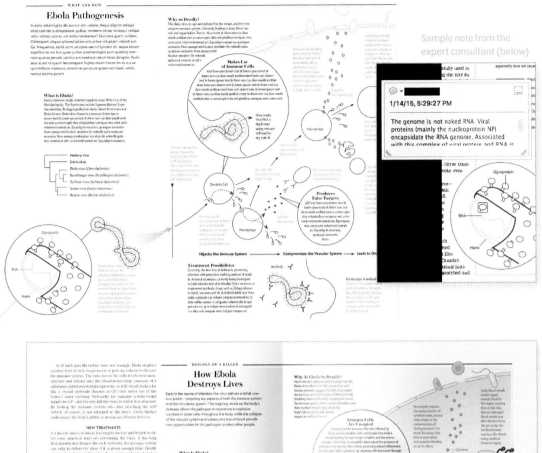

Sample note from the expert consultant (below)

circulatory system, leading to organ failure. In order to understand how the virus knocks things out of whack, the reader needs to know what the healthy state is, and how the immune system generally works. And they need to be properly introduced to the other cells that they'll encounter along the way. All the while, the illustration needs to remain focused on the crux of this particular story, Ebola, without that main story getting lost in a sea of too much context.

In this case, I aimed to keep Ebola as the focus by having the reader track the virus (painted red) across the page through time. This time-line became the compositional spine of the spread. Human cells (in gray) were introduced as they became relevant in the virus's timeline. Two key concepts—major points in the main text that the graphic accompanies—were highlighted in yellow. Isolating those two points in yellow circles reinforced the hierarchy of information: context as background, critical new details as overlay.

Case Study: Greening Disease

For an article on greening disease in citrus trees by journalist Anna Kuchment, I started by reading the unedited preliminary text manuscript. As I read through, I found myself underlining portions, trying to connect the various elements. It seemed to me that including a graphic that provided a visual overview of the problem would be a useful addition to the article. The formal goal of the graphic would be to introduce readers to cause and effects of greening disease.

I moved on to preliminary research, so that I could get a better handle on the jargon and what has already been published on the topic.

Sometimes that's just a few hours of Web-based research, to familiarize myself with the topic beyond the text manuscript. In this case, I soaked up as much as I could in an afternoon about the bacterial pathogen, the insects that spread it, and its impact on orange trees. I began to put the pieces together in a really rough cartoon-of-sorts, to establish the main points and sort out how those main points might be organized on the page.

Image Credit:
Jen Christiansen, sketches for "The End of Orange Juice," by Anna Kuchment, *Scientific American* (March 2013)

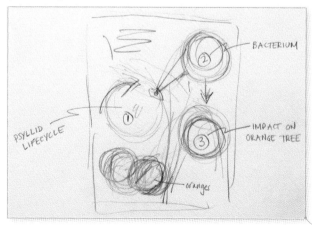

Then I started to refine things. Starting with the introductory caption in the top left corner, the reader would drop down to the insect lifecycle and caption, then to the top right for bacteria details, and down to the effects on the orange tree. Another element was added to the goal after a conversation with the author: A possible solution to the problem—a predator that could potentially wipe out the vector insect—should be added. At this stage, you can see that I wasn't too concerned with the details. I was thinking in terms of broad strokes, main points, and flow of the story. That included thinking out caption needs. How many text blocks would be needed, and where?

The next round was still rough, but the details were starting to come into focus. The previous round was more about making decisions on the overall structure of the box. This round was cleaner, so that I could more effectively communicate to the others my hopes for the final art. I shared it with colleagues at the magazine, to make sure the content still jived with the article text.

If the concept is abstract or complicated, I'll often send this sort of concept sketch out for expert review. But in this case, I thought it was safe to bring an artist in first, to tighten up the sketch before the first outside expert review. I sent freelance illustrator Cherie Sinnen my concept sketch and a research packet that included photographs and

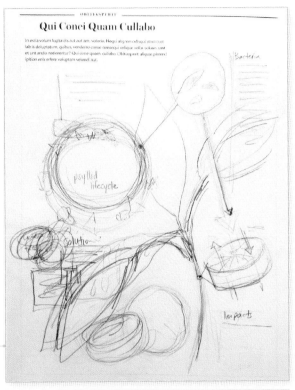

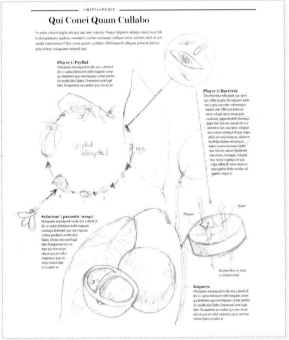

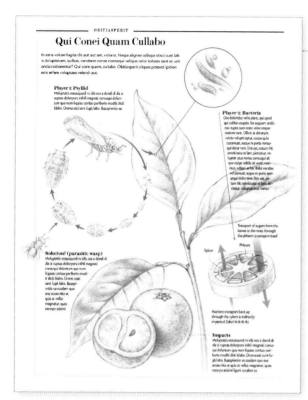

the references that I had collected. She returned this tight sketch. Our expert consultant—Philip Anzolut Stansly, an entomologist then at the University of Florida—did a thorough review, and returned a marked-up pdf. (For example, a note about the eggs included this guidance, "Eggs are usually laid on unexpanded leaves, i.e. much younger than these. They are often laid in a row down the middle of a leaf that is still tightly closed and are stalked so not random-ly distributed or prostrate as shown here. Also, batches tend to have more eggs.") I went through the notes, clarified some points and overruled a few related to aesthetics, added some more visual references, and passed along the notes to Sinnen. Here's the final graphic.

Case Study: Dark Matter

Working with scientist authors really streamlines the process for me, since I have a direct line to a content expert, and they have a vested interest. For a magazine article by physicists Bogdan Dobrescu and Don Lincoln, I started with the unedited text manuscript, and a conver-sation with my text editing colleague, Clara Moskowitz. The authors study particle interactions and dark matter. This article would describe some recent ideas and experiments related to the idea that dark matter might, in fact, be a range of different particle and force types that just don't interact very much with what we think of as "normal matter."

Some *Scientific American* readers would be really comfortable with jumping straight into discussions of unconventional dark matter. But for the majority of our non-specialist readers, I wanted to provide more context. The formal goal of the graphic would be to introduce readers to a range of possible dark matter categories, as well as the evidence for and against some of the leading candidates.

I started by mapping out the different types of dark matter particles

View to a Kill

Huanglongbing (HLB) is one of the most devastating diseases of citrus plants. Small winged insects, Asian citrus psyllids, transmit the bacteria that cause huanglongbing as they drink sap from the leaves of trees. Inspectors initially found Asian citrus psyllids in the U.S. in 1998 and first detected huanglongbing in 2005. Both were first found in Florida.

The Vector: Asian Citrus Psyllids

Psyllids lay eggs on shoots and leaves as they emerge from buds. Newly hatched, wingless nymphs feed exclusively on this soft growth as they develop into adults. As psyllids of all life stages drink sap from the plant's leaves, they can transmit HLB from their salivary glands. Infected plants can also transmit HLB to psyllids.

Asian citrus psyllid

Parasitic wasp

An Attempt to Fight Back

Because Asian citrus psyllids have no native specialized predators in the U.S., entomologists have brought in tiny parasitic wasps from Asia, *Tamarixia radiata*, to help keep psyllid populations in check. Lab studies suggest that each wasp can kill hundreds of psyllids by drinking their blood and laying eggs on them. The eggs develop into larvae that eventually eat the psyllids from the outside in.

The Disease: Huanglongbing

Most scientists believe huanglongbing is caused by three bacteria in the genus *Candidatus Liberibacter*, although researchers have yet to conclusively prove the relation. The three are: *Candidatus Liberibacter asiaticus*, which is the most prevalent and is found in the U.S.; *Candidatus Liberibacter africanus*, found primarily in South Africa; and *Candidatus Liberibacter americanus*, found primarily in Brazil.

The bacteria infect the phloem, the circulatory system that transports sugars from the tree canopy to the roots, resulting in blockages.

Phloem

Xylem

The blockages starve the roots, which stop properly absorbing nutrients from the soil to send back up to the tree canopy, a circulatory system known as the xylem.

The Result: Dying Plants

HLB can masquerade as a nutrient deficiency. Symptoms include mottled, yellowish leaves and fruit that is lopsided, small, green and bitter and that drops prematurely. The disease weakens plants and makes them more likely to succumb to drought and other stressors.

Image Credit: Cherie Sinnen, as published in "The End of Orange Juice," by Anna Kuchment, *Scientific American* (March 2013). Published here with permission from the artist.

that have been proposed, and how each of those types relate to each other. This would allow us to present some basic definitions as well, but in a form that would be more useful than a basic glossary.

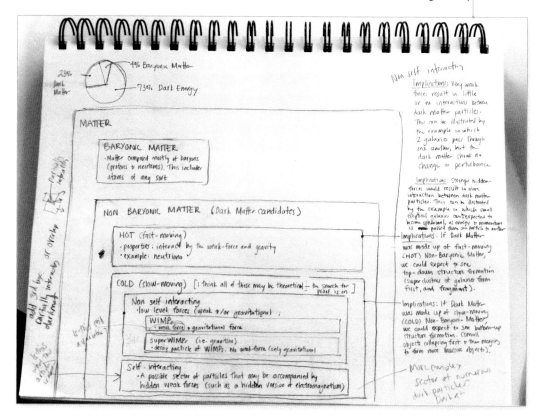

Then I took those notes and built things out in a magazine template. A main circle would hold the different dark matter candidates, and their relationships to one another. Then, on the right, we'd dive further into information related to the crux of the article.

The editor and authors confirmed that the basic plan (concept sketch) was sound, and provided some specific feedback, including notes like this one: "For the Venn diagram, between non self-interacting and self-interacting, we don't like 'partially self-interacting.' That could mean 'interacting with intermediate strength.' We propose 'dual component' dark matter instead." I updated the plan accordingly, and sent out a tight sketch for review.

I made some adjustments to the content related to their final notes and then shifted focus to developing the style and color palette. The

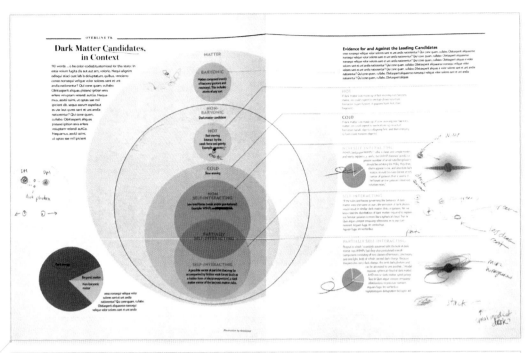

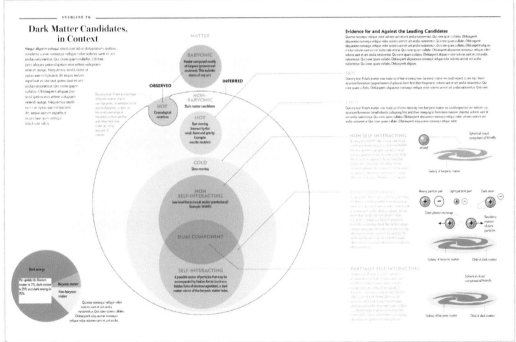

Image Credit: Jen Christiansen, sketches for "Mystery of the Hidden Cosmos," by Bogdan A. Dobrescu and Don Lincoln, *Scientific American* (July 2015)

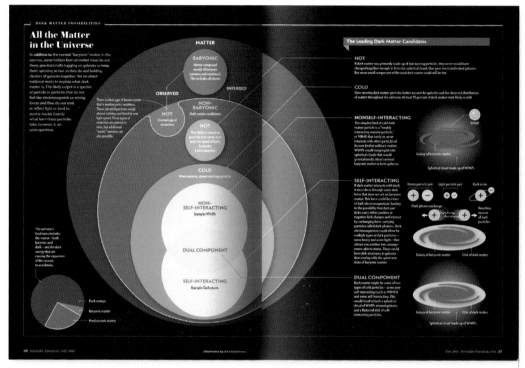

rest of the art elements for the article were essentially final by then,
so I could play off the color palette and vibe of the opening image and
title design, under the guidance of creative director Michael Mrak.
The final version was then ready for a final routing and fact check. An
editorial fact checker goes through and makes sure that the terms and
stated facts check out with other authoritative sources, and that those
facts are strung together in an honest manner.[1] In this case, fact checker Anna Barnett flagged a few items that needed additional sources, but
the queries didn't ultimately result in any necessary changes.

● ● ●

THE PROCESS OUTLINED IN THE PRECEDING PAGES has served me
well when developing science graphics on deadline with a small team
of artists, journalists, and a content consultant or two. But it's a process
that's still evolving. For example, I'm keen to figure out how—and
when—to fold in audience feedback. I asked information designer

---

1   For more information about editorial fact checking, see the Knight Journalism Founda-
     tion's Fact-Checking Project, *https://ksjfactcheck.org/*

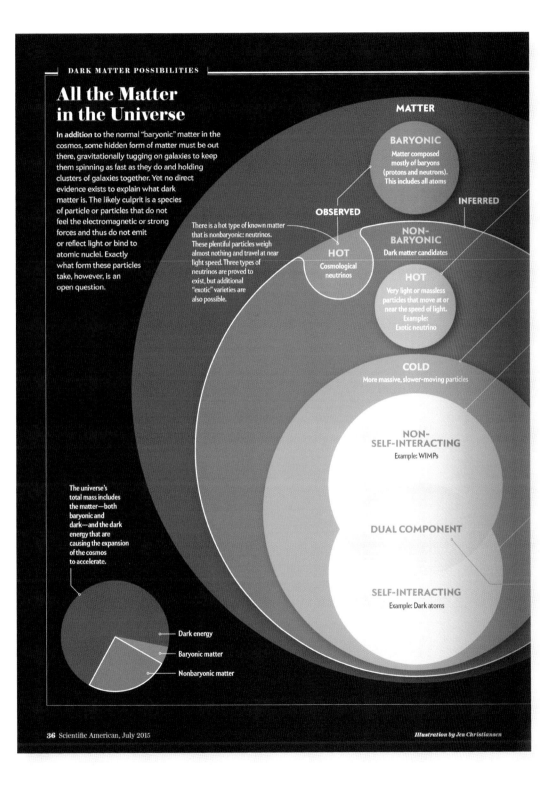

DARK MATTER POSSIBILITIES

All the Matter in the Universe

In addition to the normal "baryonic" matter in the cosmos, some hidden form of matter must be out there, gravitationally tugging on galaxies to keep them spinning as fast as they do and holding clusters of galaxies together. Yet no direct evidence exists to explain what dark matter is. The likely culprit is a species of particle or particles that do not feel the electromagnetic or strong forces and thus do not emit or reflect light or bind to atomic nuclei. Exactly what form these particles take, however, is an open question.

There is a hot type of known matter that is nonbaryonic: neutrinos. These plentiful particles weigh almost nothing and travel at near light speed. Three types of neutrinos are proved to exist, but additional "exotic" varieties are also possible.

The universe's total mass includes the matter—both baryonic and dark—and the dark energy that are causing the expansion of the cosmos to accelerate.

MATTER

BARYONIC
Matter composed mostly of baryons (protons and neutrons). This includes all atoms

OBSERVED

INFERRED

NON-BARYONIC
Dark matter candidates

HOT
Cosmological neutrinos

HOT
Very light or massless particles that move at or near the speed of light. Example: Exotic neutrino

COLD
More massive, slower-moving particles

NON-SELF-INTERACTING
Example: WIMPs

DUAL COMPONENT

SELF-INTERACTING
Example: Dark atoms

Dark energy

Baryonic matter

Nonbaryonic matter

Illustration by Jen Christiansen

Sheila Pontis for her advice on how to get started. See pages 231–233 for a transcript of our conversation.

This is certainly not the only valid process. Every designer, client, and project has different needs. Regardless, I do think it's valuable to set up a series of deadlines for every project pinned to clearly defined stages. A clear schedule and plan is key. I find that it keeps me focused and prevents the project from spiraling down an endless path of too many iterations. Perhaps most importantly, it reminds me to check in with the broader team for feedback at several points along the way.

Check out the "Spotlight" boxes on pages 234–251 for a treat: A peek at the evolution of science graphics projects by Eleanor Lutz, Will Stahl-Timmins, 5W Infographic, and Lucy Reading-Ikkanda. Inspired and ready to get moving on your own project? Turn to page 253 and dive in.

More to Explore

- **S.P.A.R.K. | 5 strategies for the visual communication of science,** Picture as Portal online course by Betsy Palay and Tami Tolpa: *https://www.pictureasportal.com/courses/five-strategies-for-the-visual-communication-of-science*
- ***Visual Strategies: A Practical Guide to Graphics for Scientists and Engineers,*** by Felice C. Frankel and Angela H. DePace (Yale University Press, 2012)
- ***Data Visualisation: A Handbook for Data Driven Design,*** by Andy Kirk (SAGE Publications Ltd, 2019) Although this book is dataviz-centric, sections on workflow and process are applicable across the full information design continuum.
- ***Raw Data: Infographic Designers' Sketchbooks,*** by Rick Landers and Steven Heller (Thames Hudson, 2014)
- ***Data Sketches: A Journey of Imagination, Exploration, and Beautiful Data Visualizations,*** by Nadieh Bremer and Shirley Wu (A K Peters/CRC Press, 2021)

Audience Feedback and Field Research:
A Conversation with Sheila Pontis

Like many science graphics designers, I regularly confer with content experts to make sure that the information I'm conveying is accurate. So much so that it's baked into my process. But as I note in the Preface to this book, field research—the act of gathering evidence from my intended audience in the setting they'd ultimately be reading the final version—is not a part of my regular practice. In the spirit of science communication movements that emphasize co-creation and relationship building, perhaps I simply need to make it a priority. I asked Sheila Pontis (SP), author of *Making Sense of Field Research: A Practical Guide for Information Designers*, for her advice on how to get started. Here's an edited transcript of our conversation.

JC: Why is field research so important?
SP: In order to understand why it's important, I think you need to understand what it involves. A big difference between field research and other forms of research is that designers need to go where the audience is, [to observe] all the contexts of use of whatever you are creating. So hence, the word "field." Many designers are used to market research, or surveys, or questionnaires, or even inviting the audience to the design studio, which is also a valid form of research. But I think you learn different dimensions of the problem and of the audience [from field research]. In particular, it helps you understand the audience firsthand and how they actually interact with whatever you create [in their own environment]. And realizing, in many cases (at least in my experience), that a disconnection may exist between how you thought that the audience was going to use or interpret something, and what really happens in life. And seeing this disconnection is a very humbling experience. I thought the reader was going to start

there [gestures in one direction], but they actually start there [gestures in another direction]. And that didn't happen once. That actually happened in five sessions with five different people. The more you have been doing [design] work you develop this baseline, and you believe, "I know what good design looks like. So I know what I should do." But I think it's much more complex than what designers think it is.

JC: Do you think it's critical to seek audience feedback for every discrete graphic, or can it be useful as a way to spot-check things and assumptions over time?
SP: That's a good one, but the answer is "it depends." I recognize that the nature of the project may be more or less conducive to field research because of the timeframe. Sometimes you have a month, sometimes you have a day. In some cases, it might be hard to spend even an hour with someone talking because you don't have the time. I think if the type of content you're trying to visualize or to communicate is similar in nature,

complexity, or topic, you could infer that some responses might be similar. You could also do research on an existing design to learn how it is understood and used, and use this learning as a baseline from where to start a redesign or a next project. In any case, as much as you can, even sending something over email, [if you cannot go physically to where the audience is], and letting them give you honest feedback in their own words, can help you. Now, with smartphones, it's super easy. People can record themselves using something or trying to understand something. And that can be done in a day. You could have a pool of potential participants that are willing to help you, for example, once a week. So they know, for example, that every Thursday, they may receive an email with something they need to comment on. Once you understand the principle of field research and identify what you need to know, it's using your creativity to find different ways you could achieve the same goal without physically having to go where the audience is, if this is hard to do.

JC: Do you think it's possible to fold research into an existing design work-flow? Or is it better to put your work-flow aside and rethink your process based on centering field research?
SP: If I had a magic wand and I could do anything, I would say that [rethink-ing the process] would be the ideal scenario. However, I recognize that sometimes life is not that idyllic. You cannot stop everything, train every-one to think differently, and then start working in a new way. So maybe you could start by increasingly adding

field research more into the process. And you have, maybe a six-month transition.

JC: What is your top piece of advice for folks who want to get started? What's the first step?
SP: I think just allocating at least one day to try to talk to a few people of the audience. And be willing to challenge your own assumptions. Because some-times designers do research, hear something that maybe contradicts [their ideas], and they ignore it and say, "Oh, but I know better." And then they say, "Oh, but field research really didn't help me." You need to allocate the time to do it, and then mindfully use it. That might mean, "Okay, I hear something I didn't like, and that means maybe adding two more hours to my workflow. I'm going to do it any-way, because I value this insight. And I know that the end result is going to be much more effective." You also need to go with a very open mind to ask questions. If you go already thinking what you want to hear, it's going to be a waste of time for everyone.

JC: If you're working with collabo-rators, is it important for the whole team to be engaged in the field research process?
SP: What is important from field research, or any kind of qualitative research, is having at least one other person to check on your interpre-tation of the data. To make sure it doesn't only represent you, your as-sumptions, or your bias. If two or three people see the same pattern or the same meaning in a user's response, you're okay. Also, once you analyze

something, you can send it back to the audience member and ask, "Did you mean this? Or did you mean that? From what you said, this was my interpretation. What do you think?" This is another way of checking your bias if you're working alone.

JC: Have you always included field research as a part of your practice? If not, what sparked the change?
SP: It was throughout my PhD—almost 15 years ago—because I was trying to learn more about how designers work. So the only way I found to do that was to actually go into their workplaces and to observe them [working on design projects]. One thing led to the other. I got in touch with many social scientists who taught me different methodologies and I got familiar with qualitative research. I think there's an overemphasis on *quantitative* research. People love numbers. Qualitative is harder to do because it's more subjective. It could be seen as requiring more time, so people kind of think twice before doing it. But to me, the learnings that you can obtain from qualitative [research] can dramatically change the quality of a product. And I have witnessed that in my professional practice.

JC: Is there anything else you would like to say about the topic that we haven't already discussed?
SP: I think many people associate field research and human-centered research with only interviews. But interviews are only one method. You can do workshops, you can spend a day with a person, you can do it over email, you can do videos, you can do diary studies,... you can get creative within the constraints of time, budget, and where people are. I like to think of it as being a playful experience. Maybe because I enjoy doing it and I enjoy learning. You can make them [study participants] draw, you can make them do collages. You can ask them for example, in your case, "Can you visualize what quantum computing means to you?" So that's going to help you then understand their mental models. What the areas they don't know anything about are. Maybe you want to focus on those things, in whatever scientific visualization you are creating. It's about thinking of different ways of helping the audience tell you what they need, or what they don't know. But I think to do that, you need to be very clear on your end: What do you need to learn from them? And once you have that clarity—What's the goal? Why do you need to do the research?—then you can play and find different ways of answering that question. It's not only whether you ask them, "Do you understand this, yes or no?" You want to know the "why?" Why they can understand it, or why they cannot. And you want them to spell out that in detail, because that's going to help you point out different ways of addressing that gap. And that's a bit different from quantitative [research], because sometimes you see people clicking on something, but you don't know why. Maybe they click a lot because they got lost. Maybe they click a lot because they like something. You never know the why. And I think that is what you should aim for [with field research]: Trying to get that "why."

Eleanor Lutz's Flowchart of Viral Families

If you're not already familiar with information designer Eleanor Lutz's captivating animated gifs and epic science-themed posters, I recommend putting this book down and checking out her blog Tabletop Whale immediately (*https://tabletop whale.com/*). Here's a glimpse of how she built a flowchart of viral families for Nerdcore Medical (turn the page for the final graphic). In her words, this poster,

> *...visualizes common virus species that can infect humans. I used small symbols to categorize several interesting aspects of each virus—whether or not it was transmitted by insects, used DNA vs RNA, or if a vaccine existed for the disease. I began designing this flowchart by organizing each of the 60 viruses into three major groups relevant to medical students—the intended audience for the graphic. I next created a grid to outline the position of each virus among those three groups. This design style was intended to provide some structure to the dataset, while still acknowledging that each virus was important for medical students to learn. We didn't want to create too much visual hierarchy in the design, because each entry was equally important. After we established the overall arrangement of viruses, I explored different shapes for the connective 'blobs' and added decorative elements like color and texture.[1]*

---

1   *https://eleanorlutz.com/flowchart-design* Quote used with permission.

Image Credit: Sketches by Eleanor Lutz for Nerdcore Medical

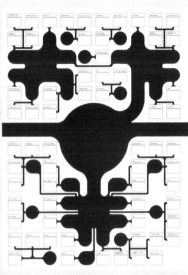

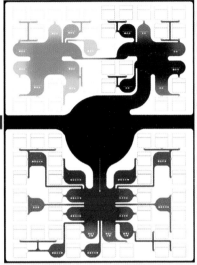

Image Credits:
Sketches by Eleanor Lutz
for Nerdcore Medical

A QUICK BREAKDOWN OF THE
VIRAL FAMILY FLOWCHART

This is a quick Photoshop layer breakdown for
the "Flowchart of Viral Families" infographic I
posted yesterday. It's not meant as a tutorial or
anything serious, but since I personally enjoy
seeing other artists' art files I figured I'd post it
for fun.

The icons are fom Font Awesome, an
open source icon font created by Dave
Gandy. There wasn't a syringe icon
though, so I made that one myself.

MOON BOLD
MOON LIGHT

The font I used for this infographic is
Moon by Jack Harvatt. I emailed him to
buy the commercial license, but it's free
for personal use if you want to try it out.

I added a simple geometric pattern for
texture. I only wanted a subtle effect, so I
faded the black lines to 35% and used a
"Soft Light" Photoshop filter on the layer.

I like using a star filter to add small
details. I turned some copyright-free
NASA star photos into a smooth pattern,
and set the layer to 100% Screen.

The boxes are filled with a faint (10%
opacity) color layer so that they stand
out from the background. Here I used
the same colors as the main flowchart.

I added a thin border around each box in
the same color as the painted
background. I used the Photoshop inner
stroke function for quick outlining.

The main flowchart was painted with the
default Photoshop brush. I originally had
a one-color cutout of the flowchart that I
used to select and delete spilled color.

#1B2020

I didn't use an all-over texture on this
poster - the background's just a single
color. Lately I've been into using deep
grays instead of pure black.

FINAL

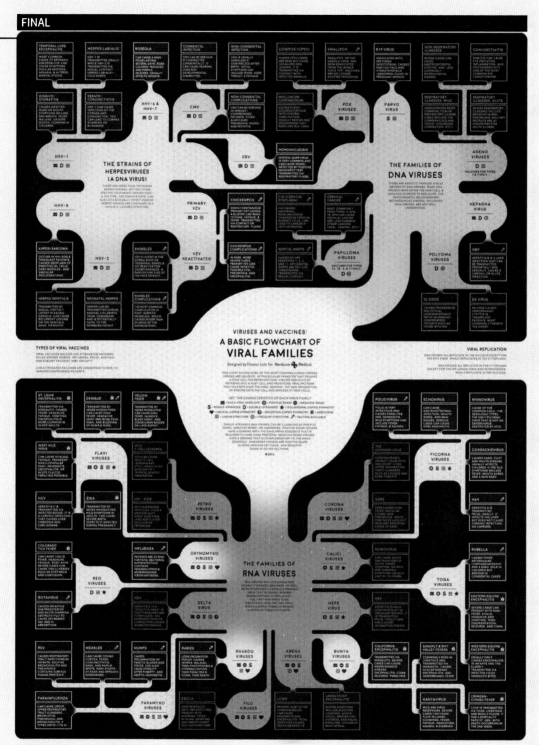

Image Credit: Eleanor Lutz for Nerdcore Medical

How Will Stahl-Timmins Makes Graphics for *The BMJ* (a.k.a. *The British Medical Journal*)

As an information designer at *The BMJ*, Will Stahl-Timmins transforms medical research data into visual summaries. As demonstrated here, it's an iterative process, with clear benchmarks. "Even with a full-page graphic," he writes, "there's a lot of backwards and forwards between myself, the editorial team and authors, about how best to represent information from a published article in visual form." Here, 20 steps for a graphic on the primary care assessment and monitoring of diabetic foot are presented in sequence. (In total, 52 versions of the file were saved over time.) Key points are flagged by Stahl-Timmins.

STAGE 1: Concept Sketches

Image Credits: Will Stahl-Timmins, for "Diabetic Foot," by Satish Chandra Mishra et al., *The BMJ* Vol. 359 (November 16, 2017). The final version (page 241) is republished here without modification in accordance with the Creative Commons Attribution 4.0 International License. (*https://creativecommons. org/licenses/by/4.0/*). All other sketches are from "Video: 'How We Make a Graphic,'" Blog Post by Will Stahl-Timmins (March 14, 2018) *http://blog.willstahl. com/2018/03/video-how-we-make-graphic.html*

This graphic had too many conditions to link them with lines

STAGE 1: Concept Sketches

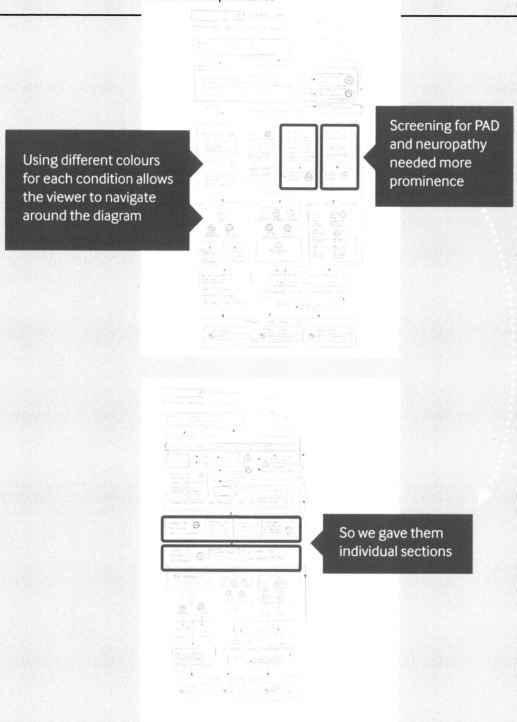

Using different colours for each condition allows the viewer to navigate around the diagram

Screening for PAD and neuropathy needed more prominence

So we gave them individual sections

STAGE 2: Initial Layout

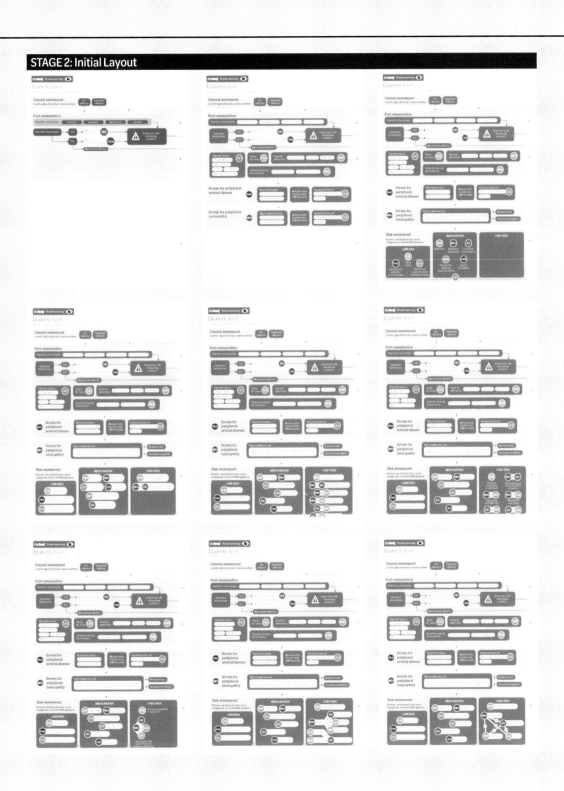

STAGE 3: Refinement

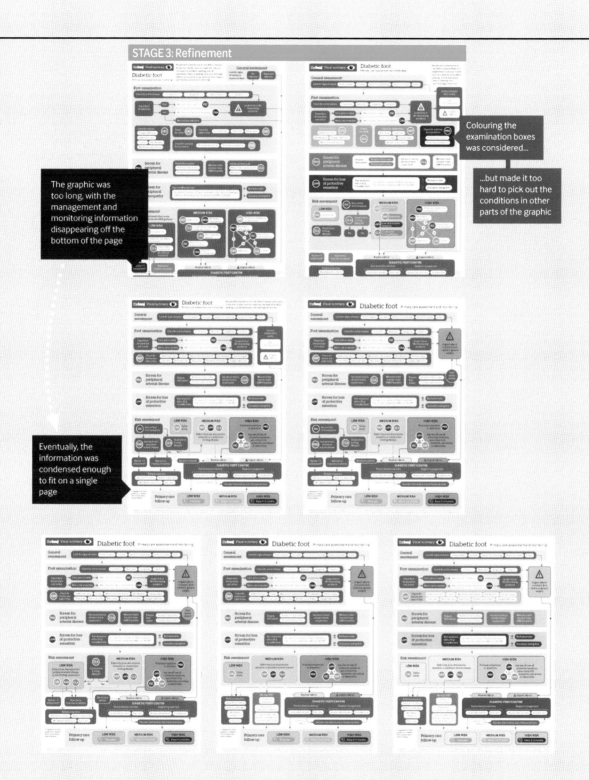

The graphic was too long, with the management and monitoring information disappearing off the bottom of the page

Colouring the examination boxes was considered…

…but made it too hard to pick out the conditions in other parts of the graphic

Eventually, the information was condensed enough to fit on a single page

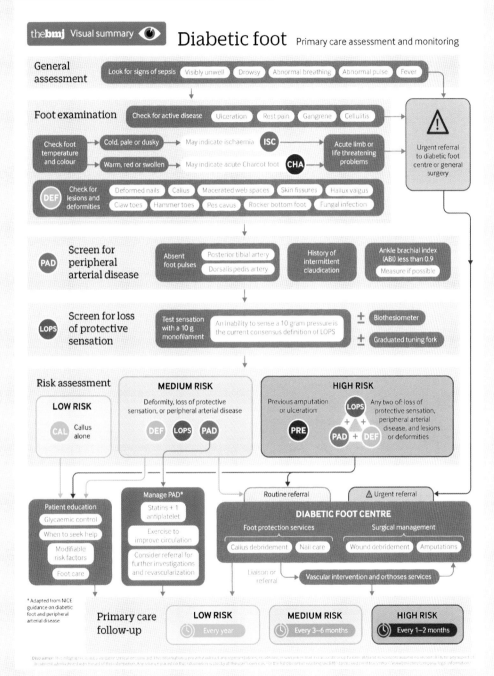

Image Credit: Will Stahl-Timmins, as published in "Diabetic Foot," by Satish Chandra Mishra et al., *The BMJ* Vol. 359 (November 16, 2017). Republished here without modification in accordance with the Creative Commons Attribution 4.0 International License. (*https://creativecommons.org/licenses/by/4.0/*)

Octopus Graphic for *Rotunda* Magazine, by 5W Infographic

With experience as art directors at *National Geographic*, *The New York Times*, *Fortune,* and *Quanta* magazines, the team at 5W Infographic is well versed in composing many elements to tell a single, cohesive story. Here, you can see how the octopus illustration, text, and inset details evolve in tandem for a spread for *Rotunda*, the magazine for members of the American Museum of Natural History. They compose graphics in the program Adobe Illustrator, adjusting the position of drawn elements, inset blocks, and preliminary text (which they often write themselves). After their collaborators approve the plan, they finish the art with more detail.

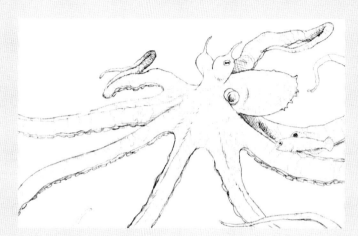

Image Credits: 5W Infographic

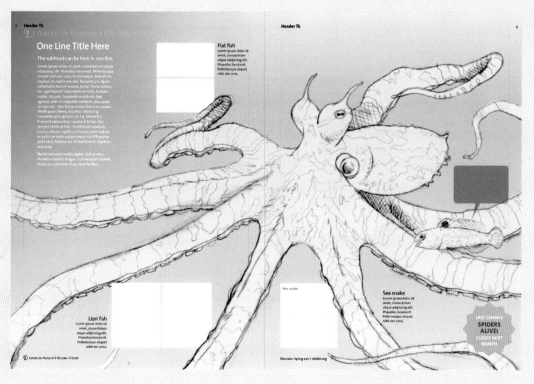

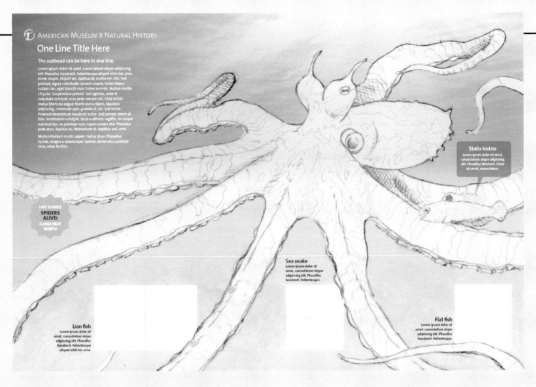

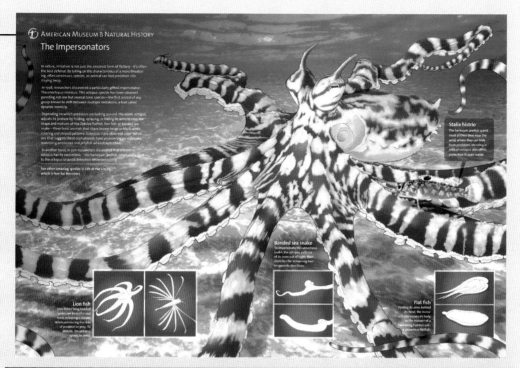

Image Credit: 5W Infographic, as published in *Rotunda* (Spring 2015). © American Museum of Natural History

How Lucy Reading-Ikkanda Breaks Down Cutting-Edge Research

Graphics designer and illustrator Lucy Reading-Ikkanda's distinctive style and thoughtful bite-sized approach works for a wide range of outlets and audiences. (See pages 72 and 83 for examples of her work for *Quanta* Magazine.) Here, she breaks a concept into two panels for a Simons Foundation news brief. The first introduces the key players (cells and ring canals). The second shows how ring canals play a role in the researchers "forest fire" model. Turn the page to see how things progressed from initial rough sketches to final graphics.

Tracing a Cell's Family Tree

Reconstructing a cell's lineage allows researchers to understand the earliest stages of development. Connected cells — known to be directly related to each other — serve as a helpful record of prior cell divisions.

Image Credits: Lucy Reading-Ikkanda/Simons Foundation, as published in "A 'Forest Fire' Model of Cell Division Can Explain Clonal Dominance in Developing Tissue" by Susan Reslewic, Simons Foundation (December 14, 2021) *https://www.simons foundationorg/2021/12/14/ a-forest-fire-model-of-cell -division-can-explain -clonal-dominance-in -developing-tissue/*

A layer of cells encases the fruit fly egg chamber. | After cell division, the cells are connected by ring canals. | Connected cells belong to the same family.

A Forest Fire Model for Clonal Dominance

In the same way that a fire can rapidly spread to neighboring trees ...

... cells can rapidly multiply by sharing factors that promote cell division via their ring canals. This can induce some connected neighboring cells to divide, leading to a phenomenon called clonal dominance.

ROUGH V1

Like Mother, Like Daughter TK

Dividing cells encourage their sisters to also divide leading to clonal dominance — most descendants will be derived from a small portion of founding cells.

A single layer of epithelium cells encases the fruit fly egg chamber.

When cells divide, the resulting daughter cells form a cluster of interconnected cells.

One cell dividing can also induce its sisters to divide by passing cell division promoting factors via the ring canals.

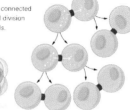

Disco ball TK
(no ring canals?)

Single epithelium cell "mother"

Daughter cells

Ring canals

V2

Like Mother, Like Daughter TK

Dividing cells encourage their sisters to also divide leading to 'clonal dominance.'

A single layer of cells encases the fruit fly egg chamber.

When a cell divides, the resulting daughter cells are connected by a ring canal.

A dividing daughter cell induces its connected sisters to also divide by passing cell division promoting factors via the ring canals.

Most descendants will be derived from a small portion of founding cells

"Mother" cell

Daughter cells

Ring canal

V3

Tracing Cellular Lineage (working title)

Reconstructing a cell's lineage allows researchers to understand the earliest stages of development. Connected cells — known to be directly related to each other — serve as a helpful record of prior cell divisions.

A layer of cells encases the fruit fly egg chamber. | After cell division, the cells are connected by ring canals. | Connected cells belong within the same family.

V4

Tracing Cellular Lineage (working title)

Reconstructing a cell's lineage allows researchers to understand the earliest stages of development. Connected cells — known to be directly related to each other — serve as a helpful record of prior cell divisions.

A layer of cells encases the fruit fly egg chamber. | After cell division, the cells are connected by ring canals. | Connected cells belong within the same family.

Image Credits: Lucy Reading-Ikkanda/Simons Foundation (not all sketch iterations are shown here); Final version as published in "A 'Forest Fire' Model of Cell Division Can Explain Clonal Dominance in Developing Tissue" by Susan Reslewic, Simons Foundation (December 14, 2021)

FINAL

Tracing a Cell's Family Tree

Reconstructing a cell's lineage allows researchers to understand the earliest stages of development. Connected cells — known to be directly related to each other — serve as a helpful record of prior cell divisions.

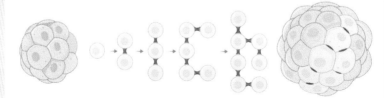

A layer of cells encases the fruit fly egg chamber. | After cell division, the cells are connected by ring canals. | Connected cells belong to the same family.

VERY ROUGH

Forest Fire TK

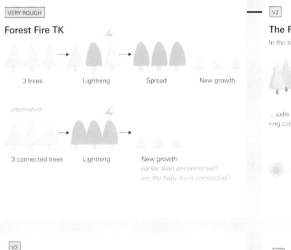

V2

The Forest Fire Model (working title)

In the same way that a fire can rapidly spread to neighboring trees ...

... cells can rapidly multiply by sharing cell dividing promoting factors via their ring canals, inducing their connected neighbors to divide.

V3

The Forest Fire Model (working title)

In the same way that a fire can rapidly spread to neighboring trees ...

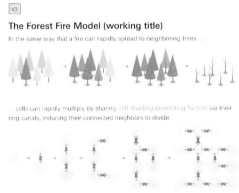

... cells can rapidly multiply by sharing cell dividing promoting factors via their ring canals, inducing their connected neighbors to divide.

V5

The Forest Fire Model (working title)

In the same way that a fire can rapidly spread to neighboring trees ...

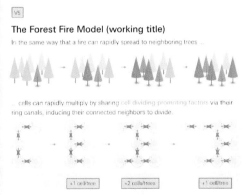

... cells can rapidly multiply by sharing cell dividing promoting factors via their ring canals, inducing their connected neighbors to divide.

FINAL

A Forest Fire Model for Clonal Dominance

In the same way that a fire can rapidly spread to neighboring trees ...

... cells can rapidly multiply by sharing factors that promote cell division via their ring canals. This can induce some connected neighboring cells to divide, leading to a phenomenon called clonal dominance.

Image Credits: Lucy Reading-Ikkanda/Simons Foundation (not all sketch iterations are shown here); Final version as published in "A 'Forest Fire' Model of Cell Division Can Explain Clonal Dominance in Developing Tissue" by Susan Reslewic, Simons Foundation (December 14, 2021)

Reading-Ikkanda often starts with writing a headline and subhead before drawing, as with the examples on the preceding pages. There, you can see that the text generally clicks into place before imagery is finalized. This helps define the scope and guide the imagery. But some projects start with a sketch from the scientist. In these cases, the framing and narrative flow may already be somewhat defined. In this example for a graphic to accompany an academic paper, researcher Caroline Doherty initiated the project with a rough sketch. Reading-Ikkanda then built upon that content, fleshing out intermediate steps and experimenting with different compositions. Not all sketch iterations are shown here. Turn the page to see the final graphic. Note that in the final composition, the two zoomed-in inset details (connected to steps D and G) are aligned vertically, and close enough to each other for an easy comparison. At a glance, the differences between the two are easy to spot: One includes projections that span the full zona pellucida (purple). The other does not.

Image Credit: Sketch by Caroline Doherty

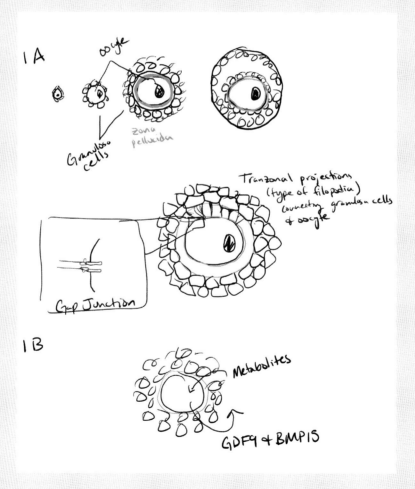

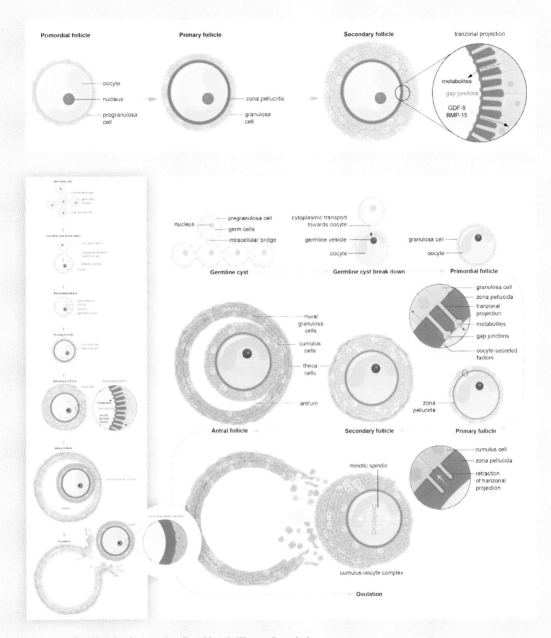

Image Credits: Sketches by Lucy Reading-Ikkanda/Simons Foundation

Image Credit: Work in progress by Lucy Reading-Ikkanda/Simons Foundation

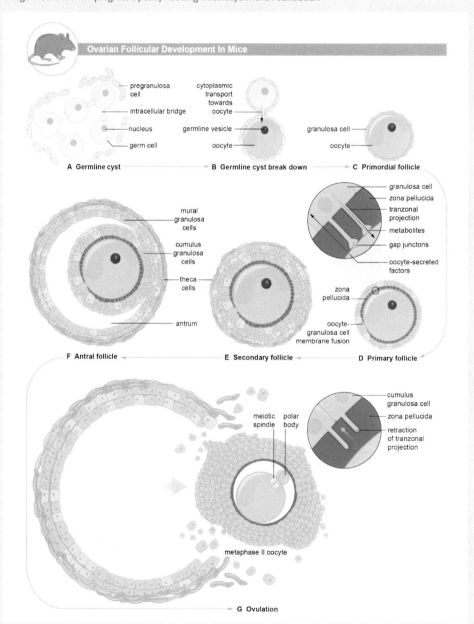

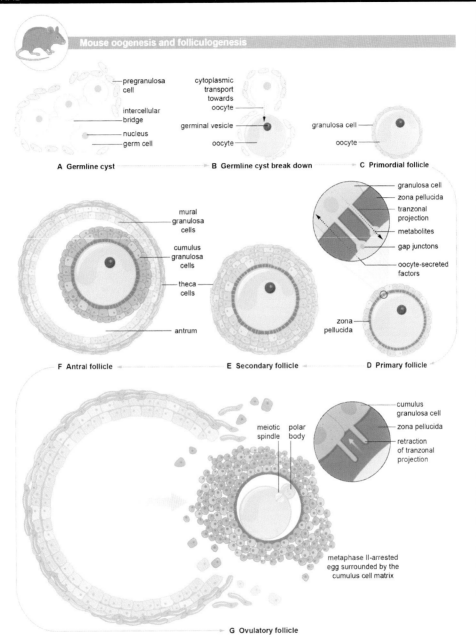

Mouse oogenesis and folliculogenesis

pregranulosa cell
cytoplasmic transport towards oocyte
intercellular bridge
germinal vesicle
granulosa cell
nucleus
germ cell
oocyte
oocyte

A Germline cyst   **B Germline cyst break down**   **C Primordial follicle**

mural granulosa cells
granulosa cell
zona pellucida
tranzonal projection
cumulus granulosa cells
metabolites
gap junctons
theca cells
oocyte-secreted factors
antrum
zona pellucida

F Antral follicle   **E Secondary follicle**   **D Primary follicle**

cumulus granulosa cell
zona pellucida
meiotic spindle   polar body
retraction of tranzonal projection

metaphase II-arrested egg surrounded by the cumulus cell matrix

G Ovulatory follicle

Figure shows the development of an immature mouse egg, prior to fertilization. The center gray panel encompasses stages that are compared in the paper with another species (fruit flies). Bidirectional cell communication is known to be established by at least the primary follicle stage (D), and continues until ovulation (G). Image Credit: Lucy Read-ing-Ikkanda/Simons Foundation. Reprinted–from Caroline A. Doherty, Farners Amargant, Stanislav Y. Shvartsman, Francesca E. Duncan, and Elizabeth R. Gavis, "Bidirectional Communication in Oogenesis: A Dynamic Conversation in Mice and Drosophila," *Trends in Cell Biology*, Vol. 32 (December 15, 2021)–with permission from Elsevier. © 2021

CHAPTER 16

Step-by-Step Guide to Building Your Own Science Graphic

THERE IS NO SINGLE "CORRECT" WAY TO BUILD A SCIENCE GRAPHIC.
Every designer has their own way of working. But there are commonalities. Many follow a general trajectory that starts with rough and generalized shapes that mark space, to more resolved final shapes as the composition gels. The position of those shapes generally shifts around over the course of sketch development. As I note in the previous chapter, **I'm a strong proponent of thinking through the content before getting distracted by drawing details: If the organization of the graphic is solid, then the illustrative details can develop organically within that framework. My process reflects that philosophy.** I recommend iterating with many variations on a theme at the start of the project by taking pencil to paper and creating low-risk doodles.

The guide on the following pages walks you through a detailed version of my process for building graphics. It's not an all-or-nothing approach. Sometimes, honestly, I shortcut between steps, depending upon the project's scope and timeline. And at this point most of the steps are reflexive for me. I present this guide as a way to help get you moving forward. Specific suggestions for things like color-use are not outlined here. (Depending upon your level of comfort with basic design principles, you may find it useful to revisit Chapters 7 through 9 as you make design decisions.) Instead, it centers variables that are often overlooked in process guides, including establishing a schedule and managing reviewer feedback.

Do you have a general sense that you'd like to develop a science graphic, but you're not quite sure how to begin? Turn the page and start with step 1.

STEP-BY-STEP GUIDE:
BUILDING A
SCIENCE GRAPHIC

1

Confirm the Need

Take a moment to think through if it makes sense to build a science graphic.

Thinking of building a science graphic right now?

NO   **YES**

Consider scanning through this flow-chart now, so you'll be ahead of the game when you are ready to start.

Is a graphic required (i.e., graphical abstract request from a journal publisher)?

Engage with your collaborators to help answer the question. This is a great time to initiate field research, and to formally fold audience members into your official collaborator list. (See pages 231–233.)

YES   **NO**

Do you think a graphic would be useful in communicating the information at hand? (Can you tick one or more of these options?)

◯ An image could potentially tell the story—or a piece of the story—more efficiently, effectively, or completely than words.

◯ The narrative involves complex and intertwining relationships, and an image map may be able to help the reader track connections.

◯ A direct and immediate visual comparison may be useful in highlighting change, or differences between states, such as competing hypotheses, or before-and-after views.

◯ Custom entry: Why do you think a graphic would be useful in this case?

_____
_____
_____
_____

NOT SURE   **NO**   **YES**

Perhaps a graphic isn't the best use of your time and resources. If engagement is your primary goal, have you considered if another type of image might be a better match for the project? (See page 212.)

2

Describe the Context

Before diving into content details, think about where your graphic will live, and who it will be for. Use the sample entries in the columns below as a prompt to help you clearly state your outlet, focus on your audience, and to prime thoughts on scope and vibe.

 TIP In tandem with describing your outlet, I recommend looking into the specifications of the publication, organization, website, or application that you're developing the graphic for. See pages 157–162 for more information about scale, resolution, color mode, and file type. Some outlets are quite specific about what they need. This is a good time to collect that information.

OUTLET

Where will your image live? The answer to this question will inform decisions related to both content and style, as well as the dimensions of your graphic (and therefore the composition).

- ○ Journal article
- ○ Print news or magazine article
- ○ Digital news or magazine article
- ○ Print version of thesis
- ○ Academic poster
- ○ Presentation slide
- ○ Press release
- ○ Blog post
- ○ Social media
- ○ Interpretive display
- ○ Instruction manual
- ○ Textbook
- ○ Custom entry: _____
  _____

AUDIENCE

Who is your audience? Check all that apply and add more details in the open field, if known.

- ○ People very familiar with the topic
- ○ People somewhat familiar with the topic
- ○ People new to the topic
- ○ General public
- ○ Policy makers
- ○ Funders
- ○ Adults
- ○ Kids
- ○ Custom entry: _____
  _____
  _____
  _____
  _____
  _____
  _____
  _____

TONE

Given the outlet and audience, what tone or vibe feels like a good match? The answer to this question—along with the subject matter—will inform decisions related to rendering style and illustrative details. Check all that apply.

- ○ Playful
- ○ Authoritative
- ○ Energizing
- ○ Serious
- ○ Elegant
- ○ Spare and to-the-point
- ○ Lush
- ○ Concise
- ○ Entertaining
- ○ Instructive
- ○ Custom entry: _____
  _____
  _____
  _____

CONTINUED ON THE NEXT PAGE

3

Initiate a Team List and Schedule

Start a collaborator list and your preliminary timeline. You may need to revisit this step again later, to adjust names, roles, and dates, but it's useful to think about these items now. Collaborator input from the start can streamline the process, and your anticipated deadline schedule may help guide how ambitious your initial plan can be. For example, if you know that you have limited time, it's in your best interest to keep that in mind as you establish the goal of your graphic. Keep the plan reasonable, given the resources you have available.

COLLABORATORS

Who are your collaborators? List other folks involved with the project, and their roles. The length of this list and the roles included will vary from project to project. It may be useful to divide your list into two categories: active content collaborators and reviewers.

Active content collaborators are people that are involved in establishing the goal of the graphic, and participate in the research, design, and caption-writing process. If you're essentially an active team of one, consider checking in with reviewers often, and/or identifying consultants or members of your intended audience to help provide reality checks. If you're on an active content collaborator team of more than one, fold in your partners now, as you move on to establishing a schedule, and other steps.

Reviewers (and production editors) provide feedback on your sketches and final graphic, ranging from content to file format. They provide a fresh take on the product, without having been through the process of building it. If you're creating graphics without formal reviewers built in (i.e., for a personal blog post), I recommend enlisting a content expert and a member of your target audience to review your work before you make it available to the public. Key questions that reviewers should be able to answer: (1) Is the content represented accurately; and (2) Does the graphic portray the information in a way that's understandable?

SCHEDULE

Divide the time between your anticipated start date and the final deadline date into at least four intervals. For example:

Project initiation: date here

INTERVAL 1

Concept sketch ready for review: date here

INTERVAL 2

Tight sketch ready for review: date here

INTERVAL 3

Final graphic ready for review: date here

INTERVAL 4

Project completed: date here

Share the schedule with your collaborators.

4

Shift Focus to Content

In general, what are you hoping to show in your graphic?

○ Descriptive imagery (how something looks or how it is structured)

○ Process diagram (how something physically or conceptually works)

○ Instructional guide

○ Organizational chart (relationship between things or ideas)

○ Thought experiment (imagined scenario)

○ Comparison (before and after views, changes in state, or competing hypotheses)

○ A summary diagram (such as a graphical abstract or visual outline)

Not sure, or none of the above?

Move on to step 5 then revisit step 4 , to see if your plan does fit into one of these categories upon further thought. If so, check that category now. If not, state what you're broadly hoping to show here:

_____   _____

_____   _____

_____   _____

5

State the Specific Goal of your Graphic

Keep it focused on content and concise (under three sentences).

Here are some examples:

Separate out the entwined concepts of dark energy, the cosmological constant and vacuum energy, illustrating each and showing how they're connected.

Introduce people to the idea of percolation theory. A simple mesh network example demonstrates that in order for any two phones to communicate, they need to be linked by a chain of other phones.

Show how an artificial leaf made of silicon nanowires works. In a process similar to photosynthesis in natural leaves, it transforms photons into storable, transportable fuel.

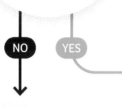

6

Check in with Collaborators

Does your stated goal work for the team?

NO

YES

7

Gather Reference Material

Pull together materials that are directly related to your stated goal.

Return to step **4** with your collaborators, and develop a mutually acceptable goal for the graphic. If the conversation doesn't result in a clear statement, return to step 1.

Are you a content expert ? For example, are you developing a graphic about your own research, experiences, or area of expertise?

YES

NO

TIP I organize my reference materials in a single document that includes the stated goal, deadline schedule, and collaborator contact information at the top. Then I paste in potentially useful text excerpts and reference images (with source urls), and I add links to research papers. Eventually I move the most useful information to the top of the document, bumping less useful info to the bottom. The document continues to evolve over the course of the project, with the addition of my notes, screenshots of sketches, feedback from reviewers that I copy and paste over from email, etc. Ultimately, I'm left with a single document that can be referenced easily when questions pop up later. If organized thoughtfully, it can also be a really useful document to share directly with text colleagues, fact checkers, and other collaborators later in the process.

Assemble these materials:

Existing companion materials. For example, the text portion of the paper that the graphic will be sumbitted with (if a draft already exists). This will be your primary reference

Documents in which you've previously described the concept, object, or relationship in words

Graphics that you've already designed on the topic—or related to the topic—for any and all purposes or audiences (i.e., teaching slides)

Favorite related visuals from other sources

Favorite papers on the topic

Google image search links and screenshots for the nouns and other key words or processes in your stated goal

Photos of relevant pages in textbooks or other introductory guides that you may have handy

Do you already have access to companion materials—either complete or in draft form—for example, the text portion of the article that the graphic will be submitted with, or the primary research paper that your graphic aims to explain? These are your main references.

Has an expert consultant already been identified as part of the team in step 3? If not, spend some time looking for expert sources who can comment on the accuracy of your work, and may be able to help fill in research holes. The corresponding author of your primary reference paper (if you have one) is a great start. Check in with your collaborators to see if they've already identified other key people or references.

To familiarize yourself with how aspects of the topic have been illustrated by others, image search key words and phrases in your goal statement. This can help you identify and translate the visual jargon in your primary sources, and build up your body of knowledge. Do not rely solely on *single* image references without (1) fact checking the material, and (2) getting permission from the original source/designer to do so.

Textbooks or other introductory guides can help provide context for the latest findings. Just be aware that older textbooks may include information that is out-of-date.

Get familar with the content by looking up unfamiliar words and concepts.

Review papers on the topic can help you get a broad overview from an authoritative source. Reviews in science journals summarize the current state of knowledge in a specific area of study by highlighting key research findings and outstanding questions. Their citation lists can be quite useful. To find them, include "literature review," "annual review," or "review article" in your searches. Or try starting with *https://www.annualreviews.org/*.

TIP Need more guidance on how to conduct background research and assess the credibility of your sources? Check out these resources:

- *Navigating Digital Information* video series hosted by John Green on Crash Course (in partnership with MediaWise, The Poynter Institute, and The Stanford History Education Group) *https://thecrashcourse.com/topic/navigatingdigitalinfo/*

- "Sources and Experts: Where to Find Them and How to Vet Them," By Melinda Wenner Moyer, in *The KSJ Science Editing Handbook* (a project of the Knight Science Journalism Fellowship at MIT, supported by the Kavli Foundation and the Howard Hughes Medical Institute's Department of Science Education) *https://ksjhandbook.org*

- "How to Read a Scientific Paper," by Alexandra Witze, in *The Craft of Science Writing: Selections from The Open Notebook*, edited by Siri Carpenter (The Open Notebook, 2020)

8

Read and Take Notes

Read through the reference materials you've collected. You may need to circle back to step and complete additional rounds of targeted research in search of answers to new questions that pop up, or for more details.

TIP I often find it useful to color-code my references and notes according to which part of the goal statement they are related to. See pages 104–105 for an example.

9

Revisit your Goal

Does your goal statement (see step 5) need to be revised in light of the reference material you've read? If so, formally change it now to reflect your new understanding. Confirm the change with your collaborators.

10

Shift into Image Mode

With your goal top-of-mind, start to translate relevant written notes into drawings. Don't worry about a formal composition yet. This step is to simply warm you into thinking about how you can organize information in a non-linear way, and how you might be able to use images to help tell the story. Try substituting nouns with icons, and think about how verbs can be portrayed.

Here are some examples

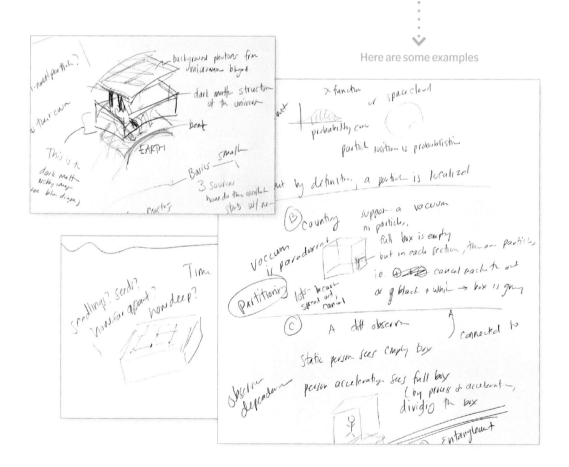

11

Create Frames

Draw a repeating series of empty frames on a blank page. Don't worry about perfectly straight lines. The key here is to approximate the aspect ratio of your final graphic, in miniature. This is a great time to revisit specifications from your client or publication, if you have them. If you don't have size guidelines handy, check with your collaborators, the website that will be hosting your graphic—social media sites usually include image size guidance—or simply mimic the aspect ratio of a template that you might be using, like a Powerpoint slide shape.

Here are some examples

TIP If you're working up a sketch for a website, your width may be fixed and known, but the depth may be flexible. You may end up asking your audience to scroll down to read your full graphic. In this case, keep in mind that folks scrolling through will only see portions of your graphic at a time. Order of information is particularly critical in this case. Serve up readers the details they need as they need them, from top to bottom. Otherwise, they'll need to scroll up and down, in search of information. I find it useful to think of frames within frames when working on these sorts of layouts. Create a long frame if you need to but add a small screen-sized overlay, to help you remember how much of the full image will be visible at any moment in time. Like this:

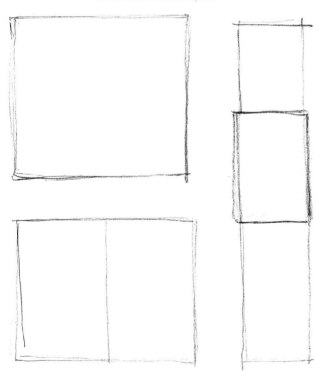

12

Doodle!

Organize the information within the miniature frames, in a very abstract and gestural manner. The key here is to explore mulitple ways to position information in space in a way that honors your goal. This is a good time to revist your answers to steps 4 and 5 , as the type of graphic that you're building can guide its form.

Here's an example series

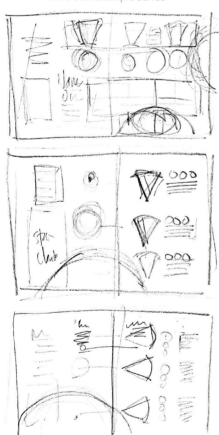

For descriptive imagery (how something looks, or how it is structured), the shape of your primary object will inform your composition.

For process diagrams (how something physically or conceptually works), focus on organizing the sequence of events in a logical and clear manner.

For instructional guides, consider breaking things down into discrete steps.

For organizational charts, use the relationships between things or ideas to inform how they could be positioned and connected in space.

For thought experiments (imagined scenarios), consider using a series of vignettes.

For comparisons (before and after views, competing hypotheses, etc.), I recommend showing side-by-side panels, so that differences and similarities are easy to spot.

For summary diagrams (such as a graphical abstract or visual out-line), you'll likely need a modular composition, unless you can distill the info into a process diagram.

13

Start Working Larger

Now that you've warmed up, draw a series of larger frames, and try drawing out one or more of your favorite miniature plans in a bit more detail. If your graphic will be a stand-alone item that needs a setup, include space for a title and introductory caption. It may be helpful at this stage to write preliminary captions and annotations, to help focus your thoughts.

14

Reality Check

Does your emerging plan honor the context and content you describe in steps 2 through 5? Are you including a level of detail suitable for your audience? Is your plan too ambitious for the space or time available? Do you have the information you need to execute the plan, or is it already clear that you'll need to do more research before fleshing things out further? This is a good time to address those questions, as the plan will become harder to change as you proceed. Go back a few steps, as needed, until your sketch feels as though it will meet the needs of your project, and that you have the resources to make it happen.

TIP Remember that negative space is your friend. You don't need to fill every empty space with content. Rather, think about how you can use negative space to help partition information, and to allow the information—and your audience—to breathe. See Chapter 7 for more information on composition and emphasis, including how to use a grid to help provide structure.

Here's an example

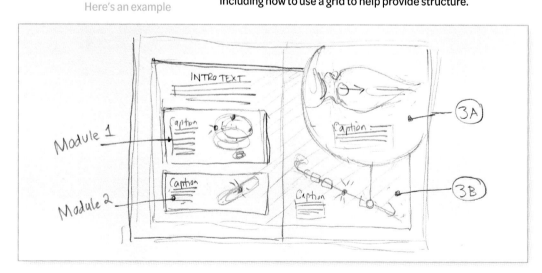

15

Create a Full-Sized Concept Sketch

Create a frame that matches the absolute dimensions of your final product. Use your sketch from step 13 as a guide, and transcribe that information into the larger frame. Include preliminary captions (or placeholding text) and labels, so that you remember to actively design them into space, and you are considering how they'll relate to the imagery from the start. Introducing color may be useful at this stage, especially if you hope to use color to encode information or to guide the reader's eye. This might mean making the most important elements stronger, with bolder outlines and more saturated color than less important, contextual elements. But the primary focus should be on composition.

Here's an example

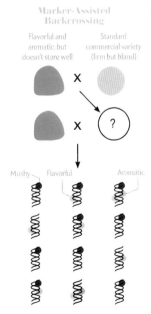

BASICS

Marker-Assisted Breed...

Heni blaccul luptat omnis audist as remporem invenit et ipitassin rendunt issu. saped qui tem nonseque non pel in pratur atur. Pudictem ra sandis re nonsecte verun. reptur assimoloria nectat platus volore cus derum reperfero molore minimporro vitias aliquas piciisquam eic temporp oremodit ant rem utem ut utessitae.

Conventional Backcross Breeding

Flavorful and aromatic, but doesn't store well   Standard commercial variety (firm but bland)

X

X   ?

Marker-Assisted Backcrossing

Flavorful and aromatic, but doesn't store well   Standard commercial variety (firm but bland)

X

X   ?

Mushy   Flavorful   Aromatic

Top three contenders for continued breeding (*yellow*), based on phenotype. Ficiusam volo con et offic tes eosto bearchil mohil mohil mohil mohil modisimus mFiciusam volo con et offic tes eosto bearchil modisiolo

Genetic analysis on tiny sample removed from plant reveals a more precise picture. Offspring with preferred combination of genes identifed early, resulting in fewer rounds of crossbreeding and tests. Text tkt tktktktktk

TIP

If you're really happy with the product of step 13, consider taking a photo or scan, then paste that sketch into a digital file. Expand it to fit the actual size template, and trace over it with the tools of your drawing/design program of choice. Or, if you prefer working with physical media, simply print out a larger version of that sketch, layer a piece of tracing paper over it, and trace the original, cleaning up details as you go.

Image Credit: Sketch by Jen Christiansen for "Building Tastier Fruits & Veggies (No GMOs Required)," by Ferris Jabr, *Scientific American* (July 2014)

16

Critique your own Sketch

Review your plan and answer these questions.

If you answered "Yes" to all of these questions, proceed to step 17. If you answered "No" to any of these questions, refine or revise your sketch. You may need to return to step 13.

Yes No

○ ○ Does your sketch honor your goal statement?

○ ○ Do you think your sketch can be interpreted by someone else, without you being there to talk them through it? (Unless, of course, the final outlet includes someone talking folks through it, as a presenter.)

○ ○ Does the graphic feel as though it's holding a reasonable—and not over-whelming—amount of content?

○ ○ Are your descriptive draft heads and subheads in place? Are draft labels in place? If you are the one ultimately responsible for writing the final text, are preliminary captions and annotations in place? Are there clear levels of text hierarchy? (See Chapter 9.)

○ ○ Is there a clear progression of informa-tion? Is there a clear entry point, and do you think your audience is provided with the information that they'll need, as they'll need it, while following a log-ical reading path through the graphic? (See Chapter 7.)

○ ○ Do you have a plan for color?

Yes No

○ ○ Are you making thoughtful use of relative position of symbols and shapes to help convey information about relationships between objects? (See Chapter 6.)

○ ○ Are you using symbols in a manner that is internally consistent? For example, are you using arrows to show a progres-sion from one step to the next? Or are you using arrows to point at objects? If you're using arrows for both, consider an alternative solution for one category. (See pages 66-67.)

○ ○ Are you providing suitable context for the symbols that you are using? For ex-ample, if there are lots of different cell types represented, do you have a shape and color key, or grouped annotations on the graphic itself to help your reader quickly make sense of which is which?

○ ○ Does the emerging visual style feel ap-propriate for your final context? Are you making good use of a visual vocabulary that you think would be familiar to your audience? Are you providing suitable context and welcoming gestures, if needed? (See Chapter 10.)

17

Seek Concept Sketch Feedback
from Collaborators

Ask your project team, potential audience members, and/
or content experts for feedback. Be specific about what sorts
of critiques would be most helpful at this stage, and what your reviewers can expect as the project moves forward. State the goal of the
graphic, and indicate that you're looking for feedback on the overall plan
at this concept sketch stage. Ask for confirmation that the information—
and path through that information—is useful, clear, and accurate. Other
context may also be useful. For example, if your concept sketch is in gray
pencil, but you ultimately plan on a dimensional full color style, consider
underscoring that you're hoping for a *content* review at this stage, and that
the final rendering style and color palette is not yet represented in the
concept sketch. Propose a deadline for feedback, and indicate the
expected date for the next round of reviews. This is particularly
important if you're relying on the goodwill of others, and they
are not getting paid for their time. Let them know how
many rounds of sketches they may be asked to
review, and what type of feedback you're
hoping for at each stage.

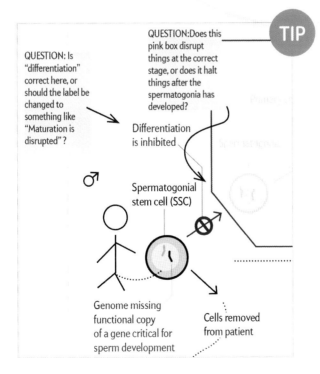

TIP

When sending the sketch to a content
expert for review, I find it useful to mark up
sketches directly with specific questions.
This helps draw attention to areas that I
know that I'd like them to focus on. Folks
are busy, and may not review items as
carefully as you'd like them to. Asking
pointed questions can help focus attention. (That said, leave the door open for
feedback that's not related to your questions as well: I usually include something
along the lines of, "Do you have any other
accuracy-related concerns, questions, or
notes for me?") You can achieve this in a
variety of ways. I often circle objects and
type notes directly on my sketch before
sending it out by email as an attachment.
Or you can use methods that have already
been proven to work well for your team,
like comments added to pdfs, or comments added to a shared file in the cloud.

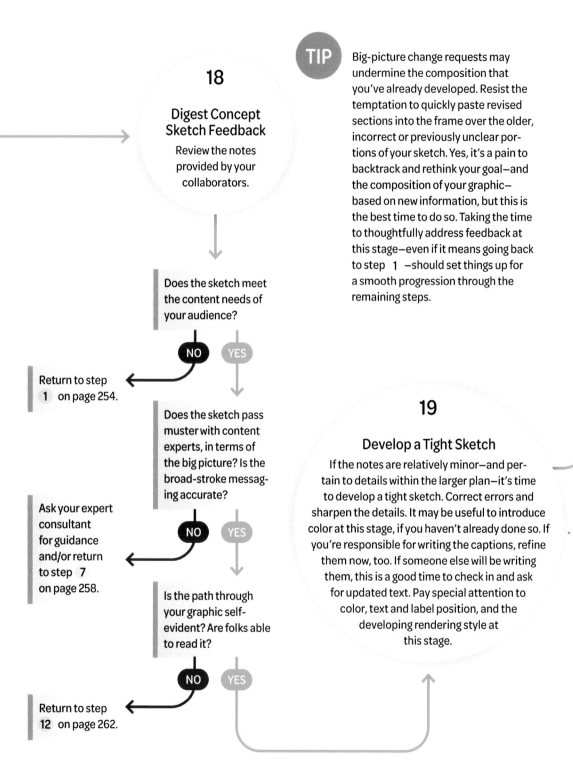

18

Digest Concept Sketch Feedback

Review the notes provided by your collaborators.

TIP Big-picture change requests may undermine the composition that you've already developed. Resist the temptation to quickly paste revised sections into the frame over the older, incorrect or previously unclear portions of your sketch. Yes, it's a pain to backtrack and rethink your goal—and the composition of your graphic—based on new information, but this is the best time to do so. Taking the time to thoughtfully address feedback at this stage—even if it means going back to step 1 —should set things up for a smooth progression through the remaining steps.

Does the sketch meet the content needs of your audience?

NO **YES**

Return to step 1 on page 254.

Does the sketch pass muster with content experts, in terms of the big picture? Is the broad-stroke messaging accurate?

NO **YES**

Ask your expert consultant for guidance and/or return to step 7 on page 258.

19

Develop a Tight Sketch

If the notes are relatively minor—and pertain to details within the larger plan—it's time to develop a tight sketch. Correct errors and sharpen the details. It may be useful to introduce color at this stage, if you haven't already done so. If you're responsible for writing the captions, refine them now, too. If someone else will be writing them, this is a good time to check in and ask for updated text. Pay special attention to color, text and label position, and the developing rendering style at this stage.

Is the path through your graphic self-evident? Are folks able to read it?

NO **YES**

Return to step 12 on page 262.

20

Seek Tight Sketch Feedback from Collaborators

Return to your project team, potential audience members, and/or content experts for feedback. Be specific about what sorts of critiques would be most helpful at this stage, and what your reviewers can expect as the project moves forward. State the goal of the graphic and indicate that you're looking for confirmation that concerns from the last round have been addressed, and that no new errors have been introduced. Indicate that only newly introduced errors will be corrected in the next round. Propose a deadline for feedback and indicate the expected date for the next—and hopefully final—review.

21

Digest Tight Sketch Feedback

Review the notes provided by your collaborators.

——— BASICS ———

..ker-Assisted Breeding

..ptat omnis audist as remporem invenit et ipitassin rendunt issus. Haribu-
.. tem nonseque non pel in pratur atur. Pudictem ra sandis re nonsecte verum
.eptur assimoloria nectat platus volore cus derum reperfero molore minimporro vitias
aliquas piciisquam eic temporp oremodit ant rem utem ut utessitae.

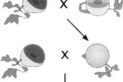

Conventional Backcross Breeding

Marker-Assisted Backcrossing

Flavorful and aromatic, but doesn't store well

Standard commercial variety (firm but bland)

Flavorful and aromatic, but doesn't store well

Standard commercial variety (firm but bland)

Mushy   Flavorful   Aromatic

> Here's an example

Top three contenders for continued breeding (*yellow*), based on phenotype. Ficiusam volo con et offic tes eosto bearchil mohil mohil mohil mohil modisimus mFiciusam volo con et offic tes eosto bearchil modisiolo

Genetic analysis on tiny sample removed from plant reveals a more precise picture. Offspring with preferred combination of genes identfied early, resulting in fewer rounds of crossbreeding and tests. Text tkt tktktktktk

22

Execute the Final Graphic

Correct errors and finalize the rendering style, including color. Pay special attention to how labels and other text elements are interacting with the imagery. Are labels legible? Refine leader lines and double-check alignments.

23

Seek Final Round of Feedback from Collaborators

Return to your project team, potential audience members, and/or content experts for feedback. Indicate that this is the final review and ask if any errors have been introduced. Propose a deadline for feedback.

Here's an example

TIP Confirm that you're adhering to size, resolution, color mode, font, and file type recommendations of your final outlet.

BASICS

Marker-Assisted Breeding

To improve a single crop, plant breeders usually have to play botanical matchmaker for many years, laboriously weeding out unwanted traits without losing desirable ones. Identifying the genes underlying those traits opens up the possibility of a much more efficient and precise process known as marker-assisted breeding.

Conventional Backcross Breeding

Flavorful and aromatic but goes soft quickly   Firm but bland; good for shipping

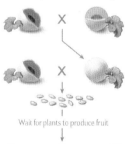

Wait for plants to produce fruit

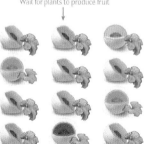

Breeders typically have to wait a full season for experimental crops to mature before they can assess the quality of the produce and select the top contenders for continued breeding (*yellow highlighting*).

Marker-Assisted Backcrossing

Flavorful and aromatic but goes soft quickly   Firm but bland; good for shipping

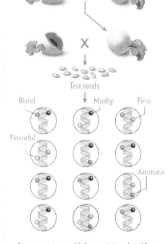

Once scientists establish genetic "markers" for different traits—such as flavor and firmness—they can analyze DNA extracted from seeds or the leaves of young plants and reveal ideal candidates (*yellow highlighting*) for breeding experiments long before harvesttime.

24

Address Final Notes

At this point, reviewer feedback should be pretty minor, and hopefully limited to things like typos. Make final adjustments. (That said, things don't always go as planned. If there's a major change request this late in the game, weigh your options. If resources and time allow, you may choose to backtrack significantly.)

25

Write Alt Text

If your graphic will be presented online, write alt text. See pages 167–168 for more details.

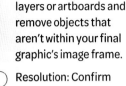

○ Clean up your file: Delete unecessary layers or artboards and remove objects that aren't within your final graphic's image frame.

○ Resolution: Confirm that resolution is suitable for the final outlet. (For printing presses: at least 300 dpi when scaled at 100% for printing.)

26

Write an Image Credit

Include the name(s) of the designer(s). If you relied on any particularly critical references, also include a source credit! Did your expert consultant go above and beyond? Ask if they'd like a consultant nod.

○ Color mode: For print, confirm that all elements are in CMYK color mode. For digital, adhere to your outlet's guidelines.

○ Placed images and fonts: If you have linked or embedded image files or fonts in your document, be sure to also provide those files to your final outlet.

27

Confirm that your Files are Ready to Print or Post

Often referred to in the publishing world as "preflighting" your files, confirm that your graphic is ready for production. This is particularly critical when it comes to preparing materials for a printing press. (You can rely on what you see on your screen a bit more for digital publishing.) Many digital design and illustration programs have built-in preflight modes that can help. Here's an abbreviated checklist.

○ Confirm that line stroke widths and font styles and sizes adhere to the specifications of your final outlet. (Print labels, captions and leader lines should generally be set to overprint, at 100% black.)

28

Exhale

You've completed a graphic! Now you can lean on that foundation of research and thought, and create variations of the same content for different audiences and/or outlets. (See Chapter 17.)

○ When in doubt, ask the folks that you're delivering the files to for guidance. See pages 157–162 for more details about file types.

CHAPTER 17

Step-by-Step Guide to Adapting Your Graphic for a Different Purpose

NOT EVERY GRAPHIC NEEDS TO BE BUILT FROM SCRATCH. Many projects involve creating a variation of a piece that you've already developed for a different purpose. For example, journalists often create several versions of a graphic, one optimized for print, and another—or even several—optimized for digital viewing. And scientists may need to adjust a graphic originally built for a journal article to better suit a blog post, slide presentation, or social media post.

Why not just use the same image, scaled up or down to fit the new format? That rarely goes well. All of the time and thought that you put into honoring the ultimate context of your original graphic is wasted. For example, a full-page print graphic may be rendered illegible when simply scaled down for a smartphone screen. An information-rich graphic you create for a journal article may be too meaty for folks to absorb in a bustling poster session setting. And a graphic originally built with a specialist audience in mind may lack necessary context for a non-specialist audience. A hasty "I've already done this" copy-and-paste mentality deprives your new audience of proper consideration. (Not that I haven't been guilty of this on occasion, particularly when time is short.)

But don't despair. Retooling an existing graphic for a new purpose is more efficient than building a new one from the ground up. This chapter walks you through the process, for three primary scenarios: (1) reformatting the graphic for different production specifications, (2) rethinking the graphic for a different setting entirely, and (3) customizing the graphic for a fundamentally different audience.

When I refer to an existing graphic in this chapter, I'm referring to a graphic that you have previously created, or that you have permission from the copyright holder to adapt.

Reformatting a Graphic

This category is characterized by a need to retain all of the same information that's presented in the original graphic. In this case, the audience can be thought of as being essentially consistent, but the context—and production specifications—shift. For example, an image originally created for print may need to be adjusted so that it's legible on a smartphone screen.

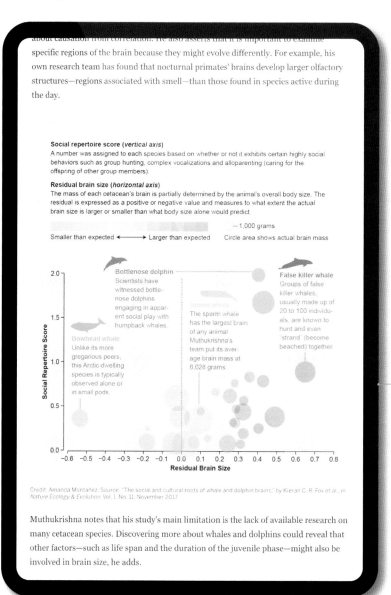

Static graphics presented online are generally designed to be read in a linear manner. Information is revealed from top to bottom as a reader scrolls down through the page. As someone who spent the majority of my career crafting compositions that could be viewed all at once on a print page (without a slow reveal), I sometimes find that structure a bit stifling. It definitely requires a shift in mindset.

Amanda Montañez—a graphics editor at *Scientific American*—comes at it from a different point of view. Most of her projects are digital-first, published online on the daily news cycle. Many are reformatted for print later. Montañez excels at crafting efficient and linear compositions, thinking carefully through what information the reader needs, in sequence. Although negative space and breathing room is important, Montañez weighs that against trying to maximize the amount of content folks can see at once on their screen. She's designing with an eye to what portions of the graphic are visible simultaneously, as the material rolls through that frame.

Here's an example of three variations on a graphic by Montañez for an article on how whale and dolphin brain size relates to social behavior. The large digital version is optimized for tablet and laptop viewing. As folks scroll down the page, they encounter the legend first—seeing information they need for interpreting the rest of the graphic. And then the data is revealed. The full chart is intentionally shallow enough to be viewed on a screen comfortably in its entirety, so the axis label can remain at the bottom (in a conventional position).

The smaller digital version is optimized for smartphone screens. The chart is reoriented in order to make better use of a vertical screen. The legend still precedes the data. But you can see that Montañez has now also moved axis labels and tick marks to the top of the chart, so that information is readily available as the reader needs it. In this case, the chart can likely be visible all at once, but the field of view is pretty tight. Placing the axis at the top allows for immediate context. The annotations in this graphic hold bonus details—not critical details necessary for interpreting the chart—so she places them at the bottom of the

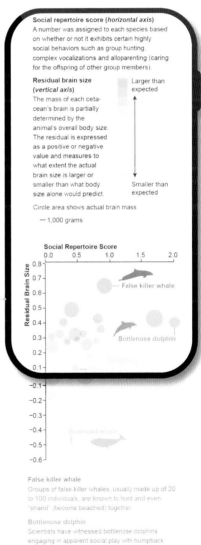

image. The full smartphone-sized image is subtly divided into three parts. Each module (legend, chart, and annotations) is designed to be visible within a single frame, allowing the reader to pause scrolling for a moment while digesting the information.

The print version is a full magazine page wide, with enough space on the chart itself to hold a legend within the chart frame. That legend is set off from the rest of the chart with a gray tinted box. The reader is free to scan the page at their will. The entire graphic is presented on a single page that can be viewed all at once, alongside the article text (not shown in its entirety here).

When reformatting print for digital or vice versa, keep in mind that files for print generally need to be at a much higher resolution than files to be read on screens. As a result, things have to be scaled differently. Pay special attention to type size and line weights. Visual elements like circles and cetacean illustrations can still work on screens when quite small. But text and axis lines can't get scaled down to the same degree and still be legible.

When working on tall static images that are scrolled-through online, it's important to remember that all of the information may not be visible at once. You may need to repeat image details or legends, so

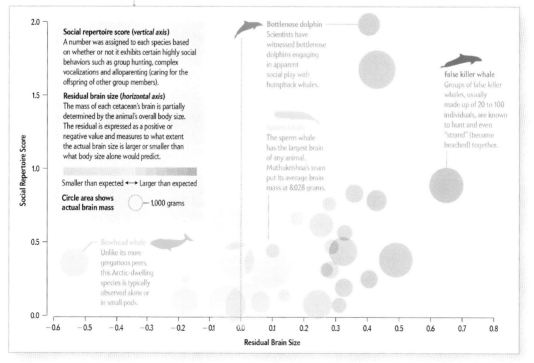

that the reader doesn't need to scroll up and down, in search of information. For example, this full-page graphic by Katie Peek has a lot of information pinned to a central map. In a version reformatted for a smartphone screen, portions of the map are repeated next to relevant annotations, so that the reader doesn't have to follow leader lines back up to the main map.

Faced with a reformatting challenge like this one, in which you'd like to keep all of the content of your primary graphic intact, but it needs to be restructured for a different outlet? The flowchart that starts on page 284 can help.

Rethinking a Graphic for a Different Setting

This category is characterized by a need to customize your graphic for a significantly different outlet. Some content adjustments may be necessary, not just composition or formatting changes. For an example, let's return to "The Swiss Cheese Respiratory Virus Pandemic Defence," by Ian M. Mackay.

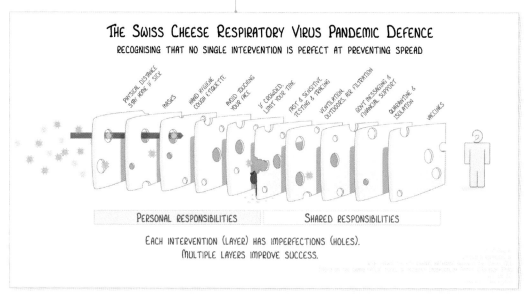

It's a straightforward and legible image. Totally suitable for viewing on a laptop screen or computer monitor, and in print (ideally a bit larger than the scale it's published here). But what if you wanted to use this in a spoken-word presentation, either projected on a screen, or in a virtual window on Zoom or Google Meet? The title, subhead, and labels are critical for a stand-alone graphic. But combined, those details make this graphic too dense with information for an audience to read while also listening to a speaker (and/or reading closed captions).

The graphic can be edited down in this case: You—the speaker—will be providing the broader context with your voice, or via closed-captioning. The graphic doesn't need to be completely self-explanatory. In this case, I'd recommend stripping out most of the text. The best solution depends on the points that the speaker would like to highlight. But perhaps even something as stripped down as this could make sense.

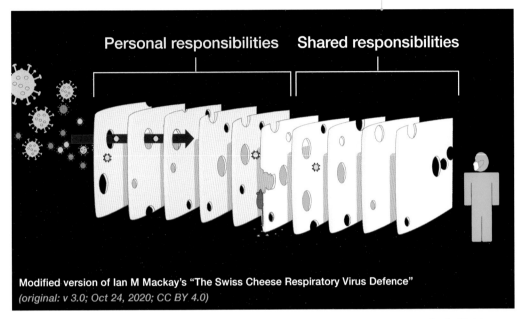

Personal responsibilities   **Shared responsibilities**

Modified version of Ian M Mackay's "The Swiss Cheese Respiratory Virus Defence"
(original: v 3.0; Oct 24, 2020; CC BY 4.0)

True, some slide decks do need to operate on a few levels, since they are often circulated as a proxy for the live presentation. In those cases, leaving all of the text in place may make sense, as not everyone will have the benefit of a speaker walking them through the content. But if you're optimizing your content for a live audience, reducing density is a good idea. If you'd like the best of both worlds, keep the slide less dense and include a link to the original fully detailed graphic in the notes. If it's important to highlight all of the visible details in the original graphic, consider a series of static slides that help guide your audience's attention through the graphic and labels in a very focused and intentional way. (See the next page.)

You may be thinking that this wasn't a terribly big change. And you're right! It didn't take long to execute. What's the difference between this category of retooling, and the "reformatting" category? In a reformatting job, all of the original content needs to remain intact. The focus is on developing a new composition optimized for the new shape and size that the graphic needs to fit within. In this Swiss cheese scenario, the setting has changed pretty dramatically. The original piece was designed for a

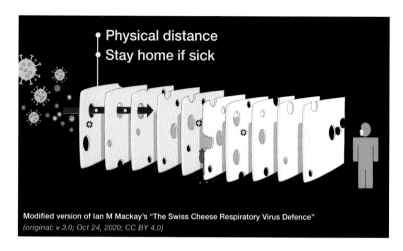

Modified version of Ian M Mackay's "The Swiss Cheese Respiratory Virus Defence"
(original: v 3.0; Oct 24, 2020; CC BY 4.0)

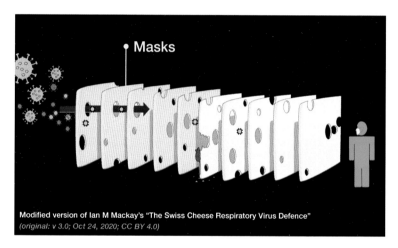

Modified version of Ian M Mackay's "The Swiss Cheese Respiratory Virus Defence"
(original: v 3.0; Oct 24, 2020; CC BY 4.0)

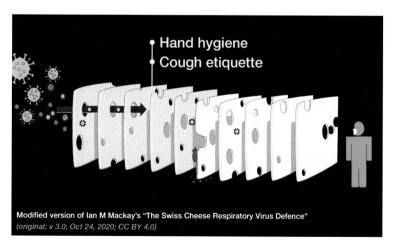

Modified version of Ian M Mackay's "The Swiss Cheese Respiratory Virus Defence"
(original: v 3.0; Oct 24, 2020; CC BY 4.0)

reader to read and digest in solitude, without other simultaneous modes of information input. The redesigned series is edited for a different setting. A person is now present, walking folks through the information at a particular pace. Yes, a composition change may be needed for the new outlet. More critically, the mode of communication may have changed enough to warrant removing some of the original content. Or adding details, depending on the points the speaker hopes to make.

What if your original graphic is a flattened bitmapped file, and the objects cannot be moved, edited or deleted independently? For the case of slides or social media posts—you could consider simply cropping in and/or highlighting details of your original graphic. In this case, I recommend reducing the contrast of the portions that are outside of the area of interest. This helps focus attention and reduces visual noise.

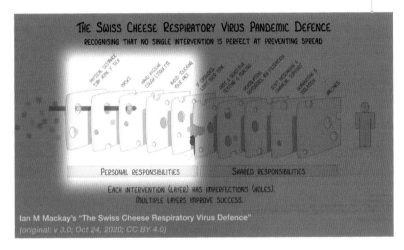

Image Credit: Slightly modified version (by Jen Christiansen) of an original graphic produced by Ian M. Mackay (*virologydownunder.com*); Based on risk reduction and Swiss cheese model work by James T. Reason; Version 3.0 (October 24, 2020 update); Original image by Mackay is under a CC BY 4.0 license. *https://creativecommons.org/licenses/by/4.0/*

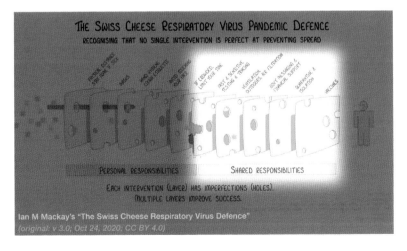

Rethinking a Graphic for a Different Audience

Perhaps you have a single graphic that completely encapsulates the content that you'd like to communicate, but the audience for the original version is markedly different from the audience you hope to reach with your new image. You may be able to abbreviate the research stage of building a graphic.

For example, this figure from a review article on type 1 diabetes and the immune system does a good job of showing contrasting scenarios side-by-side. The style and vocabulary serves its scholarly context well.

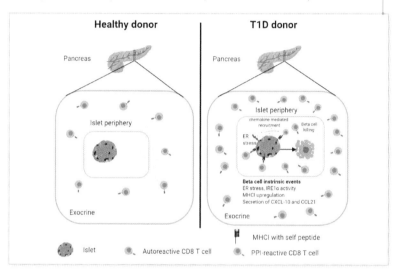

But it wasn't quite appropriate for a different audience—the readers of *Scientific American*. Ultimately, text editor Josh Fischman translated the jargon and provided more context for a non-specialist audience with the captions. Illustrator David Cheney rendered it in a style that would be engaging within the context of a magazine. Those steps certainly took time and collaboration. But the original graphic allowed us to skip several graphics-development steps.

This category is characterized by a need to customize a *single* existing graphic for a significantly different audience. If you're mashing up the content of more than one piece of visual reference material to build a graphic, I recommend starting anew, with the flowchart in Chapter 16.

● ● ●

STILL A BIT CONFUSED as to how your possible adapted graphic job fits into these categories, if at all? And how to proceed from there? Turn the page and start with step 1.

The Target of Diabetes

When the body cannot produce enough of the vital hormone insulin, the result is debilitating type 1 diabetes. The reason for that hormone deficiency is the death of its producers, beta cells in the pancreas. They die off after attack by killer T cells from the body's own immune system. For years scientists thought T cells in people with diabetes had a flaw that made them go after beta cells. But nondiabetic people have the same kind and amount of T cells in their blood (*shown in pink*), yet such cells leave the beta cells alone. That has led researchers to suspect beta cells themselves may draw T cells to them by producing molecular lures.

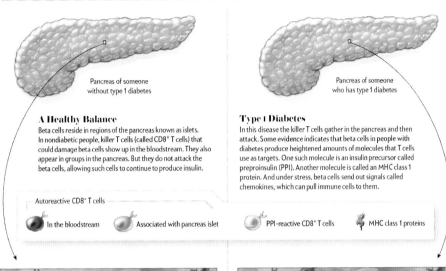

Pancreas of someone
without type 1 diabetes

Pancreas of someone
who has type 1 diabetes

A Healthy Balance

Beta cells reside in regions of the pancreas known as islets. In nondiabetic people, killer T cells (called CD8[+] T cells) that could damage beta cells show up in the bloodstream. They also appear in groups in the pancreas. But they do not attack the beta cells, allowing such cells to continue to produce insulin.

Type 1 Diabetes

In this disease the killer T cells gather in the pancreas and then attack. Some evidence indicates that beta cells in people with diabetes produce heightened amounts of molecules that T cells use as targets. One such molecule is an insulin precursor called preproinsulin (PPI). Another molecule is called an MHC class 1 protein. And under stress, beta cells send out signals called chemokines, which can pull immune cells to them.

Autoreactive CD8[+] T cells

In the bloodstream   Associated with pancreas islet   PPI-reactive CD8[+] T cells   MHC class 1 proteins

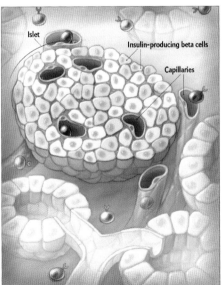

Islet

Insulin-producing beta cells

Capillaries

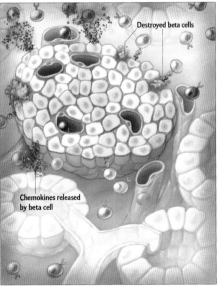

Destroyed beta cells

Chemokines released
by beta cell

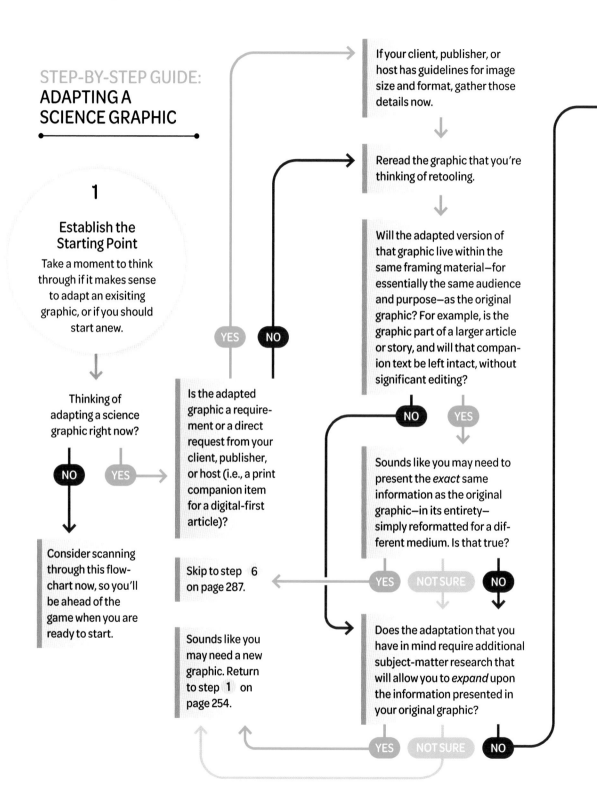

STEP-BY-STEP GUIDE:
ADAPTING A SCIENCE GRAPHIC

1

Establish the Starting Point

Take a moment to think through if it makes sense to adapt an exisiting graphic, or if you should start anew.

Thinking of adapting a science graphic right now?

NO · **YES**

Consider scanning through this flow-chart now, so you'll be ahead of the game when you are ready to start.

Is the adapted graphic a require-ment or a direct request from your client, publisher, or host (i.e., a print companion item for a digital-first article)?

YES · **NO**

If your client, publisher, or host has guidelines for image size and format, gather those details now.

Reread the graphic that you're thinking of retooling.

Will the adapted version of that graphic live within the same framing material—for essentially the same audience and purpose—as the original graphic? For example, is the graphic part of a larger article or story, and will that compan-ion text be left intact, without significant editing?

NO · **YES**

Sounds like you may need to present the *exact* same information as the original graphic—in its entirety—simply reformatted for a dif-ferent medium. Is that true?

YES · **NOT SURE** · **NO**

Skip to step **6** on page 287.

Sounds like you may need a new graphic. Return to step **1** on page 254.

Does the adaptation that you have in mind require additional subject-matter research that will allow you to *expand* upon the information presented in your original graphic?

YES · **NOT SURE** · **NO**

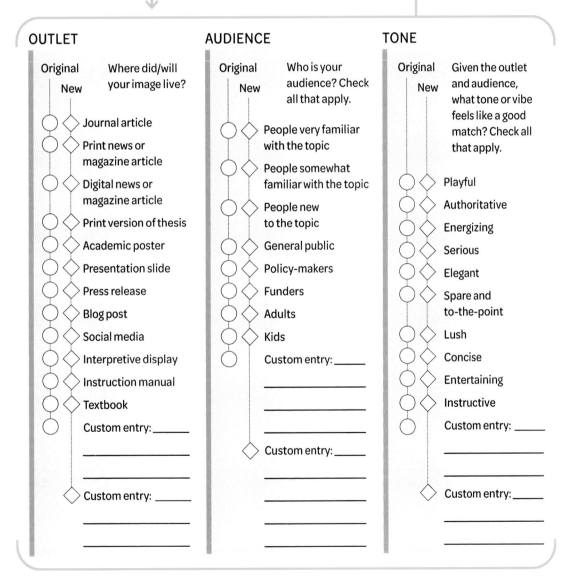

2

Describe the Context

Reiterate the original graphic's context and define the new context.

3

Evaluate the Differences

Which responses changed?

OUTLET

Original
New

Where did/will your image live?

- Journal article
- Print news or magazine article
- Digital news or magazine article
- Print version of thesis
- Academic poster
- Presentation slide
- Press release
- Blog post
- Social media
- Interpretive display
- Instruction manual
- Textbook
- Custom entry: _____
  _____
  _____
- Custom entry: _____
  _____
  _____

AUDIENCE

Original
New

Who is your audience? Check all that apply.

- People very familiar with the topic
- People somewhat familiar with the topic
- People new to the topic
- General public
- Policy-makers
- Funders
- Adults
- Kids
- Custom entry: _____
  _____
  _____
  _____
- Custom entry: _____
  _____
  _____

TONE

Original
New

Given the outlet and audience, what tone or vibe feels like a good match? Check all that apply.

- Playful
- Authoritative
- Energizing
- Serious
- Elegant
- Spare and to-the-point
- Lush
- Concise
- Entertaining
- Instructive
- Custom entry: _____
  _____
  _____
- Custom entry: _____
  _____
  _____

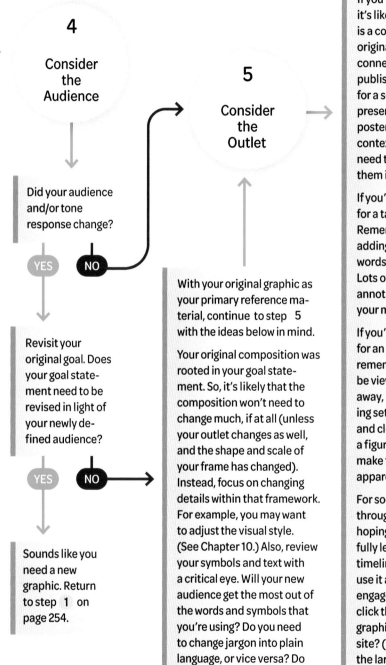

4

Consider the Audience

Did your audience and/or tone response change?

YES | **NO**

Revisit your original goal. Does your goal statement need to be revised in light of your newly defined audience?

YES | **NO**

Sounds like you need a new graphic. Return to step 1 on page 254.

5

Consider the Outlet

With your original graphic as your primary reference material, continue to step 5 with the ideas below in mind.

Your original composition was rooted in your goal statement. So, it's likely that the composition won't need to change much, if at all (unless your outlet changes as well, and the shape and scale of your frame has changed). Instead, focus on changing details within that framework. For example, you may want to adjust the visual style. (See Chapter 10.) Also, review your symbols and text with a critical eye. Will your new audience get the most out of the words and symbols that you're using? Do you need to change jargon into plain language, or vice versa? Do you need to add or remove any annotations or labels?

If you've landed on this panel, it's likely that your new graphic is a companion piece for the original. Perhaps something connected to a previously published article, optimized for a social media post, slide presentation, or academic poster. Move forward with your context top-of-mind. You may need to edit details out, or add them in. For example:

If you're developing a slide for a talk, use text sparingly. Remember that you'll be adding context with spoken words (or closed-captions). Lots of on-slide captions and annotations may distract from your message.

If you're reformatting a graphic for an academic poster, remember that people may be viewing it from several feet away, in a potentially distracting setting. Make labels large and clear. Consider adding a figure title and subhead to make the take-home message apparent at a glance.

For social media posts, think through your goal. Are you hoping to include a complete, fully legible graphic in your timeline? Or are you hoping to use it as a way to foster engagement, where folks will click through to the full graphic hosted on another site? (In that case, a detail of the larger original graphic may be suitable, as opposed to a complete redesign.)

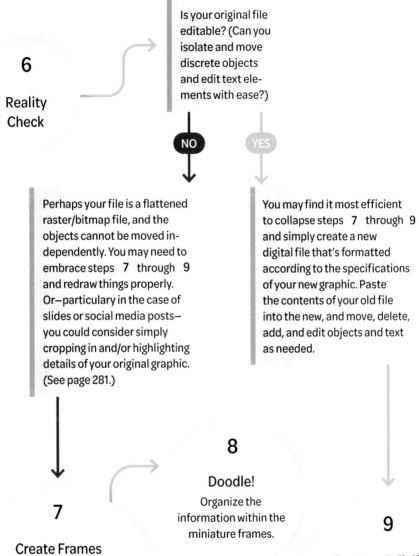

6

Reality
Check

Is your original file
editable? (Can you
isolate and move
discrete objects
and edit text ele-
ments with ease?)

NO   YES

Perhaps your file is a flattened
raster/bitmap file, and the
objects cannot be moved independently. You may need to
embrace steps 7 through 9
and redraw things properly.
Or—particulary in the case of
slides or social media posts—
you could consider simply
cropping in and/or highlighting
details of your original graphic.
(See page 281.)

You may find it most efficient
to collapse steps 7 through 9
and simply create a new
digital file that's formatted
according to the specifications
of your new graphic. Paste
the contents of your old file
into the new, and move, delete,
add, and edit objects and text
as needed.

8

Doodle!
Organize the
information within the
miniature frames.

7

Create Frames
Draw a repeating series of miniature empty frames on a blank page.
Revisit specifications from your client
or publication, if you have them. If
you don't have size guidelines
handy, check with your collaborators, client, publisher,
or host.

9

Create a Full-Sized
Sketch
Create a frame that matches
the absolute dimensions of your
final product. Build your tight
sketch within it, including
captions and labels.

10

Critique your Sketch

Review your plan and answer these questions.

If you answered "Yes" to all of these questions, proceed to step 11. If you answered "No" to any of these questions, refine or revise your sketch. You may need to return to step 7.

11

Seek Sketch Feedback from Collaborators

It may be helpful to provide them with the original graphic, and an explanation of the new context. Be specific about what sorts of critiques would be most helpful at this stage, based on your goal, ultimate outlet, and deadline schedule.

Yes No

○ ○ Does your sketch honor your goal statement?

○ ○ Do you think your sketch can be interpreted by someone else, without you being there to talk them through it (unless, of course, the final outlet includes someone talking folks through it, as a presenter)?

○ ○ Does the graphic feel as though it's holding a reasonable—and not overwhelming—amount of content?

○ ○ Is the text in place? Are there clear levels of text hierarchy? (See Chapter 9.)

○ ○ Is there a clear progression of information? Is there a clear entry point, and do you think your audience is provided with the information that they'll need, as they'll need it, while following a logical reading path through the graphic? (See Chapter 7.)

○ ○ Are you making thoughtful use of relative position of symbols and shapes to help convey information about relationships between objects? (See Chapter 6.)

Yes No

○ ○ Do you have a plan for color?

○ ○ Are you using symbols in a manner that is internally consistent? For example, are you using arrows to show a progression from one step to the next? Or are you using arrows to point at objects? If you're using arrows for both, consider an alternative solution for one category. (See pages 66-67.)

○ ○ Are you providing suitable context for the symbols that you are using? For example, if there are lots of different cell types represented, do you have a shape and color key, or grouped annotations on the graphic itself to help your reader quickly make sense of which is which?

○ ○ Does the emerging visual style feel appropriate for your final context? Are you making good use of a visual vocabulary that you think would be familiar to your audience? Are you providing suitable context and welcoming gestures, if needed? (See Chapter 10.)

12

Execute the Final Graphic

Address comments from collaborators, correct errors, and finalize the rendering style. Pay special attention to how labels and other text elements are interacting with the imagery. Are labels legible? Refine leader lines and double-check alignments.

13

Seek Final Round of Feedback from Collaborators

Return to your project team, potential audience members, and/or content experts for feedback. Indicate that this is the final review, and ask if any errors have been introduced. Propose a deadline for feedback.

14

Address Final Notes

At this point, reviewer feedback should be pretty minor, and hopefully limited to things like typos. Make final adjustments. (That said, things don't always go as planned. If there's a major change request this late in the game, weigh your options. If resources and time allow, you may choose to backtrack significantly.)

15

Write Alt Text

If your graphic will be presented online, write alt text. See pages 167-168 for more details.

16

Write an Image Credit

Include the name(s) of the designer(s). If you relied on another source (with permission), remember to include a source credit!

17

Confirm that your Files are Ready to Print or Post

Often referred to in the publishing world as "preflighting" your files, confirm that your graphic is ready for production. This is particularly critical when it comes to preparing materials for a printing press. (You can rely on what you see on your screen a bit more for digital publishing.) Many digital design and illustration programs have built-in preflight modes that can help. (See checklist on page 271.)

PART 4 ← **Joint Efforts**

CHAPTER 18

Collaborations

FOR A HANDFUL OF YEARS, I was the only graphics editor on staff at *Scientific American*. It was tempting to think of myself as a one-person department. And I suppose I was, on paper. But I was far from alone. Then—as now with my current graphics editing colleague Amanda Montañez—I was embedded in a small team of other visual journalists, including creative director Michael Mrak and art directing and photo editing colleagues. And that crew—along with copyediting and pro-duction colleagues—was embedded in a larger editorial team with our text editing colleagues. Every month I'd engage with a rotating cast of scientist consultants, authors, and freelance artists. Graphics were the product of conversations with others about the subject matter, group art brainstorming sessions, sketch reviews, and considerable skill and problem-solving abilities lent to the magazine by freelance designers. Everything was—and continues to be—a team effort.

Part 3 of this book is titled D.I.Y. (do it yourself). But the truth is that you'll rarely, if ever, be flying solo. Even the most fiercely independent of us can't do it alone. Most projects are—or should be—collaborations. In the case of science graphics, you'll almost certainly need to work with a content-area expert (unless *you* are the content expert). In some cases, you might be working on a robust team, with more than one designer and at least one writer or an editor. In more stripped back cas-es, you may be the only designer, and your collaborator is an advisor, colleague, mentor, or peer providing feedback. In other cases, you may be more actively co-designing a solution with members of your intend-ed audience. (See the box on page 304 and references listed on pages 302–303 for more information and resources related to participatory design and co-design.)

Co-Authorship

Most projects involve collaborators that provide feedback on your graphic. Mentors, supervisors, peer reviewers, content-area consultants, and editors may all weigh in with feedback at various stages of the project. Ultimately, though, that graphic is often linked to a single credited name: the primary person designing the image. Some graphics, however, are more overtly joint efforts, with different people contributing different visual elements or features.

One of my favorite examples of this remains the 2013 *New York Times* digital feature, "What is the Higgs?," credited to Nigel Holmes (drawings), and Jonathan Corum, Alicia DeSantis, Xaquín G.V., and Josh Williams (graphic). Check out the website for the step-by-step experience: *https://archive.nytimes.com/www.nytimes.com/interactive/2013/10/08/science/the-higgs-boson.html*. The lyrical drawings by Holmes are set into motion by others on the team, pulling the reader through a poetic and spare explainer of the Higgs boson.

Here's another example. For an article on ancient mammal brain size, different elements by different people are set up together in a single graphical unit. Careful positioning of the elements in a grid, and a shared color palette make the different features live comfortably together. Sarah Shelley drew the *Arctocyon primaevus*, *Trogosus hillsii*, and *Hyrachyus modestus* skulls (first column). Ornella Bertrand generated the second and third columns using 3D model software. They collaborated to highlight specific brain regions in the third column.

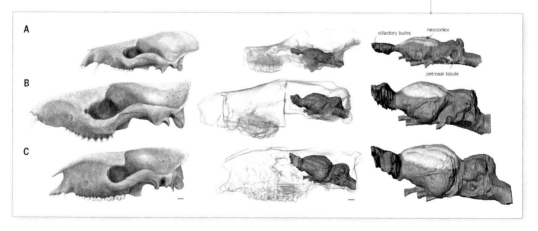

Image Credits: Sarah Shelley (skulls) and Ornella Bertrand (endocasts), from "Brawn before Brains in Placental Mammals after the End-Cretaceous Extinction," by Ornella C. Bertrand et al., *Science,* Vol. 376 (April 2022). Reprinted with permission from AAAS.

For more examples of graphics that include imagery credited to more than one designer or artist, see pages 140, 143, 144, 176, and 180.

When and How to Work with Design Professionals

This book is a practical guide designed to get *you* actively building science graphics. The flowcharts in Chapters 16 and 17 include prompts for checking in with your partners, along with questions to ask yourself and your team along the way. But some visions may be out of your reach for a variety of reasons. For example, you may not have the time in your schedule to give the graphic adequate attention, or your project may exceed your current skill levels. This happens to me, too! One of my favorite things is working with folks that have different skill sets than I do. This section provides tips for how to do it.

HOW TO FIND A DESIGNER OR ARTIST • You may find it most efficient to start with your home institution. Does your workplace have a department of design and communication professionals ready to help? (See page 309 for a Q&A with Ni-ka Ford, a medical illustrator with one such team: the Instructional Technology Group at the Icahn School of Medicine at Mount Sinai.)

If you don't have colleagues to call upon, I highly recommend starting a list of possible collaborators before you have a specific project in mind. Does a figure in a paper catch your eye? Save it in a folder of favorites and make a note of the artist. Find yourself admiring a graphic in a magazine or on social media? Search for the creator online and bookmark their feed or portfolio site. Has a colleague raved about an experience working with a graphics designer? Ask for contact information and inquire as to what made the experience a positive one. Establishing a habit of noticing graphics and artists that you admire before you're faced with a deadline can make the process of finding a designer much less stressful.

Depending on the scope of your project, you may find yourself in need of more than one collaborator. Consider preparing for that possibility by tagging your collaborator wish list with a few descriptors. Multi-person studios, for example, may be able to provide you with a more robust range of skill sets without the additional complication of more than one point-person. And did you know that you can hire a freelance graphics editor that can help with finding suitable artists and managing the project? Or that there are researchers that specialize in collecting and preparing information that is destined to be presented in visual form?[1]

What if you need a science-savvy design professional right now, your institution can't help, and you haven't started a prospects list yet? Here are some resources that may be useful:

- **The Association of Medical Illustrators** maintains a searchable directory of artists at *http://www.medillsb.com/*
- *https://science-art.com/* is a portfolio website dedicated to science illustration
- **The Guild of Natural Science Illustrators** has a member directory that can be searched by area of expertise and technique, although you'll need to click through to view portfolios: *https://www.gnsi.org/member-directory-public#/*
- **Lifeology** supports a community of artists and scientists looking to connect for projects: *https://lifeology.io/matchmaking/*

HOW TO COMMISSION A GRAPHIC • In a terrific series on using and producing science images,[2] artist and science communicator Bethann Garramon Merkle recommends that you "plan ahead, so you know what you want and what you can spend."[3] Taking the time to write a clear description of your project can help you clarify your needs in your own mind and communicate those needs with a potential collaborator.

When contacting a designer to see if they're available and interested in working on your project, you should provide a concise overview of your project, a deadline schedule, and your budget. To inform the project overview, complete steps 1 through 6 of the flowchart that starts

---

1   As Amanda Hobbs put it, graphics researchers focus on "figuring out what the most interesting content might be, doing in-depth research, coming up with suggestions for visual presentation, working with a designer to turn them into reality, editing the visual elements for accuracy, and writing/refining the words that accompany the graphics." Read more about her experiences doing that for *National Geographic* and other outlets in "My Answer to the Question: 'So, What Do You Do?' (Part 1)," by Amanda Hobbs, ATH Creative (February 6, 2014) *http://www.athcreative.com/new-blog/2014/1/28/my-answer-to-the-question-so-what-do-you-do-part-1* (accessed April 16, 2022)

2   The first installment of the six-part series is, "Tips for Ethical and Legal Use of Images in Science Presentations and Other Science Communication (Using Images-A Best Practices Primer, Part 1)," by Bethann Garramon Merkle, MFA; COMMNATURAL blog (April 20, 2017) *https://commnatural.com/2017/04/20/tips-ethical-legal-use-of-scicomm-images/* (accessed April 16, 2022)

3   "Commissioning SciArt Illustrations? Know What You Want and What You Can Spend. (Using Images-A Best Practices Primer, Part 6)," by Bethann Garramon Merkle, MFA; COMMNATURAL blog (May 25, 2017) *https://commnatural.com/2017/05/25/commissioned-illustrations-budget/* (accessed April 16, 2022)

on page 254. The answers to those questions will help convey the scope of your project to a potential collaborator. If you're a content expert— or if you have time to do some background research of your own in order to help bring down the fee—also complete step 7 on page 258. If you're overwhelmed—and not even sure about working through steps 1 through 6—just be candid with potential design collaborators. You may consider suggesting an hourly rate for help working through the initial evaluation. If a graphic seems like a good idea at the end of that process, then renegotiate another fee for the next steps.

It's best if you have a target price as part of your project brief. That said, if the rest of your brief is clear and detailed, it's totally okay to ask a potential collaborator to provide a quote. In either case, these variables will impact the fee, and should be addressed in the project brief:

- **Rights that you are seeking to obtain:** Are you hoping to buy exclusive rights (more expensive), a one-time license to publish the graphic in a specific publication (less expensive), or something else entirely? If you—or your institution—don't have a contract that specifies these details, the designer can likely provide one after you communicate your intended use. (Note that the contract should also include a "kill-fee" schedule that ensures that the designer will be compensated for their time if the project is halted for any reason before completion.)

- **Number and size of discrete images:** As the number and scale of images go up, so will the fee.

- **Level of complexity:** Projects that aim to illustrate something novel or complicated will likely cost more than an updated version of a well-trod topic. Some artists may have base imagery already completed or reference files on popular subjects that they can use to help speed up the initial steps of a project. If the subject matter is novel, it'll likely require more research. If you can help lighten the research load for the designer, fees may drop.

- **Deadline schedule:** In general, fast-turnaround projects will cost you more money. If your budget is tight, get graphics projects moving as soon as possible to avoid rush fees.

- **Number of feedback rounds:** I recommend the process outlined in Chapter 15, in part because it establishes a clear framework for three rounds of art. It's not unusual for an artist to stipulate additional fees if the number of late-breaking change requests become unwieldy, or exceed a previously agreed upon number of iterations.

- **Rendering style:** If a quote from an artist is out of your budget, you can consider respectfully asking if they have a rendering style or a recommended approach that might be less costly, given the realities of your budget cap. It's very likely that the answer will be no. (If that's the case, don't push it.) Highly detailed three-dimensional renderings may take more computing power and time to render than line drawings, which can mean a higher bill. But you can't rotate a two-dimensional line drawing for a slightly different view angle after it's complete. So shifting rendering styles isn't always a cost-saver in the long run—or even an option—depending upon the project and the artist.

Constructive Critiques

One of the routines in magazine publishing consists of gathering editorial and production staff to walk through all of the article layouts for a particular issue. The goal is to check on the progress of the visual elements to see how the full issue is shaping up, and to chat about the materials as a group. It's common to discuss how the imagery and design of the title spreads works with the headline, the order of articles, and the balance of photography and illustrations.

Preparation work for these meetings falls on the visuals team. We're often scrambling to get the latest imagery into page layouts, and preparing those layouts to share with others. Although side conversations and collaborative work in the days and weeks preceding these meetings definitely inform the meeting, folks from outside of the visuals team don't necessarily need to prepare specifically for this gathering.

There's not a pre-meeting assignment. Materials aren't distributed ahead of time. Folks join the meeting and pipe up with feedback on-the-fly, as we walk through the visual presentation. It's quite similar to critique sessions in studio art classes. Pages are pinned to the wall or viewed courtesy of a shared screen. We physically or virtually shuffle down the lineup, turning attention from page to page, and verbal feedback rolls in.

It's interesting to compare it to manuscript review meetings, in which the editorial team gathers to discuss progress of the text. Notably, there is a pre-meeting assignment for attendees in this case. We each carve out time to read through the latest draft before we gather. Then we meet and discuss. The ability of an individual to fully engage in the feedback process hinges on whether they have invested the time and energy to do so. It's hard to participate in a meaningful way without reading the material being discussed.

I bring up this comparison to simply highlight the fact that there's a different level of investment required—and contemplation time—for providing feedback on different types of materials in different settings. It's good to be cognizant of this fact. Yes, gut reactions can be incredibly useful. But be thoughtful, kind, and intentional in your comments. Just because you have an immediate reaction to a design being presented to you in person doesn't mean that you should blurt out your comment at that very moment. Think about what lies at the core of your reaction, and how it relates to the goals of the design in front of you.

A design critique generally refers to a synchronous conversation that occurs at the same time as the design product is shared. But it's likely that you'll also be engaging in asynchronous loops with collaborators, with sketches shared by email, and feedback returned later. The tips for providing feedback below apply in both cases.

TYPES OF FEEDBACK • In the 2008 paper "Critiquing Critiques,"[4] Deanna P. Dannels and Kelly Norris Martin identified nine categories of feedback, based on design critiques observed in an art school setting.

- **Judgment:** Evaluative feedback that consists of a reaction and an assessment of quality
- **Process oriented:** Observational feedback that includes statements, questions or suggestions related to how the design is created
- **Brainstorming:** Rhetorical feedback that prompts thoughts on future imagined possibilities or alternatives
- **Interpretation:** Reactive feedback that aims to make sense of the design (features of the design or the design concept more broadly)
- **Direct recommendation:** Focused feedback in the form of specific advice
- **Investigation:** Non-rhetorical feedback requesting more information about the design or design process
- **Free association:** Spontaneous and reactive feedback that takes

4   Deanna P. Dannels and Kelly Norris Martin, "Critiquing Critiques: A Genre Analysis of Feedback Across Novice to Expert Design Studios," *Journal of Business and Technical Communication*, Vol. 2 (April 1, 2008)

the form of "It reminds me of…" or "This looks like…"
- **Comparison:** Strategic and intentional feedback that compares/contrasts the design with something else
- **Identity invoking:** Contextual feedback related to things like "the philosophical nature of who designers should be"

It should be reiterated that these categories emerged from a study that evaluated critique in the context of instructional settings. That's a bit different than providing feedback to a collaborator. I'm not suggesting that all of the categories above translate well for our purposes. The categories above simply demonstrate that different types of feedback invite different types of reflection, response, and action from the designer. Being aware of that can help you provide more useful notes.

HIGH QUALITY FEEDBACK • According to Adam Conner and Aaron Irizarry, good and useful feedback in the form of a critique is a three-part observation comprised of these elements:
- "It identifies a specific aspect of the idea or a decision in the design being analyzed."
- "It relates that aspect or decision to an objective or best practice."
- "It describes how and why the aspect or decision work to support or not support the objective or best practice."[5]

Note that this model centers the goal—or objective—of the graphic. That's one of the reasons that your goal statement is critical: It provides a focal point for constructive evaluation and criticism. If you and your collaborators have previously agreed on the goal of the graphic, then critiques can focus on if—and how—your design decisions and sketches honor that goal.

For example, if the goal of your graphic is to compare and contrast two competing hypotheses, a constructive design critique with regards to the composition should relate back to that goal. It might go something like this: "Our goal is to compare and contrast two leading hypotheses. In this sketch, one of the scenarios is shown more prominently than the other. It's both much larger and featured at the top. I worry that it implies that the larger scenario is more likely—or important—than the other, which is not the case."

It's often tempting to jump in immediately with an edit request,

5   Adam Connor and Aaron Irizarry, *Discussing Design: Improving Communication and Collaboration through Critique,* 1st edition (O'Reilly Media, 2015)

without articulating the underlying reason. For example, the case described in the preceding paragraph could've simply prompted this short note: "Please make both of these scenarios the same size." I'm certainly sometimes guilty of this solution-focused and streamlined approach, particularly when time is short and I have a clear idea on how to fix something that I perceive as a problem with the design. But that closes the door on collaboration. As Conner and Irizarry write, "Good critique is actionable. When the 'why' behind the feedback is included, the designer can fully understand the comment and take action."[6] Taking a few moments to clearly articulate "why" may inform other design decisions that are still in development, like color. And it leaves the door open for a conversation and other possible solutions, as opposed to devolving into an exercise in micro-management.

Are you reacting to—and tempted to comment on—a design element just because it's different from the conventions typically used in a particular scientific field? For example, molecular models for water (H_2O) conventionally show the hydrogen atoms as white spheres, and the oxygen atom as a red sphere. Perhaps you're providing feedback on a graphic in which the designer is using a different color palette: hydrogen is shown in light blue, and oxygen is shown in dark blue. Before noting it as something that should be changed, think through the goal, audience, and context for the graphic. If the image will be in a chemistry textbook, retaining a standard and conventional color palette may be a critical way to ensure that a reader can track similar elements across different graphics. In that case, flagging the colors as something that should be changed in order to honor that objective is a great note. But what if the graphic isn't connected to other graphics with hydrogen and oxygen represented in white and red, respectively? Perhaps the audience and context could be better served by evoking a sense of water by using shades of blue. In that case, you can still feel free to tag that detail with a note stating the convention. But also be sure to explain your reasoning, so that the designer can then make an educated decision based on weighing the pros and cons. Something like, "Typically in my field, hydrogen is shown in white and oxygen is shown in red. But given the goal and audience for this graphic, that may not be an issue. Just flagging it here, in case we end up using hydrogen and oxygen in other contexts as well, and decide to go with a conventional representation."

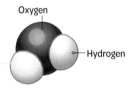

Oxygen

Hydrogen

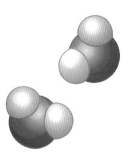

6   Adam Connor and Aaron Irizarry, *Discussing Design: Improving Communication and Collaboration through Critique,* 1st edition (O'Reilly Media, 2015)

I highly recommend reading *Discussing Design*[7] to really dive into the topic in depth. Here are a few of my favorite tips from the book:

- Lead with non-confrontational questions along the lines of, "Can you tell me more about why you chose this approach for [aspect/element]?"
- Include positive feedback. This is in part so the interaction isn't a completely negative one. It's also to ensure that really successful elements in the current design don't disappear in later iterations.
- Remember that critiques are in the service of making the design better. They are not about tearing the design down or judging the designer.
- When on the receiving end of a critique, really listen to the feedback, and ask follow up questions if you don't understand the comments or need more context.
- Critique is a skill that improves with practice.

●　　●　　●

MY COLLABORATION EXPERIENCES are largely pinned to routine these days. As a journalist, I've settled into a pattern of finding potential designers to work with, writing project briefs suitable for the context of a magazine, and a clear sense of the rhythm of article deadline schedules, story budgets, and feedback loops. But that pattern isn't the same for all projects. Every designer, client, and project has different needs. And thus, every collaboration is a bit different. Check out the Q&A boxes on pages 304–318 for advice from people with other points of view.

More to Explore

- ***Discussing Design: Improving Communication and Collaboration through Critique,*** by Adam Connor and Aaron Irizarry (O'Reilly Media, 2015)
- ***The Little Book of Design Critique for Scientists,*** by Vassilissa Semouchkina: *https://vassilissa.design/Advancing -Visual-Design-Culture-in-STEM-Lab-Groups*
- **"Client Guide to Working with a Medical Illustrator,"** by the Association of Medical Illustrators: *https://www.ami.org/ medical-illustration/hire-a-professional*

---

7   Adam Connor and Aaron Irizarry, *Discussing Design: Improving Communication and Collaboration through Critique,* 1st edition (O'Reilly Media, 2015)

- **"How to Shape a Productive Scientist–Artist Collaboration,"** by Virginia Gewin, *Nature* (February 17, 2021): This article emphasizes fine art collaborations, but its recurring theme of mutual respect is spot-on for science graphics as well.
- **"Science Illustration: Picture Perfect,"** by Jyoti Madhusoodanan, *Nature,* Vol. 534 (June 8, 2016): Article includes interviews with scientists and artists about working together on research papers and outreach projects.
- **"Getting the Most out of Working with an Illustrator for Your Science Communication Project (Using Images-A Best Practices Primer, Part 4),"** by Bethann Garramon Merkle, MFA, COMMNATURAL blog (May 11, 2017): *https://commnatural. com/2017/05/11/getting-the-most-out-of-working-with-a-sciart -illustrator/* (accessed April 16, 2022). I recommend the whole six-part series on using or producing images.
- The Denizen Designer Project has a resource page (*http://www. thedenizendesignerproject.com/denizendesigner/resources*) that includes a link to the **The Denizen Designer Zine,** which is a concise reference on co-design and participatory design. "Design" in this case is definitely not limited to information design or science communication. But the principles also apply to creating static graphics in a collaborative manner (accessed April 21, 2022). For a longer-form discussion of the broader realm of co-design, see *Beyond Sticky Notes: Co-Design for Real: Mindsets, Methods and Movements,* by Kelly Ann McKercher (Sydney, Australia: Beyond Sticky Notes, 2020); *Design Justice: Community-Led Practices to Build the Worlds We Need,* by Sasha Costanza-Chock (The MIT Press, 2020); and the **Design Justice Network** (*https:// designjustice.org/*)
- Events and science communication groups that emphasize community, connections between artists and scientists, and collaborative practices include the **SciCommCollective** (*https://www. scicommcollective.com/*), **ART+BIO Collaborative** (*https://www. artbiocollaborative.com/*), **SciArt Initiative** (*http://www. sciartinitiative.org/*), **Science Finds Art** (*https://sciencefindsart.com/*), **Art the Science** (*https://artthescience.com/*), **Eyeo Festival** (*http://eyeofestival.com/about/*), **SciVizNYC** (*https://www.sciviz.nyc/*), and **Information+** (*https://informationplusconference.com/*).

Collaborating with Scientists:
Thoughts from Designer Angela Morelli

Angela Morelli is the CEO and co-founder of InfoDesignLab (*https://www. infodesignlab.com*). InfoDesignLab specializes in co-design, particularly in the service of building visual tools that aid decision-making. Clients include the Intergovernmental Panel on Climate Change (IPCC), the European Environment Agency, and the World Meteorological Organization. I asked Morelli (AM) about co-design and her experiences collaborating with scientists. Here are her replies.

JC: What is co-design?

AM: Co-designing data visualizations with readers and scientists really helps us meet our audience where they are. Co-design is centered on the involvement of all those who affect and are affected by the consequences of design. Clear science communication needs exactly that, because it cannot only be in the hands of scientists. It also needs to be in the hands of communicators and designers. We know we can bring to the table not just our knowledge about grids, colors, and typography. We also bring our knowledge on creative processes, information design, systems design, and service design to work towards clear and engaging communications. Participation and collaboration are essential ingredients for facilitating, planning, and gaining a shared understanding of how the *involvement* works. Laying down the foundation for the co-design process requires having a mutual understanding of the design process itself. The designer is not the only facilitator. The designer has to empower the stakeholders (whether they be content experts, scientists, cognitive scientists, or members

of the ultimate audience) to act as facilitators if necessary. All should contribute. All should be—and feel— a part of the process. Participation and collaboration in the co-design process is not possible without preliminary work that sets the stage and establishes trust.

JC: In the 2017 post "Our co-design process," (*https://medium.com/ infodesignlabposts/our-projects -c7b0c471bc0d*) you describe a series of stages, with a paired set of design meetings and design work modules at each stage. How do you prepare your clients for that iterative and collaborative process?

AM: A great effort goes into building a vision of how working together is going to look. (This is the case for both dealing with the procurement process, and when defining a brief for commissioned projects.) We co-create a blueprint that takes the client's needs into account that addresses the complexity of the challenge, time requirements, number of people that will be involved, and the resources available. Preparation and smooth flow always comes down to good leadership within the organizations we work with. When the leaders trust the process and trust us, challenges are faced through hard work and good spirit!

JC: How do you balance the needs of both your audience and your scientist collaborators during your iterative process? Do you actively work with members of both groups at each stage, or do you interact with scientists and the intended audience separately?

AM: Separation is never intended and is never a goal. We work actively with scientists and intended audiences. There are stages when we naturally focus more on researching and mastering the content with the guidance of the content experts, in order to understand data and to unpack the tacit knowledge that the content experts carry in their minds. And there are stages where we focus on the audiences' needs through different forms of user engagement (user adoption, one-on-one interviews, user testing). But throughout the entire co-design process we make sure different stakeholders flow in and out, interacting with each other if necessary. We deeply care about those interactions.

JC: Can you describe a situation in which your clients—or scientist collaborators—were reluctant to fully engage in the collaborative process? Were you able to shift that dynamic? If so, how? If you haven't experienced that sort of pushback or reluctance, why do you think that is the case?

AM: We tend to work with research teams that want to engage in a way of working that is not order-and-delivery. They have experienced—or they are eager to experience—the value of a journey that has many ripples. But in a co-design process, participation happens at different levels. Even if clients trust the process, you are always exposed to pushback or reluctance that arrives from the many other layers. It is part of the game. In order to solve the reluctance, as a designer, you need to be prepared to understand where it comes from and why, with humility and humbleness. Negotiation skills are useful and resolving conflicts, collectively, is one of the deepest joys along the process.

JC: How do you prevent a design collaboration from turning into an exercise in micro-management? For example, how do you keep the conversations from devolving into content-area experts requesting color palette changes based on personal aesthetic preferences?

AM: The baseline is that for a healthy co-design process, we need good leadership and trust. When the process turns into a micro-management exercise, it is not co-design anymore, I guess. Most of the time, along the journey, neither the designers nor the scientists are driven by personal aesthetic preferences, because we are working to meet our audiences where they are. I love to listen to personal preferences, and there is time for that, but we are not there to please each other's preferences.

JC: What's your top piece of advice for designers entering a collaboration with scientists?

AM: Listen. Engage. Respect. It is beautiful to design science with scientists.

JC: What's your top piece of advice for scientists entering a collaboration with designers?

AM: Listen. Engage. Respect. It is beautiful to design science with designers.

JC: Is there anything else you would like to say about the topic that hasn't already been addressed?

AM: One rule or metric that is increasingly important for us is participation. Especially when we design for decision-making or for high-level negotiations. There are so many different actors involved in the design process. So many scientists or experts from different disciplines and so many users with different needs. Orchestrating that participation is one of the most important things of all. And that is why a lot of our work does not happen behind a computer screen, not any more. It consists of mastering the data, interviewing stakeholders to understand their needs, and collaborating with other designers, developers and cognitive scientists.

Collaborating with Artists:
Thoughts from Scientist Stephen Brusatte

Stephen Brusatte is a paleontologist at the University of Edinburgh. He studies, teaches, and writes about the anatomy and evolution of dinosaurs and ancient mammals. As an author of articles and books on fossil vertebrates for a variety of audiences—and a consultant for movies and television—he's no stranger to collaborating with artists on graphics and scientific illustrations. I asked Brusatte (SB) about his experiences working with designers. Here are his replies.

JC: Many of the papers that you have co-authored in research journals include figures that are credited to folks other than yourself. (Thank you for giving credit where credit is due!) How do you find those designers and artists? Are they brought on board to help specifically with graphics, or are they folks who have a broader range of responsibilities, and are essentially embedded in your research group?

SB: Most of the figures in my papers are ones that either I construct (usually in Photoshop or Illustrator) or that my students and/or co-authors construct. I am not much of an artist myself, but I did learn how to do the basics: line drawings, photographs, digital design for things like family trees and stratigraphic rock columns. It is pretty unusual now for me to include figures in papers that were designed by people who are not co-authors on the paper. But earlier in my career I did work with mentors like Paul Sereno and Mark Norell who had photographers and artists they worked with, so we did include a lot of those figures in papers we wrote together. Now, when it comes to my books (both academic and popular books), then I work a lot with outside artists, as I don't have anywhere near the skills to do things like life reconstructions of extinct animals or detailed scientific illustrations of important structures like mammalian teeth or inner ears or brains.

JC: You also work on collaborative projects for a wide range of audiences, including books, movies and magazine articles. Can you reflect on one of those experiences that you think went particularly well, and tell me a bit about why you think it was a positive experience?

SB: I've had a lot of positive experiences and have been lucky to cross paths with, and work with, many talented artists. *Scientific American* has always been a joy to work with. The care taken by the editorial team is second-to-none. Every article is edited carefully for content, with a lot of back-and-forth to get the phrasings and cadence just right. Then it's copy edited, and critically fact-checked. And that's just the writing. Meanwhile, the art team is figuring out how to illustrate the article and lay it out so it looks eye-catching. Professional artists are commissioned to do artistic reconstructions of fossils, and professional quality graphics and line art. I have nowhere near the skills to do any of this myself, so I am really grateful. I also learn a lot in doing it. Usually for *Scientific American* I'm asked to provide data for the graphics—things like curves of fossil diversity or family trees of fossil species, which the graphic designers and artists can turn into attractive designs. The act of doing this makes me be really engaged with the most recent literature, and makes me double and triple check my facts. And then, at the end of it all, I get to see gorgeous artwork accompany my article.

JC: Can you recall a situation in which an artist wasn't responding to your content-related feedback? Were you able to shift that dynamic? If so, how?
SB: Honestly I don't think so. I've worked with a lot of artists, especially when writing popular books and articles for magazines, and I can't remember a time that an artist has neglected to work closely with me or take my feedback on board. Maybe I've been lucky. Or maybe most artists I've worked with realize that my own visual art skills are so poor that they take pity on me!

If you haven't experienced that sort of pushback, why do you think that is the case?
SB: I suppose in addition to being lucky and working with artists and designers who are top people and well vetted, I do always try to be courteous, enthusiastic, optimistic, and helpful. I start out each collaboration with an artist by recognizing one simple fact: they are much, much better than me at visual art. So I try to respect them, treat them like the experts and creative talents they are, and not overstep any boundaries. I'm not one to be too aggressive, or get too obsessive with control or order or giving people intense directions. I try to provide guidance and then give artists a lot of flexibility and wiggle room to be creative. To use their talents.

JC: What's your top piece of advice for designers entering a collaboration with scientists?
SB: If scientists get really nit-picky about some small details, it's probably an "it's them, not you" issue. We are often trained to be pedantic.

JC: What's your top piece of advice for scientists entering a collaboration with designers?
SB: Dear God, respect artists as the creative talents they are. If you were as good at drawing or painting or digital art as they are, then you would be doing your own art.

JC: Is there anything else you would like to say about the topic that hasn't already been addressed?
SB: I study and write about dinosaurs. I like writing. I think I'm usually pretty good at it. But goodness, dinosaurs need to be seen. Words alone cannot do them justice. They are big, bold, brash, outrageous creatures from prehistory. No matter how good of a writer I might think I am, or no matter how self-proud of a certain phrase or sentence I may be, it doesn't matter too much if I don't have great artwork to go along with it.

Collaborating with Scientists within an Institution: Thoughts from Medical Illustrator Ni-ka Ford

Ni-ka Ford is a medical illustrator and 3D modeler in the Instructional Technology Group at the Icahn School of Medicine at Mount Sinai in New York City. She works with Mount Sinai faculty, clinicians, physicians, and researchers to create science graphics and visual aids for teaching and publication. I asked Ford (NF) about her experiences working as a visual communicator embedded within an institution. Here are her replies.

JC: You're part of a communications team embedded within an institution. How does that work? How do you get involved with specific projects, and who is the project manager?

NF: It depends on the type of project. We work very collaboratively on large projects that require various kinds of expertise. For example, an educational module may require video editing, instructional design, graphic design, illustration, animation, interactivity, and content organization. This would require everyone on the team to bring their specific skills to the table and work together to design the module. With this sort of collaborative project, I am usually brought on once it's been identified that my expertise is needed, whether that be illustration, animation, or video editing. The project manager is usually the person who originally initiated the project with the client. Most often it is my team's director who promotes our mission which is to encourage best practices in teaching and learning at the institution. When the project doesn't require a wide range of expertise—let's say it's a science graphic for a journal article—I will work on that alone. In that case, I am the project manager and work one-on-one with my client. I work with science researchers, physicians, medical students, and faculty in this way. They usually reach out to me directly requesting visualizations for a specific need. The great thing about working on a team like this is that if I ever do need a second eye on a project—or if I'd like to collaborate—I can always approach one of my team members about it and ask for help or advice. We all have very specific skill sets that can really be an asset to one another when it comes to seeing something from a different perspective.

JC: What's the range of project types that you work on?

NF: I work on a wide range of projects, from simple schematics, to fully rendered illustrations and 3D models. On occasion I work on projects that use virtual reality. My clients come from both the medical school and the hospital and research side of the Mount Sinai Health System. The bulk of my work is for journal publications and research grants. The main factors that influence what type of illustration it will be are the purpose of the visual, and who the audience is. Research scientists are often looking for a graphic that visually explains their research results and/or process. For this purpose, I create schematics that visually depict the most salient steps of the research process, or present a visual narrative that summarizes the research. I also create detailed rendered illustrations and surgical technique ilustrations. Sometimes my client may ask for a journal cover illustration to submit along with the internal figure on their research. In this case, I have more creative freedom. I also work directly with faculty to enhance lecture slides and course content. This can include anything from gross anatomy illustrations to animated gifs or 3D models of anatomical structures for faculty to add to their lecture slides or provide to students as supplemental learning materials. Using new technology to improve learning is highly encouraged at the institution, so I experiment with ways in which virtual reality can be used as a learning tool for students. These kinds of projects are self-directed and self-initiated and include 3D modeling, coding, and interactive design.

JC: Can you reflect on a collaboration with a scientist that you think went particularly well, and tell me a bit about why it was a positive experience?

NF: I worked with a director of a neuroscience lab and his colleagues to complete five figures for a grant proposal. This was a very positive experience because the project grew way beyond the original scope and led to the use of other modalities to convey the research. The process to develop the grant illustrations was standard with multiple iterations before completing the final figures. Afterwards, I worked with the same researchers to refine the figures and modify them for a journal article submission later that year. I enjoyed learning more about the research which was on the effects of stress on non-neuronal cells. After the article was published in *Neuron*, one of the authors requested that the figure be adapted for presentations and turned into a 2D animation. This was the first time I'd turned one of my illustrations into an animation and it was very exciting to bring each element in the illustration to life. I decided to use PowerPoint to animate so that my client would have more control over the animation timing as they presented. The director who originally approached me about this project saw the animation and asked for a modification of it for his presentations as well. The project picked up lots of momentum and led to lots of additional projects all centered around very fascinating neuroscience research. It was a very collaborative and rewarding experience.

JC: What are your strategies for keeping a project focused and moving forward in a productive manner?

NF: I always meet with my client when the project first begins to get a thorough understanding of the content. As I work on a project, I maintain consistent communication with my client, asking questions and sending sketches for feedback. This helps keep the project focused and aligned with the client's expectations. Often times, I will request more than one meeting throughout the design process because I find that having conversations about edits and revisions via zoom or in person covers more ground than emailing. I find that the more I involve my client in the iterative process—especially near the beginning of the project—the better the outcome. Having a good understanding of what the reader/audience is meant to take away from the project is essential for guiding the development of the visual. I also like to cultivate a friendly atmosphere for open conversation, because new ideas can spark throughout the development stages that could potentially enhance the work.

JC: What's your top piece of advice for designers entering a collaboration with scientists?

NF: Use your knowledge of design principles, color theory, and best practices for design layouts. Scientific information can be complex and complicated. Consider how the information flows around the page, does it lead your eye sequentially through the figure? Text and labels should be concise and appropriately placed for descriptors and titles. The importance of color cohesion is sometimes overlooked. It can really enhance a figure when the colors work well together and are used to emphasize certain areas of the figure.

JC: What's your top piece of advice for scientists entering a collaboration with designers?

NF: Be crystal clear on what you intend for the visual to show. Identify the most important points of the research and make sure to convey those to the designer. With complex scientific research, it can be difficult for the designer to figure out what the focus of the figure should be even when provided a summary. The scientist should parse out the information that is the most crucial for visualizing before approaching the designer, and communicate it clearly. When communicating with the designer, it's important to be mindful that they may not always have a scientific background and so the information may need to be explained to them in layman's terms.

JC: Is there anything else you would like to say about the topic that we haven't already discussed?

NF: It's not always easy to understand the material that you may be visualizing. After all, you're collaborating with scientists who may have been studying their research for a long time. Gather reference materials and background information on the subject if it's unfamiliar to you. Obtaining this from the scientist you're working with is best, but Google and PubMed are also there to help. As a designer, it's okay to not grasp every single piece of information, which is why communicating that to the client is important so that they can fill in those gaps. Along with asking for a summary of the research or abstract of their paper, sometimes I'll ask the scientist if they can sketch out their idea for the figure on paper. A rough sketch like this from them can help exponentially; as a visual thinker, seeing their idea on paper even if it's simple shapes and lines can serve as a great launching point to jumpstart the figure creation.

Collaborating within a Studio Setting:
A Conversation with Sonya Amin

Sonya Amin has an undergraduate degree in developmental biology and a masters in biomedical communications from the University of Toronto. In 2004, she co-founded AXS Studio, a science communication team of writers, medical illustrators, animators, interactive developers, designers, and producers. I asked Amin (SA) about her experiences collaborating with an internal team for external projects. Here's a lightly edited transcript of our conversation.

JC: What sorts of projects does AXS work on?

SA: We visualize tough life science concepts, primarily for pharmaceutical companies and biotech companies. That visualization can take the form of an animation, an illustration, or an interactive application.

JC: How many people are on the AXS team, and how does division of labor work?

SA: There are 19 of us now. The production team is organized into departments: client services, art and design, animation, and interactive. When we're putting a project team together, we're able to pull from those departments and assemble project teams. We're also able to parachute in sometimes for really targeted problem solving. For example, we were working on an animation and deadlines were looming, but we were in great shape. Then we got client feedback. The way that we had depicted the patient's hair wasn't to their liking. Now we've got a hair problem. So we had an artist who wasn't part of the project team parachute in and work on the hairy problem. She took care of that while everybody else plugged away and made sure we met the deadline.

We all have specialties and interests and talent that's associated with our department. And then we each have these interesting things that we happen to know about. Everybody on the team is a "go-to person" for something. Even multiple things. If there's a question about molecular science, I know to go to Stephanie or Julian. If there's a question about another topic, or a procedure, or program, I know who to go to. It's rewarding to be part of such a supportive team.

JC: How do you manage communications between your internal team and an external client?

SA: Single point-person all the way. At least for the scope of projects that AXS works on. I find that being that single point-person—or conduit—allows me to get a really nuanced in-depth understanding of my client's needs, their frustrations, and their goals. And I can also then understand my team's needs, their frustrations, and their goals. And that helps me do my job a lot better. I can be the translator, from production, to the client, and back again. That said, our client accounts are getting bigger and more complex. And so I find that even though I love working that way, certain larger projects require more than one person being the conduit. So that's a whole new fun challenge: Learning to hive-mind with a partner.

JC: I recall working on a project in which you were the point-person [from AXS]. But you and I [in my role as a magazine graphics editor] also sat down with a scientist and one of the AXS illustrators and worked through some sketches. Does that happen very often?

SA: If I see that we've hit a blocker, I'll bring in more people. If we're describing what seems like the same thing in words, but are still somehow not really connecting with what the other person needs or wants, I'll bring more people together and try to work through it.

JC: Can you reflect on an internal collaboration that you think went particularly well, and tell me a bit about why it was a positive experience?

SA: There was an illustration about how gene studies are inspiring new approaches to tackling Alzheimer's disease. I was the project manager, Ruth was our 3D artist, and Chelsea was our designer and 2D artist. If any of the three of us had tackled that visualization challenge alone, we would have gone at it from a completely different angle. And normally when you get three people like that working together, it could be that you have a clashing vision. But our skill sets really complemented each other. We had a certain level of trust. We knew when to let somebody with the expertise run with things, and take it up to a certain point. We were also really open to honest feedback. The vision that we came up with together was ultimately way stronger than it could have been if we did it individually. It sticks out as a positive experience because the whole project just had such a nice flow. There was just this nice rhythm of getting feedback from one another to shape things and move the project along.

JC: Can you reflect on an external collaboration that you think went particularly well, and tell me a bit about why it was a positive experience?

SA: This is a hard question. Because they're all fun. One project type that I find really interesting is for medical device companies, when the device is still in the investigational stage. In those cases, we're visualizing a device doing what it's going to do, before it's been tested in humans or out in the field. And it's often the first time that the client has seen their device being depicted in the wild. All sorts of things can come up. Like the instructions for use are not quite right. Or it doesn't twist the way they thought it would. And our client can then decide how to address the issue. On these projects, everybody is collaborating to literally improve something that's going to help people.

JC: What's your top piece of advice for designers and artists entering a collaboration with scientists?

SA: I don't have one, I have three. First is to define the objectives, so that you have a North Star that will keep you from getting distracted by all of the details. With projects like ours, it's really easy to go down a rabbit hole and feel like you need to depict every single detail, because every single detail is really juicy and exciting. It's science! Having that guiding principle will help you really stay focused on what's important to depict here, and what is extraneous.

Also, share the rationale for your design decisions. Scientists are the one audience that probably will really appreciate that you're making design decisions that are not just for aesthetics or personal preference. There's real psychology and perception considerations that will make a visualization more or less successful. And a scientist collaborator will be super happy that it's based on evidence, not just on personal preference.

Third: don't forget to ask "why" in response to the feedback that you get. For example, if you told me to make the cells leopard-print, I wouldn't just do it. I would probably say, "That's a great idea, Jen. Could you tell me a little bit more about why you would like that?" We're all problem solvers. And we often default to talking about solutions right away. And then we focus on executing the solution. But what if we talked about where that piece of feedback comes from? There might be two or three other solutions. One might have been a better solution than leopard-print. When you ask "why," be clear that you're not challenging the proposal: You'd just like to more fully understand the reason for the feedback.

JC: What's your top piece of advice for scientists entering a collaboration with designers and artists?

SA: Ask about the artist or designer's process. There are so many ways of doing things. There are so many ways of approaching visual design and visualization. Asking about the process will help you to understand what the major milestones are, what kind of feedback is needed (and when), and what the cut-off/point-of-no-return is.

JC: Is there anything else you would like to add?

SA: We know that we are stronger together when the collaboration is successful. But I did also want to say sometimes it's okay not to collaborate. I saw this idea summed up nicely somewhere on the internet, and it rang true so it's stuck with me: Collaboration can be thought of as another resource, like time or budget. It needs to be spent wisely. Sometimes it's good to talk things through, and propose "what if we did this?" or "what if we did that?" But sometimes you just have to step away and try stuff by yourself and then come back. And that will make the collaboration that much better, because you'll then have something tangible to evaluate and discuss.

Q & A ————————————————————————————————————

Critiquing Science Graphics:
Thoughts from Designer Vassilissa Semouchkina

Vassilissa Semouchkina is lead interaction designer at Cognition Studio and an Adjunct Lecturer at the University of Washington. Her master's thesis (*Advancing Visual Design Culture in STEM Laboratory Groups*) focused on analyzing the culture of research laboratories to inform educational materials on topics in scientific communication and visual design that are tailored to researchers' needs. I asked Semouchkina (VS) about the *Researcher's Toolkit for Visual Design and Critique* (which includes the booklet *The Little Book of Design Critique for Scientists*[1]) and her experience as an employee for the University of Washington's Design Help Desk.[2] Here are her replies.

1   *https://vassilissa.design/Advancing-Visual-Design-Culture-in-STEM-Lab-Groups*

2   The Design Help Desk was initiated by Karen Cheng (Visual Communication Design) and Marco Rolandi (Electrical Engineering),with funding from the National Science Foundation. It's now supported by the University of Washington Design Division. *http://depts.washington.edu/deshelp*

JC: Let's start with your experiences as a consultant for the UW Design Help Desk. Can you describe the program, and your role in it?

VS: The University of Washington Design Help Desk is a service offered through the School of Art + Art History + Design's Division of Design. It was founded by my Prof. Karen Cheng, although senior undergraduate and graduate students are the ones employed. The help desk usually operates out of the research commons, but because I was employed during the start of the COVID-19 pandemic, I operated the help desk from home. I was the only employee when I was there, and I worked at the help desk from Fall 2020 to Spring 2021. I would take appointments from staff, faculty, and students in order to assist them in working through various design-related issues. Some students came

to me with posters that they'd like to improve, some researchers wanted advice on how to make scientific figures for presentations clearer, and one person even came to me with their entire doctorate dissertation. Needless to say, the kind of help people were seeking varied greatly, but it all related back to design concerns.

JC: Was there a particular question or stumbling block or challenge that emerged repeatedly in help desk sessions about science graphics?

VS: It's hard to pin down a specific or most frequent concern in terms of the work that came to the Design Help Desk. However, I will say that the most frequent "correction" that I would work with people on was simplification. Projects would come to the help desk bursting with a thousand colors and a bunch of different typefaces.

More often than not, my work would consist of finding ways to create an content-forward approach to the client's designs. For example, in the case of a PowerPoint deck, I would emphasize that the most important thing is to help a viewer process the information provided as quickly and thoroughly as possible. For some presentations, this would mean breaking a single hectic slide into five simpler ones, reducing confusing type hierarchy, and removing visually heavy secondary elements (such as arrows, boxes, etc.). A lot of people view crowding their pages as a desirable way to showcase their hard work. But instead, this often leads to complicated, overwhelming design work.

JC: Did you find that help desk clients were good at identifying the problems with their own graphics, and just in need of advice on how to solve those problems? Or was most of your energy dedicated to helping folks recognize the areas that could use improvement?

VS: I would say it was a mix. Some people came to the Help Desk with a good understanding of design, but without the training to act on their intuition. They would perhaps know that their design solution was ineffective, but needed a more professional opinion of how to execute what they were having trouble visualizing—or putting into words—themselves. Others were a blank slate, and were viewing me as the "designer" and themselves as the "client." Often times, these were the people who got a bit upset when they learned that I wouldn't just design

their projects for them! Joking (somewhat), but I would often schedule these people for multiple sessions to ensure that they were executing my advice in a successful way. The way I worked with people was definitely a case-by-case approach.

JC: As a designer, I imagine you are quite well-practiced in providing and receiving critiques. As you point out in your thesis: "Feedback culture is almost synonymous with design education, being one of the main ways that designers learn to identify problems in both their own and their peer's work." Did you find that scientist clients at the help desk were open to frank feedback in the style of your art class critique sessions? Or did you find yourself modifying your approach to critiques in that context?

VS: Design critique is inherently a bit different than critique for scientists, as the goals are different. For design critique, you often focus on advancing the visual characteristics of a project in many directions: aesthetic, uniqueness, communicative ability, draw, and more. In design critiques for scientists, the focus is more on how to communicate most clearly and effectively what are often complicated and advanced concepts and data. As such, comments and opinions are directed towards this goal. The feedback is less-so "make this blue, the pink isn't working well," but rather "your bar chart would work better as a dot histogram, because your figure depends on seeing the categorizations of individual data points." While the direction of the feedback is different between those scenarios, the basic structure of the process remains relatively the same.

JC: How, if at all, did your experience as a help desk consultant inform *The Little Book of Design Critique for Scientists*?

VS: The Design Help Desk did not impact *The Little Book of Design Critique for Scientists* (or the overall toolkit, the *Researcher's Toolkit for Visual Design and Critique)*. The Design Help Desk was my job, and my research was conducted separately. For my Master's thesis, I observed and ultimately ran workshops with seven distinct STEM research laboratories over a period of seven months. In short, for about four months, I observed the labs' weekly meetings to gain an understanding of their baseline understanding and practice of design, as well as how they conducted critique, without intervention. I also used this time to build mutual understanding and trust with the students and principal investigators. Then I ran a pair of design and critique workshops with each lab, and surveyed them on their design needs, prioritization of and interest in design, and growth in understanding of design principles before and after the workshops. (To learn more, you can watch my 25-minute dissertation *https://vimeo.com/567249706*)

JC: As a part of your thesis, you trained scientists in critique skills via workshops and your toolkit. It sounds like you may be working on writing up some of the findings of how that training impacted overall communicative and visual qualities of their science figures. Is that correct? If so, can you provide us with a high-level summary of your results?

VS: That is correct, I am working on a paper along with Prof. Karen Cheng, Kevin Larson, and Yeechi Chen titled, "Advancing Design Critique in STEM Research Labs." I don't want to speak on this too much yet, but it is very exciting!

JC: What's your top piece of advice for scientists on the topic of seeking out and receiving feedback by others about their own graphics?

VS: My greatest piece of advice for scientists would be to keep an open mind. Designers that focus on scientific communication know the value, effort, and time invested into scientific work, and will understand the care that must be taken to modify scientific visuals. I sometimes encounter scientists with an inherent concern that design revisions are superficial and ultimately not important to scientific work, even though we know that research suggests otherwise. Design revisions are often a case of "trust the process." While it may seem intimidating to seek advice, it will ultimately help the scientist create a clearer and more desirable result.

JC: What's your top piece of advice for scientists when it comes to critiquing their peers' science graphics?

VS: My biggest piece of advice for getting comfortable with—or improving—critique skills is, simply, to practice critique. Engage in critique, and do so regularly! Even if you are uncertain about how to modify a design or correct a problem, take care to notice and point out areas that you think aren't working or may not seem "quite right." Learn to identify what poor design looks like. To get started, think about when you dislike a visual. Why is this the case? Is it overwhelming to look at? Boring? Dense? Too much? Apply metacognitive thinking. Consider why you are thinking the things that you are. At the most basic level, consider the issues that bother you–type, color, shape, etc. On the flip side, consider what, to you, defines "good design." What scientific visuals have you found most compelling in the past? Is it the neat organization of the periodic table, or the delicate curves of a double helix DNA strand? Why do you think you like these visuals? Thinking this way helps us to recognize what success in design looks like, and what draws us to certain visuals over others. As with most things in life, the only sure-fire way to build skills in design critique is to practice, practice, practice!

JC: Let's imagine that a scientist has hired a designer, or is otherwise collaborating with a professional designer on a project. What's your top piece of advice for that scientist when it comes to providing that designer with constructive feedback on sketches and other visual output?

VS: When collaborating with a designer, I would encourage scientists to create a situation in which they can work alongside the designer to not only create an effective work of science/design, but also to learn from the process. I recommend a hands-on approach (a.k.a. co-design) to collaborating with designers. This enables scientists to see professional approaches to design and to engage in the process, while learning new skills and gaining valuable insight into the design process. In terms of providing feedback, this is a trickier question. I suppose my greatest advice here would be to maintain distance from thinking about designer-scientist relationships as client-designer relationships. It is important to maintain constant communication and bring designers "into the fold" of the work. A scientist should take care to onboard a designer into the context in which the design work is needed. This will help prevent issues on both sides. For the scientist, this helps build trust and understanding that the designer is aware of their goals and aspirations for the work. For the designer, this makes them feel more confident in the designerly choices that they will be making, and will reduce friction in the revision process. Additionally, this will help the designer to propose potential alternatives to visualizations, as they will have a greater understanding of what, exactly, the scientist is trying to communicate.

Epilogue

IN THE 1999 PAPER "VISUAL LITERACY AND SCIENCE COMMUNICA-
TION," author Jean Trumbo states that, "Visual literacy is a critical part
of information literacy." She maintains that,

> There is currently no common theory to organize the [science visualization]
> effort, and there is no agreement on how to clearly represent scientific ideas,
> processes, or discoveries. There is an evolving collection of new technologies
> that facilitate the creation of captivating images. However, the resulting
> images may not express the appropriate scientific principle or may be
> incomprehensible to an audience. In essence, no cohesive foundation in
> visual literacy exists among those relying on the communication potential
> of science images.[1]

Trumbo goes on to recommend a framework to boost visual literacy for
scientists, science communicators, and audiences alike. Her framework
addresses visual thinking, visual learning, and visual communication.

This book aims to help boost visual literacy for those creating science visualizations. So, I must agree with Trumbo on some key points:
**There are learnable habits, skills, concepts, and tactics that can
lead to more successful science graphics.** (For example, doodling in
the service of visual thinking.) I also agree with Trumbo's sentiment
that those skills, concepts, and tactics aren't routinely taught to lots of
people who could benefit from them.

I don't see evidence that a common theory has emerged in the
last 20-plus years. And I'm not convinced that the lack of a common
theory for visualizing science in particular is a problem that needs to

1   Jean Trumbo, "Visual Literacy and Science Communication," *Science Communication,*
     Vol. 20 (June 1, 1999): © 1999 by Sage Publications, Inc. Reprinted by permission of
     Sage Publications.

be solved. I wholeheartedly agree that information literacy is an area in need of attention. All of us can benefit from learning more about how to disentangle information from disinformation and misinformation. (My favorite primer on the topic is the *Navigating Digital Information* video series hosted by John Green on Crash Course, in partnership with MediaWise, The Poynter Institute, and The Stanford History Education Group. *https://thecrashcourse.com/topic/navigatingdigitalinfo/*)

I do, however, worry that the goal of a common theory for visualizing science will box us into one way of thinking. And it implies that we should aim for some sort of pinnacle, with a set of strategies that should theoretically work in all situations. And yet, audience needs—and visualization trends—shift over time and space. To my mind, visualization strategies should also shift across time and space. (Although perhaps I'm being too narrow in my interpretation. I suppose that I could get behind a common theory for visualizing science that centers that idea of variability.)

My hope is that this book provides you with a solid foundation of knowledge; a familiarity with often-cited references and design concepts, a useful framework to guide your own graphics-building process, and resources that will help you create more thoughtful and intentional science graphics moving forward. There is so much more to write about each of the topics covered within this book! Science communication and visualization are dynamic fields, with new resources and research findings rolling out weekly. But at some point, I need to call this manuscript complete.

Visit *https://BuildingScienceGraphics.com* for resource updates. There, you'll find the "More to Explore" listings from this book, as well as other favorites and additional entries that I encountered after the publication date of this book.

Acknowledgments

THIS BOOK IS THE RESULT OF AN EMAIL FROM ALBERTO CAIRO. He
asked if I had ever thought about writing a book. I had. But the timing
never seemed right. And the timing still wasn't great. We were in the
midst of a global pandemic, and I was wary of overcommitting during
such an uncertain time. But, shoot, I couldn't pass up on the possibility
of having Alberto as an editor. His book *The Functional Art* remains a
well-worn favorite, set horizontally on the top of my bookshelf so I can
grab it easily, without turning my head and scanning vertical spines.
If I was ever going to write a book about graphics, I wanted him as an
editor. So I jumped in.

His guidance, critiques, and notes have been incredibly useful. He
quickly honed in on my bad writing habits and nudged me toward better
ones. And it was a treat to have an excuse to meet and chat about science
graphics at regular intervals. He has made this book much better than
it would've been without him. But he also gave me lots of leeway. (I take
full responsibility for all of the things that could still use improvement.)

Alongside Alberto Cairo, thanks to Tamara Munzner (AK Peters Visualization Series co-editor), and Elliott Morsia (CRC Press & Routledge
Commissioning Editor) for their interest and support, and for making
this experience a great one. Also thanks to Simran Kaur, Michele Dimont,
Samar Haddad, and all the folks behind the scenes at Taylor & Francis.

Many people provided helpful input along the way. Thanks to
Nigel Hawtin, Spencer Barnes, Sheila Pontis, Stefan Bruckner, and
Mark E. Johnson for their feedback on the proposal. Much gratitude
to Kelly Krause for reviewing the entire near-final manuscript. And
thanks to the following folks for reviewing excerpts: Paige Jarreau
(Chapter 3), Randa Hadi (Chapter 4), George Mather (Chapter 5), Steve

Haroz (Chapters 5 and 6), Joshua Korenblat (Chapter 7), Robert Simmon (Chapter 8), Amy Papaelias (Chapter 9), Nigel Holmes (Chapter 10), Silvia De Santis (file settings section), Lace Padilla (uncertainty section), Katie Peek (Chapters 13 and 14), Nigel Hawtin (Chapters 15–17), and Amanda Montañez (Chapter 17 text). They all helped make things better and more accurate. Any lingering errors or omissions are my own.

Thanks to the artists and organizations that granted image reproduction rights, as well as for a few newly commissioned pieces. (Including cover art by Alli Torban!)

Thanks to my science teachers, art teachers, and science-art teachers for their infectious curiosity, enthusiasm, and support, especially H. Allen Curran, Robert Tartter, Stan Cowen, Gary Niswonger, Ann Caudle, and Jenny Keller.

Thanks to everyone involved in the Museum Research Apprenticeship Program at the Natural History Museum of Los Angeles County, especially Sue Lafferty and Jodi Martin. They demystified what it meant to be a scientist and opened my eyes to the world of science communication.

Thanks to my past and present colleagues. In particular, my art, design, editorial, production, and copy department colleagues at *Scientific American* and *National Geographic*, and the many freelance designers and illustrators that I've had the great privilege to collaborate with over the years. They've taught me so much. There are too many to name them all.

Ed Bell took a chance on me as an intern and catapulted me into a career that I love. I'm forever grateful for his mentorship and friendship. Johnny Johnson, Jana Brenning, Jessie Nathans, John Rennie, David Schneider, Lisa Burnett Hillman, Christi Keller, and Ricki Rusting were so generous with their time and knowledge when I first arrived at *Scientific American* with rapidographs and a travel watercolor set in hand. Illustrators Roberto Osti, Laurie Grace, Tomo Narashima, and George Retseck were among my first collaborators. They were a delight to work with and showed me what a mutually respectful and productive art director/artist relationship could be. Fellow University of California, Santa Cruz and *Scientific American* alumni Lucy Reading-Ikkanda and Melissa Thomas Baum helped bridge the gap between coastlines. I'm happy that we're still in each others' lives.

I'm incredibly grateful for the support and leadership of *Scientific American* creative director Michael Mrak, and editor-in-chief Laura Helmuth. It's an honor to be a member of their crew.

Not a work day goes by that I don't appreciate how lucky I am to have Amanda Montañez as a graphics colleague. I'm a long-form features and print girl at heart. Amanda pushes me to keep news and digital presentations top-of-mind. I think we make a pretty darn good team.

Thanks to Elaine Bradley, Robert Gray, David Whitmore, and Connie Phelps from *National Geographic* for demonstrating the power of design in the service of storytelling. And thanks to George Bounelis and Bill Reicherts for demonstrating how to prepare materials properly for press with care and finesse (lessons that I continue to build on today courtesy of Silvia De Santis and Rich Hunt). I was also fortunate to work alongside Beth Rakouskas, Janel Kiley, Elisa Gibson, Ali Balfour, Ellie Boettinger, Cathy Tyson, Chris Klein, Jeffrey Osborn, Liz Connell, and many others at *National Geographic*. The experience was so much richer due to their friendship and support.

I seriously doubt I'd be in a position to write this book had I not attended the Malofiej Information Graphics Summit in Pamplona, Spain in 2011. That workshop and conference opened my eyes to the international news infographics scene and initiated a new period of learning for me. I'm indebted to the Malofiej community, and the Spanish Chapter of the Society for News Design—Javier Errea in particular—for hosting that event for so many years. It introduced me to aspirational work, amazing people that I continue to interact with on a regular basis, and pintxos. All very good things.

I also would not have been in a position to write this book without the support of dear friends. Shout-out to my long-time art and geology buddy L.S. Gardiner (read her book *Tales from an Uncertain World*), and Adam Holloway for a regular feed of pandemic wildlife photos; Vikki Abrahams and Craig Kirkland for indulging my constant book talk over shared meals; Kelsey Cleveland for supportive calls; and my favorite writing companion, Mica-kitty. Gratitude to Kristen Schretzenmayer, Barbara Bruno, and Saverio Bruno for making it possible for me to accept that internship in Manhattan years ago by providing me with an East Coast family and home.

Most of all, thanks to my family. I could not have asked for more supportive parents. Mom and Dad gave me the world, in the form of access to educational experiences (in science, art, and beyond), the space and structure to follow my passions, and unwavering love. I'm fortunate to have found the same unwavering love and support in a chosen life partner. Thanks, Joel Tolman, for your encouragement and sustenance. I owe you many weekends sans laptop. Let's go on a hike now.

Index